Fashion
TALKS

Fashion
TALKS

Undressing the Power of Style

Edited by

Shira Tarrant and Marjorie Jolles

Cover photo: © Roman Rozenblyum, www.romanroze.com.

Published by State University of New York Press, Albany

For information, contact State University of New York Press, Albany, NY
www.sunypress.edu

Production by Eileen Meehan
Marketing by Kate McDonnell

Library of Congress Cataloging-in-Publication Data

Fashion talks : undressing the power of style / edited by Shira Tarrant and
    Marjorie Jolles.
        p. cm.
    Includes bibliographical references and index.
    ISBN 978-1-4384-4320-1 (pbk. : alk. paper)
    ISBN 978-1-4384-4319-5 (hardcover : alk. paper)
    1. Women's clothing—Social aspects.   2. Clothing and dress—Social aspects.
3. Fashion—Social aspects.   4. Feminism—Social aspects.   I. Tarrant, Shira, 1963–
II. Jolles, Marjorie.

GT1720.F37 2012
391'.2—dc23   2011036641

10 9 8 7 6 5 4 3 2 1

To Emilie Tarrant I give all my love. Gratitude goes to the rest of my family, as well. For Marjorie Jolles—your conscientious, engaged, enthusiastic, and smart co-editing means this book is a far better collection than it could have been otherwise. Plus, it's been a lot of fun. My former students, Jennifer Sheik and Audrey Silvestre, provided valuable feedback on early essay drafts. You two will certainly recognize improvements on these pages that have a lot to do with your insights. High five to Roman Rozenblyum for serendipity and a vibrant cover image. Roll call: Cathie Roberts, Rebekah Spicuglia, Jennifer Pozner, Nancy Schwartzman, Micky Hohl, Andrew Lopas, Shawna Kenney, and Judith Grant—thank you in so many ways. I'm sure you each know why. Finally, big thanks to my dog Pickle for taking me on walks in the park that cleared my head and nourished my soul.

—Shira Tarrant

Love and thanks go to Matthew Pearson, whose furious styles in so many domains of life are my constant inspiration. I'm especially grateful to Shira Tarrant for the idea of this book, her friendship, and the inimitable snap, crackle, and pop of her writing. I thank the students in my *Fashion: The Politics of Style* courses at Roosevelt University for their sharp questions and close readings, and Michelle-Marie Gilkeson for proofing assistance. Warmest thanks go out to the many members of my family, local and far-flung, for their enthusiastic interest in this project (Fiona Jolles, you were the most enthusiastic of all!). And for transformative conversations about style, ideology, and the pleasures and labors of writing, I'm forever indebted to my invaluable mentors Chuck Dyke and Laura Levitt, and my brilliant friends Katherine Mack, Audrey Nezer, Allison Page, and Bryan Sacks.

—Marjorie Jolles

Contents

I
Dressing the Body: The Politics of Gender and Sexuality

II
Fashion Choices: The Ethics of Consumption,
Production, and Style

Illustrations

Acknowledgments

This collection grew out of presentations at the 2008 National Women's Studies Association conference and the 2009 meeting of the Cultural Studies Association. We are grateful to the panelists and audiences at both events who provided valuable, spirited feedback and affirmation of fashion's significance for feminism.

We also thank the contributors to this volume for their creativity, enthusiasm, and insightful scholarship on such diverse, pressing matters in fashion and feminism. We are grateful to Andrew Kenyon and Larin McLaughlin, our editors at SUNY Press, for their early and steady support for this project. We thank Kathryn Adèle Hardy Bernal for permission to reprint Image 7.1 and Image 7.3; James George Stratton Percy for permission to reprint Image 7.2; Bevan Ka Yan Chuang for permission to reprint Image 7.4; Arabesque Sheilas and Abayas for permission to reprint Image 8.1; and Diana M. Pho for permission to reprint Image 12.4.

Our colleagues and students at California State University, Long Beach and Roosevelt University have inspired us with their tireless and passionate engagements with feminism. We thank them for their contributions to our own feminist theorizing, for challenging us so productively, and for doing it all with such style.

Introduction

Feminism Confronts Fashion

Marjorie Jolles and Shira Tarrant

Fashion. We love it. We hate it. We debate it.

But why does fashion matter?

Beyond the clothes that line our closets or the photo layouts we flip past in glossy magazines, fashion is also the site of specific philosophical tensions. Fashion is symbolic, expressive, creative, and coercive. It is a powerful way to convey politics, personalities, and preferences for whom and how we love. Fashion encourages profound rebellion and defiant self-definition. Yet fashion can simultaneously repress freedom by controlling or disciplining the body, and by encouraging a problematic consumer culture.[1]

Fashion creates collective identity, but also restricts individual voice. Fashion provides ways to resist hegemony and communicate identity in the face of cultural and political pressure. At the same time, though, fashion is an integral part of this very conformist culture itself. In other words, fashion contains the potential for pleasure and subjugation, expression and convention. This book neither defends nor condemns fashion. Instead, these essays grapple with how fashion both enables and constrains expression in ways that are uniquely raced, gendered, classed, sexed, and bound to national and cultural histories.

Taking up this tension from a feminist perspective reveals how fashion—like power—is neither inherently good nor bad. What matters is how it is *used.* Consider sociologist Fred Davis's point that black lace at a funeral means something quite different than black lace on a negligee.[2] Or that wearing a pair of overalls in Manhattan evokes quite a different response than wearing overalls on a farm. What fashion *means* depends on context, but

I

also on whose interests it serves, what its audiences and practitioners bring to their engagement with it, and how it protects and transforms social divisions.

The problem is that fashion's liberatory possibilities are easily co-opted. Clothing manufacturer American Apparel pilfers support for sexual expression by turning a political ideal into exploitative billboards of its own. Or take the popularity of "green" style.[3] The belief that sociopolitical or ecological improvement can be achieved through alternative channels of fashion and style invites a potentially empty promise of empowerment-through-consumerism that is more emblematic of backlash than progress. We can try going DIY, but that comes with a set of problems, too.

Etsy.com, the hugely popular online emporium of handcrafted goods, provides a space for independent producers to sell their one-of-a-kind, hand-made wares to consumers. Etsy's mission is to "enable people to make a living making things, and to reconnect makers with buyers" in order to "build a new economy."[4] In promoting a DIY aesthetic, Etsy also advocates a certain feminist ethics in reconfiguring the relationship between production and consumption, emphasizing—rather than erasing—the humanity of labor.[5] Notwithstanding the big chance to make hand-embroidered messenger bags *and* work outside an oppressive capitalist system, the problem, writes Slate.com blogger Sara Mosle, "is that on Etsy, as in much of life, the promise is a fantasy. There's little evidence that most sellers on the site make much money."[6]

Tossing our hands in the air and making a beeline to the closest Big Box, corporate-chained, sweatshop-supplied clothing rack does nothing to dislodge the status quo, either. That is the conundrum. Even if we attempt to reject it, none of us can opt out of fashion and style (or global capitalism) completely.

Living in an increasingly visually mediated and commodified world means that having one's own style is compulsory. It is a core component of self-expression and self-realization. We need look no further than our TVs for contemporary mythologies about identity, expression, and transformation as evidence of their cultural sway. Makeover shows of every type abound, whether the focus is on stylizing the corporeal body (*What Not to Wear*), the business (*Tabatha's Salon Takeover*), or the home (*Extreme Makeover: Home Edition*).[7]

Sociologist Anne Cronin describes this cultural mandate to self-express as an ideology of "self as project," in which consumerism and self-styling make possible the (historically masculine) Enlightenment ideal of personal authenticity.[8] Each of us engages with fashion and style whether we want to or not. We might not all read *Vogue*, but we still get dressed in the morning.

And once we're dressed, we carry with us into the day the sartorial significance of race, class, gender, sexuality—as well as issues of global politics, domination, imperialism, exploitation, and free will. This collection of essays uses explicitly feminist lenses for analyzing this paradox of fashion and style.

Feminism and Fashion

Feminism—and feminists—have a bad rap when it comes to fashion. We're accused of being frumpy, unattractively braless, and inexcusably hirsute. Contemporary feminists who reject this characterization and attempt to bring sexy back sustain charges of being duped by the patriarchy into wearing provocative, self-objectifying outfits and mistaking this for empowerment. (Note both the Catch-22 and the assumption that feminists are women.)

Feminists' own ambivalent relationship to fashion and attempts to transcend the politically loaded project of creating personal style prompted philosopher Cressida Heyes to point out that "refusal on the part of the feminist subject to style herself in any way—to be uninvolved, neutral, or natural—is impossible."[9] More to the point, fashion has a long history as a source and resource for feminist discourse. Think, in no particular order, of Amelia Bloomer, leather chaps, myths about bra burning, politics of the Afro, and women's fight to wear pants at work. There are Hooters uniforms, rainbow flags, beauty pageants, shaved heads, bondage gear, boi styles, and high femme frills. Think sweatshops, Wal-Mart, outlet malls. Consider designer knock-offs and the workers who make them. As a vast commercial enterprise and the realm where imagination intersects ideology, fashion is never far from politics—no matter how hard fashion discourse tries to distance itself from the political by invoking its familiar keywords: fantasy and escape.

In Judith Butler's famous formulation of gender as a series of performative acts, she puts special emphasis on style as the very "language . . . for understanding gender," cautioning that to be styled is not the same as being "self-styled, for styles have a history, and those histories condition and limit the possibilities."[10] Style functions not as a celebration of the self overcoming the social, but rather as proof of the self's fundamental sociality. Style includes the habits, practices, mannerisms, tastes, codes, and stances, all informed by implicit values, that make up the "lifelong project of giving shape to human existence," as author Ladelle McWhorter puts it.[11] Feminism is a powerful tool for decoding fashion's political meaning and for acknowledging one's embeddedness in these systems of meaning.

So we are suspicious about arguments that naturalize stereotypes about gender by marking femininity as artifice and masculinity as substance. *Fashion Talks* rejects conflating fashion with femininity. Furthermore, we find it curious that a multibillion dollar global industry can be a driving economic powerhouse and simultaneously dismissed as a silly cultural accessory—as "just" fashion.

Just witness the connection talk-show host Don Imus made between black hair and sexual promiscuity when he referred in 2007 to the Rutgers women's basketball team as "nappy-headed hos." Journalist Jenee Desmond-Harris explains in *Time* magazine, "Just as blond has implicit associations with sex appeal and smarts (or lack thereof), black-hair descriptors convey thick layers of meaning but are even more loaded. From long and straight to short and kinky—and, of course, good and bad—these terms become shorthand for desirability, worthiness and even worldview."[12]

In 2009, comic Chris Rock picks up these issues in his film, *Good Hair*, a positive sign that critical analyses of beauty, race, identity, fashion, and style are now flung onto the mainstream agenda. Clearly, fashion evokes the politics of beauty and along with it brings the complicated politics of sexuality.

We have a long history of trying to manage and organize our sexual fears and desires, and one of the ways in which this is done is through the vehicle of fashion as expression, and through fashion as a tool for social control. Feminism is committed to understanding these efforts at management and organization.

The Essays

Section I—Dressing the Body: The Politics of Gender and Sexuality

Fashion Talks begins with Astrid Henry's essay, "Fashioning a Feminist Style, Or, How I Learned to Dress from Reading Feminist Theory." Henry poses the problems with stereotypes that feminism has involved at best a dismissive disregard for the subject or worse, an acrimonious disdain for beautification of the body and stylized presentations of self. The author concludes that entirely different avenues are possible that remain true to both the expressive and political self.

Because feminism takes a critical look at constructions of *gender*, not only of women or femininity, fashion is a crucial vehicle for understanding men, masculinity, and sexual identity. In "Dressing Left: Conforming, Transforming, and Shifting Masculine Style," Shira Tarrant takes up the mutability of masculinity and the ways by which fashion reflects this instability, or the constructed characteristics, of gender. Tarrant's essay questions whether it is possible to successfully transform, subvert, or transcend stereotypes and rigid expectations about masculinity, manhood, and male sexuality given the context and impulses of consumer capitalism.

Renee Ann Cramer's essay, "The Baby Bump Is the New Birkin," grapples with the meaning of pop culture's obsessive attention to pregnant celebrity bodies, as seen through their maternity fashions. Ironically, while appearing to "celebrate" the fertile body with bump-hugging looks, the fashions (and media coverage) of pregnant celebrities exert power to naturalize and normalize a certain narrative of pregnancy and motherhood. Now, through highly visible and stylized reproduction, mainstream media once again puts forth unattainable standards that women are expected to achieve. Pregnant celebrity carries status and acclaim while sifting and sorting women into racially coded Good Girl and Bad Girl labels.

"Fashion as Adaptation: The Case of *American Idol*," is an innovative use of evolutionary theory by Leslie Heywood and Justin R. Garcia to understand fashion trends as adaptive responses to cultural change. Such adaptations can be retrogressive as well as progressive, novel or normal, as the authors observe with the example of *American Idol,* Season 8. In the finale, Kris Allen, with this more "traditional" style of American masculinity, beat out Adam Lambert, whose glam-rock masculinity signaled queerness and stylistic innovation that Americans ultimately did not find *Idol*-worthy. A feminist-evolutionary approach to the contest between Allen and Lambert—as manifested in their competing styles—can provide fresh thinking about fashion as a vehicle for making social change and a primary scene of ideological contests.

Denise Witzig's "My Mannequin, Myself: Embodiment in Fashion's Mirror" compares the way the self is positioned in two sites of fashion spectacle: the high-art space of the museum exhibit and the commercial, democratic space of the shopping mall. Witzig's framing of these two modalities for "doing fashion" points to the ways our relationships to fashion are simultaneously embodied and disembodied, real and idealized, projecting backward to the past through nostalgia and periodization by situating oneself as a consumer of fashion history, and gesturing to the future in the act of shopping. While the museum would seem more conducive to disembodied experience than the department store dressing room, Witzig notes several ironies. The shopper is permitted to revel in disembodied fantasies of an improved future self, while the museum-goer is frequently brought back to the body both through the sensual appeal of the work on display and in negotiating crowded public space. Witzig's analysis sheds fresh light on feminist debates surrounding specularity, consumerism, and so-called high and low culture.

In "Life's Too Short to Wear Comfortable Shoes: Femme-ininity and Sex Work," Jayne Swift analyzes how debates around femme style have shifted from the feminist sex wars of the 1980s and 1990s to contemporary feminist political divisions and debates about sexual agency in sex work and neo-burlesque scenes. Poised in high-heeled shoes, Swift writes from the position of a queer femme sex worker, eager to forge more of a conceptual and political alliance between two subjectivities often kept both separate and silent in feminist discourse. Swift complicates feminist association of comfortable shoes with liberation, observing that wearing uncomfortable shoes in love, work, and politics enables an embodied understanding of the femininities and feminists often least visible in feminist political discourse.

In "Japanese Lolita: Challenging Sexualized Style and the Little-Girl Look," Kathryn A. Hardy Bernal questions the competing interpretations of the Japanese "Gothic and Lolita" subculture and the distinctive so-called gothloli style that mixes youth, doll-like looks, and feminist defiance. This trend vividly evokes childlike innocence, but does so toward politically and sexually subversive ends. Bernal highlights how the gothloli plays into a fantasy of the sexualized girlish woman, but uses that very position—and its highly suggestive fashions—to stage a provocative form of cultural protest against rigid sexual and social roles for women. Existing on the edge of objectification and autonomy, the gothloli pose a fashion dilemma that reveals the inherent political tensions of sexuality.

Section II—Fashion Choices: The Ethics of Consumption, Production, and Style

The essays in Section II introduce fashion's ethical dimension by highlighting the competing values that are invoked by style. Veiling, bridal gowns, and steampunk cosplay, for instance, raise important issues about the limits of our freedom to wear whatever—or to be whomever—we want. Paying special attention to the local settings and political conditions under which fashion choices are made, the authors in this section question the asymmetries of power and varying degrees of agency and restriction that are both reproduced and possibly transformed by fashion.

Section II begins with Jan C. Kreidler's essay, "Glam *Abaya*: Contemporary Emirati Couture," which grapples with the tension that erupts when fashion trends mix sexuality with modesty, and the mash-up when so-called modernity faces tradition. Kreidler takes readers to the United Arab Emirates where emerging trends in fashion reflect profound economic and social changes in the Gulf region. Among wealthy Emirati, Kreidler observes that veiling styles are becoming increasingly *haute*. Fashioning *abayat* in attention-getting, often overtly sexualized ways seems to throw into question what some consider to be the "true" meaning of veiling practices: to show modesty and deflect (masculine) sexual attention in heteronormative economies of desire. While significant in terms of understanding the range of global fashion and the varying ways in which gendered politics play out on women's bodies, there is also much to be learned through attention to this paradox of simultaneously hiding women's bodies in ways that draw attention to female sexuality, women as gatekeepers of sexual desire, and presumed male sex-right access to women's bodies.

Evangeline M. Heiliger poses questions about social justice through consumerism in "Ado(red), Abhor(red), Disappea(red): Fashioning Race, Poverty, and Morality under Product (Red)™." Heiliger highlights the making of the consumer in the act of consumption, noting the tension evoked when "shopping for social change" reinstates hierarchies among people and nations. Using the popular Product (Red) apparel line as an example of ethical consumerism in the sphere of fashion, Heiliger expands the meaning of "fashionable" in her reading of the ways Product (Red) makes shopping for a cause stylish. The cultural capital that accrues to the ethical shopper becomes an integral part of the success of (Red), drawing the first-world consumer simultaneously closer and farther away from the third-world Others, including the producers of (Red), whom her consumption acts are meant to support.

Catherine Spooner investigates the complex relationship between femininity and fur in "The Lady Is a Vamp: The Cultural Politics of Fur." Analyzing Cruella de Vil in both the original 1956 depiction in Dodie Smith's novel, *The Hundred and One Dalmatians,* and subsequent iterations in film adaptations, Spooner finds that fur functions as a powerful symbol for non-maternal feminine wickedness, lust, and vanity. This symbolism extends beyond Cruella de Vil to contemporary icons of feminine and feminist style, as revealed by attitudes about fur and fashion, feminist discourses of animal rights, and debates over fur in the fashion industry.

Shifting from the politics of fur to the politics of weddings, Elline Lipkin poses important questions about Judeo-Christian marriage rituals. In "Something Borrowed, Something Blue: What's an Indie Bride to Do?" Lipkin grapples with whether we can fully jettison the heteronormative and patriarchal foundations of marriage just by calling our own wedding fashions and rituals "alternative." With the passage of legislation around the United States both legalizing and de-legalizing marriage rights for same-sex couples—along with powerful arguments against the normalizing force of marriage by numerous queer scholars—Lipkin's essay reminds us of the politics deeply embedded in how we literally fashion love.

Authors Diana M. Pho and Jaymee Goh investigate the production of hybrid identity through steampunk, a style that takes its cues from times past. Borrowing elements of Victorian fashion, Gothic romance, and even cyberpunk and sci-fi, steampunks find pleasure and novelty in making something new from something old. The elements that steampunks borrow, however, are saturated with meaning from their colonial origins. In "Steampunk: Stylish Subversion and Colonial Chic," Pho and Goh therefore question whether steampunk can, in the present, fully override the past, or if the past remains with us, even in new combinations. In particular, Pho and Goh wonder about the vestigial impact of steampunk's colonialist influence on steampunks of color who are members of historically colonialized groups.

In "DIY Fashion and Going *Bust*: Wearing Feminist Politics in the Twenty-First Century" Jo Reger argues that examining appearance norms, specifically those of fashion, is key to understanding how contemporary feminists conceptualize the political. Reger explains that through dress, contemporary feminists embrace and reclaim aspects of femininity and sexuality. Reger draws on theories from fashion, feminism, and social movements, utilizing content analysis of the popular feminist magazine *Bust*. Reger argues that contemporary feminists attempt to create an oppositional fashion as a form of political protest. This is done through a style that resists a consumer culture, privileges individuality, and incorporates sexuality. However, this resistance through fashion is made problematic with the commodification of style and the perception that dress is an inadequate (and therefore controversial) form of feminist activism. Reger concludes by discussing how contemporary feminists continue to present a form of social resistance written out on the body and expressed both communally and individually.

Finally, in "Stylish Contradiction: Mix-and-Match as the Fashion of Feminist Ambivalence," Marjorie Jolles asks "what a feminist looks like," and gets her answer in the popular trend of mix-and-match. Jolles detects traces of a contemporary feminist celebration of personal contradiction in the ways modern American femininity is performed in fashion. Drawing from popular and public culture, Jolles finds that this contemporary feminist reconfiguration of the self as collage has been absorbed in mainstream fashion rhetoric, whereby women are encouraged to mirror their inner heterogeneity with exaggeratedly eclectic looks. Taking a critical look at contradiction as something to be used rather than just celebrated, Jolles asks readers to consider what political and material contexts might be shaping contemporary notions of the feminine and feminist self as inherently split, ambivalent, and contradictory.

Together, the essays in this book make clear that fashion is both a tool of agency and source of constraint. In addition, fashion is, crucially, about time. Fashion is both temporally self-aware ("new for spring!") and historicized, marked by time ("those legwarmers are so '80s!"). As Fred Davis observes, "the very same apparel ensemble that 'said' one thing last year will 'say' something quite different today and yet another thing this year."[13] The success of fashion is that it strikes the right note between familiar and new—fashion evokes nostalgia, fashion celebrates innovation.

Uniforms, fads, fashion icons, and creative cues shift over time. The Vivienne Westwoods and Jason Wus, the RuPauls and Lady Gagas of the world will come and go, and there will always be a new fashionista, It-designer, or style icon to herald new trends. What remain intractable and politically pressing are the bigger issues at the heart of this collection that the icons and iconoclasts of a particular moment represent: globalization, cultural imperatives of self-expression, dilemmas of sexualization that trade on racial and gender politics, co-optation and cultural appropriation, and visual rhetorics of social change. These essays provoke critical thought about the cultural and political life of fashion while challenging binary assumptions that force us to pick a side when it comes to issues of consumption and production, tradition and modernity, sexuality and innocence, novelty and normalcy, authenticity and irony, autonomy and conformity, and embodiment and ideas. *Fashion Talks* uses twenty-first-century trends and styles to grapple with the philosophical paradox between freedom and expression, conformity and constraint: political tensions that are captured by fashion, yet transcend it.

Notes

1. See Susan Bordo, *Unbearable Weight: Feminism, Western Culture, and the Body* (Berkeley, CA: University of California Press, 1993) and Susan Bordo, *Twilight Zones: The Hidden Life of Cultural Images from Plato to O. J.* (Berkeley, CA: University of California Press, 1997); Anne Hollander, *Seeing Through Clothes* (Berkeley, CA: University of California Press, 1993); Angela McRobbie, "Bridging the Gap: Feminism, Fashion and Consumption," *Feminist Review* 55 (1997): 73–89; Marianne Conroy, "Discount Dreams: Factory Outlet Malls, Consumption, and the Performance of Middle-Class Identity," *Social Text* 54 (1998): 63–83; Anne M. Cronin, "Consumerism and 'Compulsory Individuality': Women, Will, and Potential," in *Transformations: Thinking Through Feminism*, eds. Sara Ahmed, et al. (London: Routledge, 2000), 273–287.

2. Fred Davis, *Fashion, Culture, and Identity* (Chicago: The University of Chicago Press, 1992), 8.

3. See, for example, Theresa M. Winge, " 'Green Is the New Black': Celebrity Chic and the 'Green' Commodity Fetish," *Fashion Theory: The Journal of Dress, Body & Culture* 12, no. 4 (2008): 511–524.

4. Etsy.com, "What is Etsy?" http://www.etsy.com/about.php.

5. It is worth noting that roughly 96 percent of Etsy producers/sellers are women, whose average age is 35. The majority of sellers are college-educated, middle-class, and married. Sara Mosle, "Etsy.com Peddles a False Feminist Fantasy," *Slate,* June 10, 2009, http://www.doublex.com/section/work/etsycom-peddles-false-feminist-fantasy.

6. Ibid.

7. Shira Tarrant, "New Blouse, New House, I Need a New Spouse: The Politics of Transformation and Identity in Television Makeover and Swap Shows," in *Fix Me Up: Essays on Television Dating and Makeover Shows*, ed. Judith Lancioni (Jefferson, NC: McFarland Publishing, 2010), 171–181.

8. Cronin, "Consumerism and 'Compulsory Individuality,' " 275.

9. Cressida J. Heyes, *Self-Transformations: Foucault, Ethics, and Normalized Bodies* (New York: Oxford University Press, 2007), 134.

10. Judith Butler, *Gender Trouble: Feminism and the Subversion of Identity* (New York: Routledge, 1990), 139.

11. Ladelle McWhorter, *Bodies and Pleasures: Foucault and the Politics of Sexual Normalization* (Bloomington, IN: Indiana University Press, 1999), 190.

12. Jenee Desmond-Harris, "Why Michelle Obama's Hair Matters," *Time*, September 7, 2009, http://www.time.com/time/magazine/article/0,9171,1919147-1,00.html.

13. Davis, *Fashion, Culture, and Identity*, 6.

1

Dressing the Body

The Politics of Gender and Sexuality

Chapter 1

Fashioning a Feminist Style, Or, How I Learned to Dress from Reading Feminist Theory

Astrid Henry

The suit was gold and black, a shiny, iridescent weave that caught the light. It achieved the greatest of thrift store miracles: its skirt and jacket had together survived their long journey, from the department store where they had originally been purchased in the early 1960s, to the give-away bag where they ended up a decade or two later, to the used clothing bins where they were sorted, to the rack at my local vintage store where I had snatched them up. What first caught my eye was the jacket. It bore a striking resemblance to the one Madonna wore in *Desperately Seeking Susan*—the one that she eventually traded for a pair of boots and that Rosanna Arquette's "Roberta" bought in order to emulate Madonna's "Susan." It was the summer of 1985, and I had just seen the film and was in love with all things Madonna. I already owned a wrist full of black rubber bracelets, knee-length black leggings, and pointy-toed, black flat boots just like the ones Madonna wore in the "Lucky Star" video. Now I would have my very own *Desperately Seeking Susan* jacket, just in time for my departure for New York where I was about to start college.

Throughout college my Madonna obsession remained intact, but my style went through some changes. The gold-and-black vintage suit was now worn with 1950s-style prescription glasses, as I modeled myself after a character from an old *Perry Mason* rerun to create what I dubbed my "court stenographer" look. Later, the suit moved to the back of my closet, and a faded Black Sabbath T-shirt would be worn—ironically, of course, as I was no heavy metal fan—with rolled-up jeans and combat boots. When graduation day finally came, I wore a flowered, vintage shift dress with heavy men's shoes, the toes of which were filled with toilet paper in order make them fit. And of course I wore a lot of black, the look of all Sarah Lawrence students in the 1980s.

I tell this story because my introduction to feminist theory was both literally and symbolically connected to fashion, and this connection has also shaped my development as a feminist theorist. As an undergraduate, I explored feminist ideas with the same approach that I took to scrounging in thrift stores: discover something, try it out, see if it fit, and if it did, make it a part of my style. I tried on Marxist feminism, psychoanalytic feminism, and Mary Daly. Some theories suited other people more than me, some fit well, and some were just uncomfortable. The writings of the Redstockings and other radical feminist groups of the late 1960s and early 1970s were a perfect fit: I loved the bold, daring, and outrageous language of their manifestoes.

The fashion of the women who wrote these feminist works also captivated me. Looking at photos from the 1968 Miss America protest, it wasn't just the words on their demonstration signs that caught my eye: Look at those great dresses! That necklace is amazing! I wish I had a pair of sandals like that! These were hip feminists, women who were definitely in on the joke as they paraded a crowned sheep down the Atlantic City boardwalk to "parody the way the contestants (all women) are appraised and judged like animals at a county fair."[1] They were protesting the confines of traditional femininity, but they were doing it with flair and with great outfits. I admired them for their style—both in politics and in clothes.

Andrea Dworkin best represents how feminist ideas and fashion came together to shape my feminist identity and how they intertwine to pose important theoretical questions. When I discovered Dworkin's work in college, I quickly read everything by her that I could get my hands on. She seduced me with her over-the-top rhetoric and her unmitigated view of gender relations. I remember sitting in my dorm room reading *Intercourse*, her 1987 book about, well, sexual intercourse, in which she describes heterosexual intercourse as a fundamental part of male domination of women: "intercourse distorts and ultimately destroys any potential human equality between men and women by turning women into objects and men into exploiters."[2] Her language was combative and direct, offering no room for exceptions. "[G]etting fucked and being owned are inseparably the same." "[M]ost men have controlling power over what they call *their* women—the women they fuck. The power is predetermined by gender, by being male."[3] As a young feminist trying to develop my own writing voice, my own style of expression, I found Dworkin's certainty and confidence compelling.

Shortly after this discovery, I saw a picture of Andrea Dworkin. She was fat and did nothing to disguise this fact. Wearing her trademark overalls and with hair that looked like it hadn't been brushed in a while, she exemplified a certain kind of feminist style that, like her writing, seemed to say, "I don't give a fuck what you think of me." Her defiantly un-coiffed image corresponded to her ideas on femininity, first articulated in *Woman Hating*, in which she writes: "Plucking the eyebrows, shaving under the arms, wearing a girdle, learning to walk in high-heeled shoes, having one's nose fixed, straightening or curling one's hair—these things *hurt*. The pain, of course, teaches an important lesson: no price is too great, no process too repulsive, no operation too painful for the woman who would be beautiful."[4] The cost of femininity, the cost of beauty, was pain, and here was a woman who said, "I'm not going to be part of this system."

As Ariel Levy writes, "When most people think of Andrea Dworkin, they think of two things: overalls and the idea that all sex is rape."[5] As a college student, I already wondered about the relationship between these two things, the overalls and the ideas, and since then I am increasingly convinced of the connections and conflicts between clothes and feminist theory. In her 2002 autobiography, *Heartbreak: The Political Memoir of a Feminist Militant*, Dworkin only mentions her signature style once, in the preface,

Image 1.1. Andrea Dworkin.

when she writes: "So here's the deal as I see it: I am ambitious—God knows, not for the money; in most respects but not all I am honorable; and I wear overalls: kill the bitch."[6] While her memoir chronicles her life from childhood, it contains no further details as to what made her decide to wear—apparently almost every day—this particular clothing item. Yet in the brief, prefatory self-portrait, overalls are mentioned with ambition and honor: central to how she defines herself ("the deal as I see it") and to the opposition she faces, whether real or imagined ("kill the bitch"). Designed to protect one's shirt from dirt, overalls are a particularly utilitarian form of clothing, an item not usually associated with either ambition or honor. Were the overalls meant to downplay her ambition, to signal that she wasn't in it "for the money"?[7] Overalls were also originally designed for men, and unlike other styles of pants they seem deliberately asexual, disguising the body behind their denim. Were Dworkin's overalls meant to indicate that she had successfully stepped outside of what Sandra Bartky terms the "fashion-beauty complex," with its required vigilant self-monitoring of female bodies and appearance?[8] Thinking back to what first captivated me about Dworkin's writing, I find Dworkin's fashion choice is as much a rejection of social norms of "women's wear" as her writing is a rejection of liberal pleas for equality. But her flippant aside about wearing overalls suggests that clothes nonetheless express something important about a theorist, even one who critiques the social conventions of feminine style.

As an undergraduate, I went through my Dworkin phase—I even had a pair of overalls—but ultimately neither her rhetorical nor her fashion style stuck with me. The overalls, I concluded, were horribly unflattering; they had a way of making me (or *anyone*) look shapeless, and the style made me feel like a kid. Overalls looked good on little children and on Andrea Dworkin, but not on me. I still preferred vintage women's clothing, with its evocation of the glamorous (if prefeminist) good-old-days when people never left the house without being "dressed." Dworkin's arguments also lost their sway. Her view of penetrative sex bore little relationship to my own experience; her view of men as inherently different from women made little sense to me. And then there was her writing style with all of its unqualified arguments. ("Strong writing but repetitive argument," my undergraduate self wrote on the inside cover of *Right-Wing Women*.) What had originally captivated me now troubled me. I found myself seeking other types of feminist theories: ones that could ask complicated questions without providing easy answers; ones that could express ambiguities, contradictions, and a lack of certainty; ones that could address female pleasure as well as female oppression. And, yes, ones that would take note of the significance of clothing.

In fact, the case of Andrea Dworkin points to a fundamental divide within feminist thought since its inception: whether to focus on women's oppression and lack of power or whether to focus on women's agency and potential.[9] As one scholar notes in summing up this divide:

> On the one hand, feminism is about the oppression of women. Women are not treated fairly in the world, and feminism attempts to remedy that: feminism thus necessarily speaks of women's misfortune. If women were not disadvantaged and disempowered, there would be no need for feminism. On the other hand, feminism is about women's potential. If feminism could envision only women's lack of power, it would be a recipe for hopelessness rather than a dream that energizes us to change our lives and make the world better for women. Thus, feminism must speak of women's possibilities. If women were always and everywhere completely downtrodden, there would never have been any feminism. This is the double foundation of feminism.[10]

As Dworkin's work illustrates, this debate has been most visible in feminist theorizing on sexuality, articulated as a divide between the dangers and pleasures of sexuality.[11] One position argues that sexuality is dangerous for women: central to the maintenance of female oppression, a site of coercive power over their lives, and filled with violence and bodily harm. Another asserts that sexuality is pleasurable for women: central to definitions of selfhood, a site of human connection and joy, and a venue by which to exert agency and self-expression.

While the pleasures and dangers of fashion may have lower stakes than those of sexuality, the feminist debates around fashion are constructed around similar questions of women's agency and autonomy. Many feminists have argued that fashion is a means of controlling women and keeping them trapped in a feminine, and thus subservient, position in relation to men.[12] This view is already expressed in 1949 when Simone de Beauvoir in *The Second Sex* writes that for a woman: "The purpose of the fashions to which she is enslaved is not to reveal her as an independent individual, but rather to cut her off from her transcendence in order to offer her as prey to male desires."[13] Beauvoir's critique was repeated by the second-wave feminists who came after her a generation later. In her 1984 book *Femininity*, for example, author-activist Susan Brownmiller describes feminine fashion as central to maintaining gender difference and thus female oppression. As she writes, "To the Western mind the grouping of men in trousers and women in skirts is something akin to a natural order, as basic to the covenant of masculine/feminine difference as the short hair/long hair proposition." She adds, "I suppose it is asking too much of women to give up their chief outward expression of the feminine difference, their continuing reassurance to men and to themselves that a male is a male because a female dresses and looks and acts like another sort of creature."[14] Throughout her discussion of clothes, Brownmiller makes a strong case that when women wear trousers they are challenging the gender binary, obscuring the differences between men and women and thus, according to her argument, lessening the oppression of women.[15] Women wearing pants, it would seem, is central to eliminating sexism. Thus, as Brownmiller puts it, in the 1970s "it became a feminist statement to wear pants."[16]

Brownmiller's argument in favor of pants recalls Dworkin's justification for overalls and shows that the clothing we deem "unisex"—and thus gender neutral—has traditionally come out of men's wardrobes. For all intents and purposes, when we say androgynous clothing we mean male clothing, even though the common definition of androgynous is something "neither distinguishably masculine nor feminine."[17] In other words, when a woman dresses "like a man" she becomes androgynous, but when a man dresses "like a woman" he becomes feminine. Men's clothing worn by women thus symbolizes a rejection of femininity on two levels: as its masculine opposite *and* as its "gender-free" alternative. When some second-wave feminists "argued that

Image 1.2. Simone de Beauvoir.

it was necessary to reject feminine fashion by adopting masculine dress," they were claiming both the "masculine privilege" that came with such clothing and the feminist vision of a gender-free world that it symbolized.[18] This turn to masculine/androgynous fashion solidified the idea that it is *feminine* clothing—and all the accoutrements of femininity, including shoes, jewelry, and makeup—that stands in the way of women's liberation.

As someone who loves dresses, skirts, and high heels, I've always been puzzled by this form of feminist thinking on fashion. Why reject the variety and beauty of feminine clothing in favor of the drab uniform of traditional masculine dress? Or, to quote Natasha Walter, why "demand from women that they become clones of the least imaginative male dressers"?[19] Yet I recognize my position—that is, my ability to don feminine fashion styles without anxiety—is largely generational. Third-wave feminist Jeannine DeLombard captures this generational difference when she writes, in her essay "Femmenism": "Unlike my first- and second-wave predecessors, no one force-fed me femininity. On the contrary, I had to fight for it tooth and nail."[20] As I think back to that vintage gold-and-black suit I wore in college, I remember the stiffness of its fabric, its lack of elasticity, and the way the skirt made it hard to walk too fast or with my usual clunky stride. If I had grown up in the 1950s and been required to wear a skirt every day to school, would I love them the way I do today? Forced to dress in a feminine style, perhaps I would have reached for the trousers celebrated by Brownmiller or for the overalls endorsed by Dworkin. As the passage from DeLombard illustrates, one generation may be "force-fed" femininity, while the next is prescribed androgynous jeans and T-shirts. Growing up in the 1970s and the 1980s, I was surrounded by different standards of proper female dress. Traditional femininity provided one style to emulate, while feminism provided another. Wendy Chapkis notes that feminism created a "set of standards against which we can measure ourselves and find ourselves wanting: those of the model feminist. The model feminist haunts us with her lack of concern over being attractive."[21] In other words, for those of us who were raised after the 1960s, the rebellion that an earlier generation found in pants, practical shoes, and short haircuts could now be found in girlie skirts, stiletto heels, and long hair.

While the masculine dress imperative became one of feminism's fashion tenets in the 1960s and 1970s, many "ideologies about dress that have circulated within the women's movement seem never to have been made explicit," writes Elizabeth Wilson.[22] Moreover, adds Pamela Church Gibson, "there has been no real academic confrontation" over the relationship between feminism and fashion "as there has in the case of, say, pornography."[23] While feminist debates about fashion and sex seem to share some of the same concerns, one of these debates has been much more visible than the other. Ironically, it is clothing that has remained "in the closet" while sexuality in all its forms has been openly debated by feminists over the last forty years. As in the feminist debates about sexuality, however, the arguments about fashion are divided into what appear to be two mutually exclusive positions, with no apparent middle ground between them. Wilson sums up these two sides in *Adorned in Dreams: Fashion and Modernity*: "the thesis is that fashion is oppressive, the antithesis that we find it pleasurable; again no synthesis. In all these arguments the alternatives posed are between moralism and hedonism; either doing your own thing is okay, or else it convicts you of false consciousness."[24]

In addition to criticizing femininity as oppressive, late-twentieth-century feminist theory also faults fashion for its artifice and its expense. The argument against artifice is rooted in a 1960s ideal in which what is good is what is "natural." Fashion and other forms of "artificial" adornment take us away from our "natural" state. What this "natural" state entails, however, is rarely made clear. Linda Scott argues in *Fresh Lipstick: Redressing Fashion and Feminism* that "[e]xactly what counted as natural was only defined in negative terms: 'natural' is what we would look like if we did not wear corsets, hoop skirts, lipstick, push-up bras, or whatever the latest bugaboo happened to be. The alternative was presumed to be self-evident. 'Natural' is what we would look like if we weren't forced to spend so many hours and use so many products making ourselves presentable. 'Natural' is the absence of artifice."[25] As Wilson explains with added precision, this approach privileges "the 'natural' as superior to the 'artificial' (as if the concept of human culture were not artificial)," and has "confused the natural with simplicity, and so the uncorrupt."[26] Femininity, in this view, exemplifies "artificiality," while masculinity—apparently always unadorned and therefore absent of artifice—represents the "natural." This position was quickly critiqued by other feminists who argued that there is no "natural" or "pure" realm to which feminists can retreat from the socially-constructed fashion system. As Scott so astutely puts it, "What is natural for human beings is artifice."[27]

Adding a layer of political critique about artifice and authenticity is the monetary cost of fashion. This critique of fashion's expense stems from the larger socialist critique of capitalism and consumerism. In this argument, the material costs of participating in fashion culture are too high—no matter the psychological costs for a woman's self-esteem. According to Angela McRobbie, "The original argument was that the academic left including feminists too often felt the need to disavow their own participation in some of *the pleasures of consumer culture* for the reasons that these were the very epitome of capitalism and also one of the sources of women's oppression. This produced a culture of puritanism giving rise only to guilty pleasures."[28] Spending any amount of money on clothes, under this logic, contributes to the consumerist system that oppresses women. Yet, if we follow the anti-consumerist feminist argument to its logical conclusion, it doesn't necessarily lead us to a world in which we would all end up wearing trousers or overalls. As one writer notes, "a feminist whose main motivation was to put as little time and money into [her clothes] as possible should presumably go around in the first and cheapest thing she could find in a jumble sale, even if it happened to be a shapeless turquoise Crimplene dress with a pink cardigan."[29] In other words, there is no necessary link between low cost and masculine dress. If thriftiness were the only driving force behind the anti-consumerist approach, we would see much more variety—and presumably much more traditionally feminine clothing—in the "model feminist fashion" style.

Feminists who have written about fashion since the 1980s have stressed the ways in which the women's movement of the 1960s and 70s produced its own "strict dress codes."[30] Ironically, while much of the early second-wave critique of fashion was directed at its prescriptive feminine norms, these critiques created their own fashion imperative: "Blue jeans, sensible shoes and an unmasked face."[31] Some argued that the idea of a singular fashion style to which every good feminist should now conform seemed to go against the greater freedom and diversity of expression sought by the women's movement. Elizabeth Wilson points out that "[i]f liberated dress meant doing your own thing, no one ever commented on how strange it was that everyone wanted to do the *same* thing."[32] An inevitable backlash against this prescriptive norm emerged, leading us out of what sociologist Lynn Chancer has called feminism's "protest stage," where beauty is "viewed as indeed part and parcel of women's general subordination," and into a "beauty myth stage," in which the goal has been to democratize, diversify, and reform our notions of beauty.[33]

Since the mid-1990s, feminists of all generations have argued for a more inclusive and expansive vision of beauty—as well as of feminist style—rather than a wholesale rejection of beauty or fashion as inherently oppressive to women.[34] There has been a "perceived and gradual relaxation of feminist attitudes to dress over the past twenty years," writes Pamela Church Gibson, adding that "as the effects of feminism are increasingly felt within the dominant culture, and the struggles are no longer felt to be taking place from the margins, so the sense that women must declare themselves through an oppositional style has faded."[35] Part of this shift in attitude can be attributed to the cyclical changes built into the lifespan of both fashion *and* feminist theory. As Coco Chanel once famously said, "fashion is made to become unfashionable." Theory, too, goes in and out of fashion. Anti-femininity theory seems as dated today as the bell bottoms once worn by its advocates. Yet if the comparison between fashion and theory holds true, then theory, like fashion, can also come back into style. My love of late-1960s radical feminist manifestoes, then, may be like my passion for 1960s vintage clothing: both occurred in the late 1980s when these things were already out of style.[36]

Along with a renewed interest in femininity—in both its ironic and sincere forms—the last two decades have also witnessed an increasing examination of masculinity by feminist and queer scholars, such that we no longer treat masculinity—nor masculine clothing—as an un-gendered norm, as Susan Brownmiller appears to do in *Femininity*. Scholars in the field of masculinity studies have called our attention to the ways in which masculinity, like femininity, is a gender role with its own norms, values, and fashion rules, thus making it impossible to view clothing deemed "masculine" as "natural" or artifice-free. Poststructuralist theory in a variety of forms has increased our awareness of the fact that there is no "outside" to which feminists can retreat to escape the signification of clothing. Yet "it is never possible simply to 'opt out' of the discourse of dress. No one can dress in a way that signifies nothing."[37] One may be "fashion indifferent," an "anti-fashionist," or crazy about fashion. But regardless, writes Gibson, "Whether women follow current trends, ignore them and create their own style, are relatively uninterested in 'fashion' as such, or have little, if any, money to spend on clothes, they nevertheless, by the simple act of getting dressed in the morning, participate in the process of fashion."[38] And finally, a growing awareness of the performativity of all gender identities—whether feminine or masculine, normative or transgressive—has lessened the meaning of any one particular "costume" worn in any one particular performance of gender.[39] We are all performing gender whether we are wearing cocktail dresses or overalls.

I first read Brownmiller's *Femininity* as an undergraduate, and when I recently returned to my heavily-underlined copy of the book I was struck by a passage which I had not only underlined twice but had also put a large star next to in the margins. The passage reads: "Whatever a woman puts on, it is likely to be *a costume*, whether it is fur, white lace, a denim skirt or black leather pants."[40] My college-self agreed with Brownmiller's negative view of costumes, which Brownmiller sees as part of the artificiality of feminine clothing. Yet, I also enjoyed wearing costumes, putting together outfits for different occasions, seeing each day as an opportunity for a new look. As I reread this passage in Brownmiller today—and having worn all the "costumes" she lists, with the exception of white lace—I am struck by what was missing in much of the feminist theory I read as a college student in the late 1980s. Where was the pleasure, the fun, and the joy in dressing? Where was the sense of adventure that came from putting on a variety of outfits? As Brownmiller herself notes, "Straight-legged pants are boring. One cannot take on a new identity by changing trousers."[41]

In my junior year I discovered a book that changed my view of feminism—and of feminism's relationship to fashion. The book was Wendy Chapkis's *Beauty Secrets: Women and the Politics of Appearance*, published in 1986. In it, Chapkis both presents and analyzes interviews she conducted with women about their relationship to their bodies, to beauty, and to fashion. Citing Brownmiller's lament that she "mourn[s] her old dresses" and misses "the graceful flow of fabric, the gentle, gathered shapes and pretty colors," Chapkis asks, "How did women's *liberation* end up on the side of the sensible over the sexual, the 'efficient, upright, and honest' over the colorful and fun? Though women did not create the opposition between the sexy and the self-respecting, the sensuous and the serious, we often—even in our rebellion—have accepted these qualities as mutually exclusive."[42] Chapkis' *Beauty Secrets* offered a new way to view the relationship between my two great loves, feminism and fashion, and provided me with a theoretical paradigm by which to combine them. She stressed the value of fashion diversity within feminism, making it clear that there is no one right way to dress as a feminist:

> The practical, functional and comfortable are beginning to assume their rightful place in a woman's closet. . . . But perhaps now, as our culture slowly makes room for women's needs and desires, our wardrobe can expand to include elements of style beyond those appropriate to battle dress. It will be an indication of our growing strength if accessories suitable to a feminist fashion come to include rhinestone earrings and metal studs, leather ties, silver shoes, a strapped on dildo or a lacy bra, lipstick shining sensually on a mouth framed by a downy moustache, a brightly colored skirt worn comfortably over hairy legs of either sex. Such a move toward a more colorful revolution would serve to enhance our awareness that liberation is more than a settling of grievances and remind us that pleasure and creativity are among the goals and tools of our long term political project.[43]

Chapkis helped me to understand that the pleasure—including sexual pleasure—that came from clothing did not have to be denied in order for one to be a critical, leftist feminist; more than that, she stressed that pleasure—both in fashion and in sex—is valuable in and of itself.[44]

The memoirs of feminist theorists show that, even if they just wear overalls, feminists use clothes to define their identities and the eras that have shaped them. Nancy Miller says that "it's precisely the personal details of skirts, hair, shoes that make cultural history come alive: the inclusion of those daily issues of style that define a moment in a collective social pattern."[45] Take, for example, Audre Lorde's 1982 "biomythography," *Zami: A New Spelling of My Name*. In it, Lorde routinely describes the clothing that she wore at different points in her life, as well as the clothing worn by others.

Clothing details are also central to her depiction of 1950s lesbian culture in which "[c]lothes were often the most important way of broadcasting one's chosen sexual role."[46] In one passage, for example, Lorde describes the different types of clothing that made up her early adulthood wardrobe:

> When I lived in Stamford, I had worn old dungarees and men's shirts to work. . . . When I lived in Mexico, I wore the full peasant skirts and blouses so readily available in the marketplaces of Cuernavaca. Now I had my straight clothes for working at the library—two interchangeable outfits of skirts, sweaters, and a warm-weather blouse or two. I had a pair of shoes for work, and a flamboyantly cut woolen suit which I had made out of the old coat my sister had give me to wear at my father's funeral . . . I had very few clothes for my real life, but with the addition of Muriel's quixotic wardrobe, we developed quite a tidy store of what the young gay-girl could be seen in. Mostly I wore blue or black dungarees which were increasingly being called *jeans*. I fell in love with a pair of riding pants which Muriel gave me, and they became my favorite attire. They became my uniform, along with cotton shirts, usually striped.[47]

With its detail about Lorde's different outfits for her different "selves," this passage evokes one of the major themes of *Zami*, namely that "we could not afford to settle for one easy definition, one narrow individuation of self. At the Bag, at Hunter College, uptown in Harlem, at the library, there was a piece of the real me bound in each place, and growing."[48] Throughout her memoir, Lorde uses clothes to symbolize these "pieces" of herself, and her eclectic and expanding wardrobe reflects her theory of the complexity of identity.

In *Zami*, Lorde also celebrates the artifice of clothes, such as when she dresses up in costumes to go on city adventures with her high school best friend Gennie. "We took hours and hours attiring each other," Lorde writes, "sometimes changing entire outfits at the last minute to become two different people . . . Bandits, Gypsies, Foreigners of all degree, Witches, Whores, and Mexican Princess—there were appropriate costumes for every role, and appropriate places in the city to go to play them out."[49] Rather than viewing these costumes as obstacles to discovering her true self, as Brownmiller might suggest, Lorde sees them as giving her and Gennie the opportunity to "play out" different roles and live out different experiences. As such, clothes are central to her process of self-discovery.

A particularly memorable scene involving clothing comes early in the memoir, when Lorde is just four years old. Sitting on the steps outside of her Harlem apartment building, young Audre notices an even younger girl, *can be seen as a way to justify, but is a carefully considered study of...*

"gaudy" or oppressive clothes as well as the consumerist lifestyle needed to maintain...

Toni, who is wearing "the most beautiful outfit I had ever seen in my not quite five years of clothes-watching": "an unbelievable wine-red velvet coat with a wide, wide skirt that flared out over dainty little lisle-stockinged legs. Her feet were clad in a pair of totally impractical, black patent–leather mary-jane shoes, whose silver buckles glinted merrily in the drab noon light." Toni also sports a "white fur muff" that Audre slips her hands into and that enables her to feel the warmth of Toni's skin.[50] This erotic description of the encounter between the girls forms an early memory—or is it a self-created "myth"?—that foreshadows teenage Audre's coming out as a lesbian. It also evokes Lorde's classic 1978 essay, "Uses of the Erotic: The Erotic as Power," in which she describes "the power which comes from sharing deeply any pursuit with another person," including the "sharing of joy."[51] *Zami* provides an important illustration of how women can share joy, and thus find power, through wearing and sharing clothing.

Another feminist who has used the memoir genre to write extensively about fashion is bell hooks. In *Wounds of Passion: A Writing Life*, which chronicles hooks's experience as both an undergraduate and graduate student, hooks describes her "passion" for fashion. As she writes, "My motto is 'I die for style.'" She continues: "I am especially into fashion. Since I don't have any money, I buy all my clothes and everything else at secondhand stores. Fabrics and fibers intrigue me. I always wear scarves, made from huge blocks of stunning cloth. . . . Silk, cotton, linen, and cashmere—these are my favorites. To find the best things in secondhand stores, I must always be looking. . . . I am into sex and clothes, so I choose clothes made of natural fibers that are earthy and sensual.[52] In *Wounds of Passion*, hooks links her three passions—writing, sex, and fashion—through sensuality and an aesthetic appreciation of beauty, whether that beauty is found in words, a lover's body, or a beautiful item of clothing.[53] Although she claims that "No one writes great poetry about fashion," she attempts to do so in her memoir by using words to bring the erotic power of clothes to life, as in this description of a blouse: "I've found this tight pink rose-colored silk blouse that just has a luscious edible quality to it. When I'm buying it I imagine someone's lips pressed against the coolness of pink silk, sucking gently leaving a stain of wetness that will not spread but stays in place."[54] Tight, pink, and silk, this blouse is a decidedly feminine piece of clothing, deliberately chosen to evoke desire rather than repel it.[55]

My own approach to feminist theory, and to fashion, took a new turn when, as a graduate student, I first read the work of feminist theorist Jane Gallop. Her writing is bold like Andrea Dworkin's and, like Dworkin, she writes about sexuality in an explicit way. But in every other respect, Dworkin and Gallop represent different types of feminism—and different types of feminist style. This is particularly evident in Gallop's writings on the male body, which greatly contrast with Dworkin's views in *Intercourse*. In order "to affirm a woman's desire," Gallop writes that we need to see male sexuality beyond its "idealized" phallic form, the drive to possess and dominate described by Dworkin.[56] If Gallop demands what she terms "bodily masculinity" to affirm women's heterosexual desire, she also appropriates feminine clothing as an expression of women's power.[57] In a preface to an essay on the female body in feminist theory, she describes what she wore when she first presented the work at a colloquium at Columbia University, where she was to be the only feminist speaker: "I dressed in a manner that bespoke the body as style, stylized sexuality. I wore spiked heels, seamed hose, a fitted black forties dress and a large black hat. I was dressed as a woman, but as another woman. . . . I was in drag. My clothing drew attention to my body but at the same time stylized it, creating a stylized body. The fit between the paper and the look, the text and the performance was articulated unconsciously, and it worked."[58] Aware that her body would be on display—a display that would be reinforced by the focus of the talk itself—Gallop performs über-femininity, a stylized performance that calls attention to both the artifice and sensuality of feminine clothing. Her deliberately feminine performance as *the* feminist speaker at the colloquium also echoes what she elsewhere describes as the need to affirm "confusion" and "contradiction." In writing in such a way as to tease out these ambiguities, Gallop provides an important model of how to "do" feminist theory.[59] She also exemplifies how to bring one's whole self into one's writing, clothes and all.

Now a professor myself, I continue to love fashion in a way that sometimes makes me feel like I am in the wrong profession. "Academics are still the worst-dressed middle-class occupational group in America," according to fashion historian Valerie Steele.[60] I teach at a small liberal arts college in the Midwest where most people, male or female, dress five days a week as though it is "casual Friday," and where my attention to style sometimes seems to violate an unwritten code of conduct. I also confront the long-standing debate over whether a woman's interest in clothes detracts from her intelligence and professionalism, something Susan Brownmiller discussed twenty-five years ago in *Femininity*: "Serious women have a difficult time with clothes, not necessarily because they lack a developed sense of style, but because feminine clothes are not designed to project a serious demeanor."[61] Brownmiller's argument can be seen today in the advice given by Emily Toth in her "Ms. Mentor" column for the *Chronicle of Higher Education*. "Today, except in really cold climates, dresses and skirts (knee-length or longer) are a woman's professional uniform. Ms. Mentor also recommends jackets or vests, which connote authority. Young women should not model themselves on fashion magazines, movies, or TV."[62] Interestingly, Toth's advice is for academic women to dress in *feminine* clothing (dresses and skirts) but to make sure that this clothing is dowdy enough (skirts longer than knee-length, *quelle horreur*) so as to "connote authority"—presumably because overt sexuality takes away from one's authority. "If it's a choice between being chic or frumpy, I think it benefits academics more to be frumpy," says Toth. "If you look like you spend too much time on your clothes, there are people who will assume that you haven't put enough energy into your mind."[63]

As a lifelong *Vogue* reader who has also spent considerable time and energy improving my mind, I find Toth's opposition between style and substance not only unnecessary but actually quite wrong. As Jane Gallop has said, "There's a stupid impression that a lack of style signifies seriousness, but anyone who comes from a literary sense of things knows that style is often the best way to convey complicated things."[64] Contrary to Toth, I believe that a lack of style in clothing may signify a lack of style in other parts of one's life, including one's writing. Style in fashion and in prose is important. I was thus delighted when, in the late 1990s, I came across an article in *Vogue* entitled "The Professor Wore Prada," written by the feminist scholar and Princeton professor Elaine Showalter. While some have criticized Showalter for publishing "an embarrassing essay" in which she admits to her love of clothes and clothes shopping, I identify with Showalter and her open display of fashion passion.[65] As Showalter writes, "For years, I've been trying to make the life of the mind coexist with the day at the mall, and to sneak the femme back into feminist."[66] While, so far, I merely read about high-end

Image 1.3. Turban by Prada, Spring/Summer 2007.

designer fashion—I only recently got tenure, after all—I look forward to one day wearing couture as part of my feminist style. I am particularly interested in the Simone de Beauvoir-like turban that Prada showcased during its Spring/ Summer 2007 collection.

So far Prada hasn't come out with any overalls.

Notes

1. Judith Duffett cited in Alice Echols, *Daring to be Bad: Radical Feminism in America, 1967–1975* (Minneapolis, MN: University of Minnesota Press, 1989), 93. It was at this August 1968 protest that feminists threw bras, girdles, high-heeled shoes, and other "instruments of torture to women" into a "Freedom Trash Can," which they had originally intended to set on fire but ultimately didn't because of a prohibition by the Atlantic City fire department. Much of the media coverage of this event focused on the possibility of bras being set on fire, and thus the now infamous euphemism "bra burners" was coined even though no bras were ever set on fire. For more on the Miss America protest, see Echols, *Daring to be Bad*, 92–101.

2. Andrea Dworkin, *Intercourse* (New York: Free Press, 1987), 10.

3. Ibid., 66, 126 (emphasis in original).

4. Andrea Dworkin, *Woman Hating* (New York: Dutton, 1974), 115 (emphasis in original).

5. Ariel Levy, "The Prisoner of Sex," *New York Magazine,* May 29, 2005, http://nymag.com/nymetro/news/people/features/11907.

6. Andrea Dworkin, *Heartbreak: The Political Memoir of a Feminist Militant* (New York: Basic Books, 2002), xvi.

7. In her memoir, Dworkin chronicles her rising success as a national and international speaker, and mentions that she ultimately was able to get what she "needed" in terms of reimbursement, including "the best hotel I could find" and "a first-class ticket." While she faced accusations that such demands suggested she was a "capitalist pig," she learned "that the more money I was paid, the nicer people were . . . when work fell off, when the speaking events dried up, when someone was nasty to me, I just raised my prices. It was bad for the karma but good for this life." Dworkin, *Heartbreak*, 141–143.

8. Sandra Lee Bartky, *Femininity and Domination: Studies in the Phenomenology of Oppression* (New York: Routledge, 1990), 39–43. See also Susan Bordo's point that "The general tyranny of fashion—perpetual, elusive, and instructing the female body in a pedagogy of personal inadequacy and lack—is a powerful discipline for the normalization of *all* women in this culture." Susan Bordo, *Unbearable Weight: Feminism, Western Culture, and the Body* (Berkeley, CA: University of California Press, 1993), 254 (emphasis in original).

9. Dworkin cited in Jennifer Baumgardner and Amy Richards, *Manifesta: Young Women, Feminism, and the Future* (New York: Farrar, Straus and Giroux, 2000), 137.

10. Jane Gallop, *Feminist Accused of Sexual Harassment* (Durham, NC: Duke University Press, 1997), 69.

11. See Carole S. Vance, ed., *Pleasure and Danger: Exploring Female Sexuality* (Boston: Routledge & K. Paul, 1984).

12. For more on the feminist protest against fashion, see Diana Crane, *Fashion and Its Social Agendas: Class, Gender, and Identity in Clothing* (Chicago: University of Chicago Press, 2000), 124; Fred Davis, *Fashion, Culture, and Identity* (Chicago: University of Chicago Press, 1992), 175–78; Joanne Hollows, *Feminism, Femininity and Popular Culture* (Manchester, England: Manchester University Press, 2000), 139–143; Natasha Walter, *The New Feminism* (London: Little, Brown and Co., 1998), 83–105.

13. Simone de Beauvoir, *The Second Sex*, trans. H. M. Parshley (1952; New York: Vintage, 1989), 529. As Carolyn Beckingham writes, while Beauvoir provides a strong critique of feminine fashion, "Every photograph I have seen of her as an adult shows her wearing strongly coloured lipstick and nail varnish." She adds, "Perhaps it would have been socially impossible when *The Second Sex* was first published, but why did she not take up jeans and a scrubbed face in the seventies?" Carolyn Beckingham, *Is Fashion a Woman's Right?* (Brighton, England: Sussex Academic Press, 2005), 12.

14. Susan Brownmiller, *Femininity* (New York: Ballantine Books, 1984), 83, 79.

15. As Brownmiller writes, "Trousers are practical. They cover the lower half of the body without nonsense and permit the freest of natural movements. And therein lies their unfeminine danger." Brownmiller, *Femininity,* 83.

16. Ibid., 80.

17. *The American Heritage College Dictionary*, 3rd ed., s.v. "androgynous."

18. Hollows, *Feminism, Femininity and Popular Culture*, 140; Brownmiller, *Femininity*, 86.

19. Walter, *The New Feminism*, 102.

20. Jeannine DeLombard, "Femmenism," in *To Be Real: Telling the Truth and Changing the Face of Feminism*, ed. Rebecca Walker (New York: Anchor Books, 1995), 33. See also Jennifer Scanlon, who writes, "a number of third wave writers react negatively to what they see as the second wave's call for androgynous performances of gender and its rejection of decidedly feminine fashion practices." Jennifer Scanlon, "Sexy from the Start: Anticipatory Elements of Second Wave Feminism," *Women's Studies* 38, no. 2 (2009): 129. For more on third-wave feminists' embrace of femininity, see the discussion of "Girlie culture" in Baumgardner and Richards, *Manifesta*, 126–166.

21. Wendy Chapkis, *Beauty Secrets: Women and the Politics of Appearance* (Boston, MA: South End Press, 1986), 171.

22. Elizabeth Wilson, *Adorned in Dreams: Fashion and Modernity* (1985; Berkeley, CA: University of California Press, 1987), 230.

23. Pamela Church Gibson, "Redressing the Balance: Patriarchy, Postmodernism and Feminism," in *Fashion Cultures: Theories, Explorations, and Analysis*, eds. Stella Bruzzi and Pamela Church Gibson (London: Routledge, 2000), 352.

24. Wilson, *Adorned in Dreams*, 232.

25. Linda M. Scott, *Fresh Lipstick: Redressing Fashion and Feminism* (New York: Palgrave Macmillan, 2005), 11. See also Naomi Wolf who writes, " 'Natural' and 'unnatural' are not the terms in question. The actual struggle is between pain and pleasure, freedom and compulsion." Naomi Wolf, *The Beauty Myth: How Images of Beauty Are Used Against Women* (New York: William Morrow and Company, Inc., 1991), 273.

26. Wilson, *Adorned in Dreams,* 235.

27. Scott, *Fresh Lipstick,* 12. I completely agree with Scott's critique of how *some* feminists have embraced the "natural" over the "artificial." I disagree strongly, however, with Scott's suggestion that the overwhelming majority of feminist scholars over the last thirty years have also supported the "natural is better" view. Scott need only turn to Wilson's *Adorned in Dreams,* published twenty years prior to Scott's book, to find an excellent feminist critique of the idealization of the "natural." Scott appears to willfully ignore years of feminist scholarship on fashion—including by Wilson, Angela McRobbie, and others—so that her naïve, anti-fashion feminist scholar "straw woman" can stand up.

28. Angela McRobbie, "Bridging the Gap: Feminism, Fashion and Consumption," *Feminist Review* 55 (Spring, 1997): 75 (emphasis added).

29. Janet Radcliffe Richards, *The Sceptical Feminist: A Philosophical Enquiry* (London: Routledge & Kegan Paul, 1980), 184.

30. Danzy Senna, "To Be Real," in *To Be Real: Telling the Truth and Changing the Face of Feminism,* ed. Rebecca Walker (New York: Anchor Books, 1995), 16.

31. Chapkis, *Beauty Secrets,* 177.

32. Elizabeth Wilson adds, "In so far as feminists have dressed differently from other women (and most have not) their style of dress has still borne a close relationship to currently circulating styles." Wilson, *Adorned in Dreams,* 240 (emphasis in original). See also Natasha Walter's question: "How can we trust feminism's traditional promise to release us from the demands of fashion when it seems to trap us into such a precise range of sartorial responses?" Walter, *The New Feminism,* 100–101.

33. This second "beauty myth stage," according to Chancer, is followed by a third: the "beauty debate stage" where feminists argue "whether we are 'for' or 'against'" various beauty practices, such as plastic surgery. Lynn S. Chancer, *Reconcilable Differences: Confronting Beauty, Pornography, and the Future of Feminism* (Berkeley: University of California Press, 1998), 155. See also Wolf, *The Beauty Myth.*

34. See Ophira Edut, ed., *Adiós, Barbie: Young Women Write about Body Image and Identity* (Seattle, WA: Seal Press, 1998); Michelle Tea, ed., *It's so You: 35 Women Write about Personal Expression through Fashion & Style* (Emeryville, CA: Seal Press, 2007). For more on the generational shifts within feminist thinking on fashion, see Beckingham, *Is Fashion a Woman's Right?,* 13; Chancer, *Reconcilable Differences: Confronting Beauty, Pornography, and the Future of Feminism,* 152; Scott, *Fresh Lipstick,* 7–8.

35. Gibson, "Redressing the Balance," 349, 351.

36. For more on the relationship between fashion cycles and life cycles, see Margaret Morganroth Gullette, "The Other End of the Fashion Cycle: Practicing Loss, Learning Decline," in *Figuring Age: Women, Bodies, Generations,* ed. Kathleen M. Woodward (Bloomington, IN: Indiana University Press, 1999), 34–55.

37. Scott, *Fresh Lipstick,* 12.

38. Gibson, "Redressing the Balance," 161–162.

39. See Judith Butler, *Gender Trouble: Feminism and the Subversion of Identity* (New York: Routledge, 1990).

40. Brownmiller, *Femininity,* 101 (emphasis added).

41. Ibid., 181.

42. Ibid., 81; Chapkis, *Beauty Secrets,* 131 (emphasis in original).

43. Chapkis, *Beauty Secrets,* 177.

44. See Chapkis's point that "Artifice-free functional clothing is genderless and often comfortable. It is also unquestionably sensible attire for many activities. But what would functional clothing look like if our intended activity is sex? Mightn't a lacy bra or sheer stockings have erotic appeal less because they are symbols of female *powerlessness* and more because they are familiar symbols of female *sexuality*?" Chapkis, *Beauty Secrets,* 133 (emphasis in original).

45. Nancy K. Miller, *But Enough About Me: Why We Read Other People's Lives* (New York: Columbia University Press, 2002), 57.

46. Audre Lorde, *Zami: A New Spelling of My Name* (Freedom, CA: Crossing Press, 1982), 241. See also the final "Afrekete" chapter of *Zami*, in which Lorde describes in detail the clothes worn by "beautiful Black women in all different combinations of dress" at a party in Harlem.

47. Ibid., 208–209.

48. Ibid., 226.

49. Ibid., 88.

50. Ibid., 38, 37, 38–39.

51. Audre Lorde, "Uses of the Erotic: The Erotic as Power," in *Sister Outsider: Essays and Speeches* (Trumansburg, NY: The Crossing Press, 1984), 56.

52. bell hooks, *Wounds of Passion: A Writing Life* (New York: Henry Holt, 1997), 162, 195–196.

53. See also bell hooks, "Beauty Laid Bare: Aesthetics in the Ordinary," in *To Be Real: Telling the Truth and Changing the Face of Feminism*, ed. Rebecca Walker (New York: Anchor Books, 1995), 157–165.

54. hooks, *Wounds of Passion*, 196–197.

55. It worth noting that the two feminist memoirs I've chosen to write about here are by African-American writers. Like its "sex wars," feminism's "fashion wars" seem to have taken place primarily between white women, and women of color's relationship to fashion has been noticeably missing in discussions of feminist dress. For more on the whiteness of feminism's "sex wars," see Astrid Henry, *Not My Mother's Sister: Generational Conflict and Third-Wave Feminism* (Bloomington, IN: Indiana University Press, 2004), 97. See also Jane Gerhard, *Desiring Revolution: Second-Wave Feminism and the Rewriting of American Sexual Thought, 1920 to 1982* (New York: Columbia University Press, 2001), 115.

56. Jane Gallop, *Thinking Through the Body* (New York: Columbia University Press, 1988), 131 (emphasis added).

57. Ibid., 132.

58. Ibid., 92.

59. Ibid., 132.

60. Steele cited in Alison Schneider, "Frumpy or Chic? Tweed or Kente? Sometimes Clothes Make the Professor," *Chronicle of Higher Education*, January 23, 1998, http://chronicle.com/article/Frumpy-or-Chic-Tweed-or/65194. For more on fashion in academic life and academic women's apparent struggle between exuding intelligence or fashionableness, see Rachel Toor, "Can't We Be Smart and Look Good, Too?" *The Chronicle of Higher Education*, April 3, 2009, http://chronicle.com/article/Can-t-We-Be-SmartLook/9397.

61. Brownmiller, *Femininity,* 101.

62. Emily Toth, *Ms. Mentor's Impeccable Advice for Women in Academia* (Philadelphia: University of Pennsylvania Press, 1997), 124.

63. Toth cited in Schneider, "Frumpy or Chic?"

64. Gallop cited in Schneider, "Frumpy or Chic?"

65. Jane Chance, "The F-Word as 'Fashion': Gendering the Sophomore Survey," *College Literature* 28, no. 2 (2001): 77.

66. Elaine Showalter, "The Professor Wore Prada," *Vogue,* December 1997, 80.

Chapter 2

Dressing Left

Conforming, Transforming, and Shifting Masculine Style

Shira Tarrant

An attention-grabbing movie still from the 2009 summer flick *Brüno*, features an all-male military battalion dressed in uniform and marching in formation.

And by "uniform," I mean butt-hugging hot pants and tight baby Ts.

In the eponymously titled mockumentary, Brüno—played by a self-consciously fey Sacha Baron Cohen—has lost his job as fashion It-boy and embarks upon a series of escapades to restart his career. The short-lived box-office flop controversially (and some would say offensively) went to the heart of propriety and expectations of masculinity by messing with both gender and sexuality through fashion and style.

For instance, at the same time captivating and hilarious, each soldier in the promotional still is lined up and "dressing left." While this photo depicts militaristic uniformity, the stylized presentation of these troops and attention to every detail simultaneously confronts military standards of man-hood by rejecting hypermasculine warrior wardrobe in favor of sassy little soldier get-ups. The troops' barely-there hot pants highlight their collective phalli, simultaneously signifying embodied masculinity while introducing a subversive sexual element.

In plain English, *Brüno*'s troops dressed like fags. Or one version of male homosexuality, anyway, that first melds sexuality with gender and then wraps it up in effete wardrobe. The twist is the unlikely military backdrop that we associate with aggressive manhood, the kind of masculinity that says, "I don't back down" and an anatomical emphasis that provokes our cultural metaphors and biofantasies about rock-hard manhood.[1]

But this essay is not about Brüno. It is about the mutability of masculinity and the ways by which fashion reflects this instability, or the constructed characteristics, of gender. This essay takes up the gendered anxieties and the tensions between agency and constraint, stasis and change: ambivalence that is at once deeply personal, philosophically heady, pragmatically grounded, and both encouraged and reined in by consumer capitalism. Examples of conforming, transforming, and shifting masculine styles mark ways in which masculinity (and its symbols) are both challenged and strengthened in these representations. And while assumptions about the meanings of masculinity

Image 2.1. Brüno.

and femininity are deeply entrenched in our politics and laws, our religions, schools, and our mythologies, these gender ideologies are also deeply reinforced through our fashions and styles.

The paradox is that while masculinity is semiotically styled and entrenched, its expression through fashion is also temporal, temporary, changeable.

We think of the color pink as gentle, soft, and feminine. The so-called color of girls. Blue, on another hand, is thought to be "solid, firm, and tough—adjectives we link with boys"[2] and, by extension, with masculinity. But the current pink-is-for-girls and blue-is-for-boys assumption wasn't the norm in the United States until the 1950s. Prior to that, these colors and their associated traits were reversed. According to Jo Paoletti, an expert in textiles and American studies, "people used to think that pink was masculine because it was a muted version of red, representing strength, the planet Mars, war, fire, and blood." Blue was considered feminine because "the color evoked peace, harmony, water, the sky, and Heaven."[3]

This temporal aspect of gender and fashion is again starkly obvious in seventeenth century France, when a man's man wore high-heeled shoes, velvet jackets, frilly lace shirts, and rosy blush with white powder makeup. Far more recently, fashionable-if-flouncy signifiers of masculinity were emulated by musicians like the New York Dolls and David Bowie (as Ziggy Stardust), circa 1972. The cover photo of the Dolls' 1973 inaugural album features platform heels on the gentlemen that many girls (including this one) might covet.

While a fashion flashback to the men-in-tights, glam-rock era is certainly possible, for now (Billie Joe Armstrong's guyliner notwithstanding) men's big hair and big shoes remain on mainstream hiatus. These masculine styles that take gender-bending cues from women's fashion are replaced by twenty-first-century emo-hipster style, the nonthreatening appeal of skinny jeans on young men, and the jerkin' dance crews popular in Los Angeles, but quickly spreading across the country.

And while this brief romp through fashion history provides a foundation for understanding that masculine looks have always been somewhat in flux, the point is to shine nuanced light on our current cultural moment. Masculinity has ironically held onto its hegemony not through stasis, but actually by constant, if subtle and strategic shifting. This is particularly prescient given the narrative of Western masculinity suggesting that since the Great Masculine Renunciation of the mid-eighteenth century, which cast off wardrobes of "scarlets and purples, satins and velvets, lace and embroidery,"[4] men have worn suits and that has been that. A few contemporary examples illustrate that such has not been the case. The symbols of masculinity in fashion are far more diverse.

Image 2.2. New York Dolls album cover, 1973.

Image 2.3. Jerkin' in skinny jeans.

Compare, for instance, those modern dandies of the 1970s and non-threatening masculine fashions of the 2010s with the image of rugged manhood and even violent masculinity, epitomized by the stylized swagger of Clint Eastwood as Dirty Harry, the body armor of buff and brawny rapper 50 Cent, or the don't-mess-with-me masculinity of prison-inspired tattoos, a specific fashion statement of its own.

These images illustrate how fashion and style are a source for reinforcing dominant or hegemonic norms of masculinity, and stereotypes of hypermasculinity. These masculine constructions are overlaid with signifiers of race, class, ethnicity, sexuality, and age. Visual representations of black men in the cultural mainstream of music "videomercials" and fashion ads, for instance, "often rely on a particularly overdetermined image of black masculinity," expressed mainly as nihilistic attitudes and vigilante street life.[5] This sort of presumptive imagery about gender and race, like the stylized pose of 50 Cent, is at odds with the class status and social access that real-life fame provides. But where fashion has the potential to both reify and disrupt the stereotypes of masculinity, its very mutability also suggests that

Image 2.4. Rapper 50 Cent.

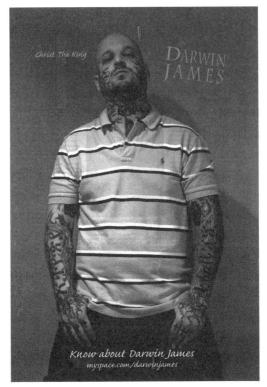

Image 2.5. *XXL Magazine*, May 2009.

fashion can shift the traps and insistence of gender by providing avenues for progressive cultural possibilities. The question is how far we'll be able to go in achieving meaningful change given the context of capitalism that profits by intentionally shifting the imagery of masculine style and consumer desire.

Undressing Assumptions of Masculine Style

In her analysis of masculinity in *Men's Health* magazine, sociologist Susan M. Alexander comments that "branded masculinity," rooted in consumer capitalism, tears men down to build them back up by selling muscles, money, and wardrobe. "Corporate profit," Alexander writes, is "enhanced by generating insecurity about one's body and one's consumer choices and then offering a solution" to achieving masculinity by combining a solid physique "with a fashion sense and the appearance of financial success." The lure is that becoming a "real man" can be accomplished through purchasing products and services offered by particular corporate brands.[6]

Historian Kenon Breazeale similarly argues that consumption practices construct masculinity, but emphasizes much earlier marketing patterns. Nearly 100 years ago, *Esquire* magazine brilliantly and intentionally created a consuming male audience and the image of stylish masculinity. This was, albeit, a class- and race-bound prototype, by which the trappings of whiteness and upper-class aspirations were melded with masculinity as hegemonic norms. Breazeale explains that the crisis of the Great Depression from 1929 into the early 1930s reshaped attitudes about masculinity, desire, and consumption. The key trope of American masculinity moved from responsibility to leisure. This shift coincided with a time when modern American commercial culture came into being.

Esquire seized this moment by capitalizing on a sense of loss (masculinity was no longer defined by responsibility) to create a new and marketable male identity. Economists and industrial engineers got together with ad agencies and the result was a new pseudoscience called consumption engineering. The idea behind it was that "real profits lie in constantly organizing taste in new ways"[7]—or constantly constructing wants and needs. In other words, *Esquire* intentionally promoted through editorial and advertisement the notion that taste, wants, and needs can be fulfilled by consuming, by purchasing and owning, or using goods and services and products. Breazeale argues that this logic of consumption still drives our culture today.[8]

This new theme of masculinity, the man of leisure (think: Hugh Hefner's bathrobe), is about wealth and refined taste. He likes good food and good booze, and *Esquire* could "help" by dedicating itself to streamlining the ideology-image-consumption triumvirate. *Esquire* set out to become the first magazine that appealed to men as consumers by using a systematically developed editorial formula. The iconography of consumption meant that spaces (e.g., shops and boutiques), purchased goods, and the activity of "shopping itself—were consistently encoded as feminine" especially notable during the turn-of-the-twentieth-century British Victorian era from 1860 to 1914.[9] With consumer culture taking strong hold on both sides of the pond, consumption was linked early-on to adorning the body, an activity further associated with stereotypes about the undesirable frivolousness of female vanity. By the time *Esquire* hit U.S. newsstands in 1933, shopping was already perceived as a girly activity, and feminine equaled bad, so *Esquire* intentionally convinced men that consumption was masculine by distancing manly activities from anything hinting at the feminine.

Esquire achieved this distance by establishing men's consumption tastes as distinct from women's tastes, and by demonstrating that men do consumption better. Everyday men lacking sufficient cash could still buy the signifiers of wealth and style through forgery, fakes, and debt. Luring the middle-class consumer relied on the embedded rules of socioeconomic status, rules promoting the notion that rich men are a cut above other men—and certainly better than women. They choose better liquor. (They drink fine Scotch, aged and on hard rocks; that is to say, serious products. Nothing frivolous, pink, or frothy.) Men know good food when they taste it—always steak (substantial), never yogurt (lightweight). *Esquire*'s practice simultaneously exploited the feminine (e.g., pin-up type artwork in the magazine) and denied the feminine (e.g., barbequing *is not* a housewife's work) to establish the masculine. *Esquire's* gendered approach, Breazeale asserts, was founded on denigrating women to create men as consumers and by constructing "masculine taste" as better. Editorial messages that accompanied ad space constructed femininity as lack. To be feminine meant that something was missing, whether this was good taste, proper consumption, or a penis.

In the twenty-first century, contemporary cultural shifts such as decreasing ratios of men-to-women enrolled in universities, or the relatively higher rates of male job loss echo changes and gender anxieties that emerged in the early 1930s during the Great Depression. As the Great Recession started in 2007, economic downturns dethroned the rugged individualism of advanced capitalism and the related man-as-breadwinner identities.

Set against this backdrop, consumption opportunities serve as remasculating tools and perpetuate the *Esquire* model of masculinity with Harley Davidsons, lifted trucks, Docker's "Wear the Pants" ad campaigns,[10] and pimping that ride with Bulls Balls or Truck Nutz, a phallic fashion statement achieved by attaching larger-than-life hanging scrotums to the tailgate region of one's car. These are each examples of masculinities-expert Michael Kimmel's hypothesis: The "gap between this atavistic ideal masculinity and the modern breadwinner role produces an identity crisis that men have tried to resolve through consumption. In other words, men whose work lives [were once] structured by conditions of hierarchy . . . now compensate for their resulting masculine anxieties" through shopping, leisure, and particular conspicuous consumption decisions.[11]

But no matter how influential the marketing messages of masculinity, none of these gender pronouncements are ever carved in stone. And when it comes to fashion, we find a robust source for reinforcing hegemony, but simultaneously opportunities for challenging or subverting dominant norms of masculinity.

The question is whether any transformation of masculinity and gender ideology can fully be achieved or whether we're looking at a constantly moving target. When men pose for fashion layouts or walk the runway, these masculine bodies on display both reinforce and transgress the rules of gender.

As philosopher (Susan Bordo) describes, "It's feminine to be on display." Yet while women internalize the conventions of femininity by learning "to anticipate, even play to the sexualized gaze, trying to become what will please, captivate, turn shame into pride," men are taught to dodge that attention.[12]

Men come under scrutiny of a particular kind—especially brown men, black men, criminally suspect men, or expressively gay men. But the very definition of masculinity means getting off the hook when it comes to relentless sexualized scrutiny. The message of masculinity is, "Get out of range of those eyes," Bordo writes. "[D]on't let them catch you—even as the object of their fantasies (or, as Sartre would put it, don't let them 'possess,' 'steal' your freedom)."[13]

Enter an unresolved tension: In the act of watching, we see masculinity reinforced through the physical presentation of bodies with smooth striated muscles, cold stares, or dimpled behinds (to use Bordo's description). Yet the quality of so-called passivity that is used to describe femininity, and that is propped up in contrast to (masculine) activity, "hardly describes what's going on when one person offers himself or herself to another. Inviting, receiving, responding—these are active behaviors too, and rather thrilling ones," Bordo writes.[14] We are *watching*. And it is in this act of watching, of putting the male body on display—and in a man's act of displaying himself—that the philosophically gendered position of the gazer and the gazed-at is tested.

To presume that *real* activity requires taking, invading, or aggressing, presupposes a macho bias, Bordo suggests. What's more, this synchronism is paradoxical: The male body can both reinforce masculine norms in its presentation of a certain corporeal image while the act of presenting the self can push back against this.

There is active engagement with placing oneself on display. Self-display is not merely a position of passive reception. Fashion ads, magazine layouts, or simply getting dressed in the morning (e.g., skinny jeans and a studied hollow hipster posture) can be done in ways that suggest vulnerability and availability for others. But the decision to represent the self as vulnerable is an active one.

It's all drag. But it's a drag that costs more to some than to others. Autonomy, freedom—even bodily safety—are deeply connected to gendered identity, how we perceive the stylized self, the ways in which we present this self to others, and how others filter these images through their own particular lenses of understanding about race, class, gender, age, power, and sexual orientation. Media and pop culture are powerful teachers in showing us how to do these things. When it comes to fashion advertising, nothing is accidental. Nor are these issues of power and identity or identity ambivalence purely the realm of philosophical conjecture. It is not by happenstance that black models, or black male celebrities hawking fashion, are positioned in a hard-stare showdown with the camera. It is not by chance that "come hither" languid posing is reserved for very young men.[15] As Bordo points out, the image of black male face-off is a clear nod to social prejudice, while young draped bodies reflects our cultural standards of sexual enticement and availability. Picture two older, black men filling in for the white gentlemen of Image 2.6. Imagine an effeminate preppy-looking young white man giving a cold stare to the camera as in Images 2.4 or 2.5. Changing the race, age, gender, class, or sexuality positioning challenges our socialized expectations. While our cultural standards of masculinity, raced maleness, and men's sexuality are shifting, there is still cultural gate-keeping that remains in place.

Again, though, none of these signifiers remain static. Advertisers shift strategy and push the envelope of convention when they see that social changes have already made consumers ready to receive new images, Bordo explains. Dual marketing, or gay window dressing, plays on the fact that

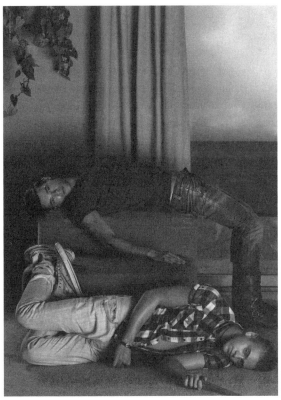

Image 2.6. *Vogue Men International Paris*, Spring–Summer 2009.

viewers read masculinity and sexuality in multiple ways.[16] This might involve a dreamy, hairless, smooth-chested and shirtless young man showing off a line of jeans, for example. Media studies expert Danae Clark explains that dual marketing strategies mean the homosexual possibilities exist at the same time the "straight" reading is never entirely erased.[17]

An Azzaro ad for Chrome cologne, for instance, features two adult white men and one white male little boy. They are smiling broadly, each in his blue shirt. The background color is blue, the fragrance is tinted blue—all visual code for The Man Color. Yet this ad also serves as an example of dual marketing. Gay men may see this ad as two dads and their son. Is this a portrait of a three-generation dynasty? Or could this be the cover image for a book titled *My Two Gay Dads*?

Similar questions about mutability, meaning, and style are exemplified by a 2009 television appearance on the Kids Choice Awards. Teen singing sensation Miley Cyrus emerges from behind the curtain to greet her fans wearing a one-shoulder draping orange mini dress. Next to Cyrus is Dwayne Johnson, formerly known as the popular WWE pro-wrestler and ultimate he-man, The Rock.

The "joke" at the Kids Choice Awards is Cyrus finding that Johnson is waiting on-stage in a matching, identical dress. With his tattooed biceps and heavy quads, Johnson seems an unlikely customer for this upscale version of a Forever 21 frock. But Johnson is not only in drag; he's in teenage girl drag.[18] He's not wearing any old dress; he's wearing Miley Cyrus' dress. And while Johnson is in drag, he also plays it off as caveman fashion. His Miley Cyrus-wig is offset by a manly unshaven five o'clock shadow. Johnson simultaneously reinscribes a warrior masculinity while pushing against the boundaries of mainstream masculine expectations. Dwayne Johnson's drag simultaneously loosens a vice-grip on manly stereotypes while shoring up a buff, exaggerated masculinity.

Yet if the staged scene at the Kids Choice Awards was a set-up for laughs, this humor deflects as much as it reveals. Johnson is both transgressing stereotypes and remasculating at the same time, and the viewer is left to wonder if either is entirely achieved.

Remasculating and the Masculinity Mash-Up

If masculinity is constructed, we know from the work of Judith(s) Butler and Halberstam that gender can also be deconstructed. Both theorists acknowledge the limitations of this process. That is to say, gender performance is informed or bounded by the normative structures within which it occurs. Judith (Jack) Halberstam also comments that masculinity cannot be reduced to the physical male body. The existence of what Halberstam calls "female masculinity" means that we must account for tomboys, butch lesbians, and other gender benders.[19] And when it comes to embodied men, we're beginning to see more options and varieties of masculinity available to invent and to emulate. Still, these new options must not be understood as existing in some "free" space having escaped the constraints of gender, but as existing within the shifting registers of gender representation.

Even while women are increasingly assuming the ranks of the armed forces, U.S. military presence in Afghanistan, Iraq, and around the globe continues to promote a form of dominance ideologically associated with manhood and masculinity. At the same time, a report from the Radcliffe Public Policy Center finds that 71 percent of men between the ages of twenty-one and thirty-nine are willing to give up pay and promotions if, in exchange, it means "they could have more time to spend with their families."[20] Eating disorders, once the primary purview of feminine peril, are now increasingly affecting men. The *Los Angeles Times* reports that in 2007, the first national study on eating disorders indicates that 25 percent of all anorexic, bulimic, and binge-eating adults are men.[21] This change coincides with a growing presence of visually objectified men in mainstream media.

We live in shifting times when it comes to the meanings of manhood and masculinity, gender and sexuality. Ads, movies, fashion, and style instructions directed toward men reflect this cultural ambivalence. For every *American Gangster* there's a *Superbad* McLovin; Arnold Schwarzenegger's take-no-prisoners Terminator tactics stand in contrast with The Dude's easy-going slacker ethos in *The Big Lebowski*.

Yet, to repeat a theme: in the face of increasing options and shifting meanings about masculinity, there remains a tension between personal expression and gender norms. In terms of fashion, this pertains to *what* is being worn as well as to *how* this stylized self is presented.

And, if gender deconstruction is nice for some, it is unnerving for others. The mere suggestion of guyliner, man hugs, murses, mandals, or bromance is enough to threaten masculine norms, or evoke hostile, defensive response. When this happens, there is a safe fashion fix for remasculating. Bricolage means the guy-thing is always there for us to revert to. Its signifiers are clear. If we want them to be, its gender boundaries are as reliable (and unyielding) as bondage gear or boxing gloves.

Bricolage—using an item for something besides what it was meant for—transforms objects from one use to another for symbolic purposes. By the time little boys are in preschool, write Ellen Jordan and Angela Cowan in their essay, "Warrior Narratives in the Kindergarten Classroom," some are using dolls as weapons or toy baby carriages as racecars.[22]

Bricolage doesn't end by kindergarten. One fashion layout from a 2009 issue of *Esquire* features a man wearing floral shorts and complementary flowered oven mitts. But lest the message be a feminized one (where cooking is female), these potholders are transformed from a tool for nurturing and sustenance, to a symbol of masculine aggression. The model wears these oven mitts as he would a pair of boxing gloves. We see the floral motif and infer the link with the feminized kitchen, yet we can also be reassured he is not a sissy. Floral or not, this guy is not backing down.

The copy reads, "Afternoon Barbecue." If kitchens are domestic feminized space, barbecues are clearly the domain of masculinity. In this fashion statement, feminine and masculine signifiers hint at changing gender politics and fissures in our myths about domestic ideology. For instance, estimates on the number of U.S. men who are considering full-time, stay-at-home fatherhood as an option range from 27 to 56 percent of those surveyed.[23] Once upon a time, this figure—at least admitted in public—would have weighed in very, very low.

Image 2.7. *Esquire*, May 2009.

Joe Jonas of Jonas Brothers fame circa 2009, visually exemplifies these possibilities of change in a *Teen Vogue* feature. His skinny jeans present a popular image that veers from the prison-inspired, gang-perpetuated, surfing/skatepunk sagging crowd of guys.[24] Jonas's necklace, trim physique, and sideswept bangs evoke a nonthreatening version of masculinity. The spread includes a similar image of Will Cameron Jr., apparently at a fashion show and surrounded by female friends, also featuring sideswept bangs. Cameron elects to take up less space by crossing his legs at his knees and keeping his elbows tucked toward his side.

A Marc Jacobs ad (also in *Teen Vogue*) features a lithe young man in a couture gown. Where sexual availability and stylistic vulnerability were previously the domain of women, an Armani ad from a 2009 issue of *Vogue Hommes International* focuses on a man in a dark-blue suit and tie, applying red lipstick pencil to match his similarly red painted fingernails.

Remasculating through fashion mash-up is the wardrobe equivalent of the mullet: business on the body and party on the lips. Or, to mix metaphors, a little bit country (squire) and a little bit (flaming) rock 'n' roll. In the end we get visuals that confront and surprise our expectations of manhood and begin partially shifting meanings of masculinity through the semiotic power of fashion. At the same time, bricolaged oven mitts, jewelry, or even Donald Trump's bright pink neckties, evoke broader questions about whether a stylized, feminizing touch "does" anything to masculinity. It is still possible to read these images as reconsolidating masculine power, just by absorbing traces of previously un-masculine culture. In this sense, the conundrum of gender remains.

This is a powerful instance of the postmodern dilemma: Denying the role of individual or collective agency in constructing masculinity means ignoring the active autonomy of a thinking, sentient society. At the same time, agency in the context of consumer capitalism means that none of us are ever completely immune from the push and pull of market forces. Consumer capitalism creates a shifting goalpost: Gender identity is purchased yet can never be completely achieved. At the same time, marketers and media intentionally create a consuming male identity. Both points are instructive. "The image of masculinity constructed purposely to sell a brand-name product also shapes the way men see themselves and others. [At the same time,] changing ideas of masculinity signal that significant transformation of the social structure is under way." For several decades social theorists have commented on the shift in Western societies from "a modern industrial culture based on production to a postmodern culture informed by the consumption of products, ideas, and knowledge."[25] (Jacques Derrida's 1966 work on structure and discourse and Jean Beaudrillard's 1981 *Simulacra and Simulation* are chief among them.[26]) As Alexander notes, the attendant change in masculinity and gender roles is unmistakable. The multiplicity of masculine gender displays found in the overlap of contemporary fashion and pop culture is exposed as capitalist hegemony. Alexander continues by writing that branded masculinities are purposely constructed by multinational companies to increase sales and profits "at the expense of any authentic understanding of what masculinity really means today."[27]

In other words, what is "real" masculinity, anyway? The fashionable hallmarks of masculinity shift with time and space. If we're searching for the real, perhaps we're left only with simulacra. To quote philosopher Jean Baudrillard, "It is no longer a question of imitation, not of reduplication, nor even of parody. It is rather a question of substituting signs of the real for the real itself."[28] If this is the philosophical puzzle, then what can fashion reveal? What window of insight into contemporary moments and possible futures does masculine style provide?

Queer Style and Female Masculinity

The fashioned body is the canvas for what sociologist Fred Davis calls our "identity tensions"[29] and the ambivalences of gender. These questions of masculinity play out on cisgendered male bodies—meaning when gender identity syncs up with the sex one is assigned at birth. But they are performed, as well, on the drag king circuit, on genderqueer and transgender bodies, and on female bodies that playfully—or powerfully—add a splash of masculine style to the semiotic repertoire. Expressions of masculine style as a reflection of masculine gender rests along a continuum, not a binary.

As author Parisa Parnian writes in her essay, "Style Outlaw," the way clothing is used on the body does not always "correlate with traditional ideas of femininity and masculinity."[30] That's what it means to queer fashion, or to queer anything, really.

The 1995 movie, *Tank Girl*, based on the 1980s British comic series, is an electrifying example of queer style and female masculinity. Fighting dystopian forces of evil, the anti-heroine rattles the world with an up-front attitude, sovereign sexuality, and a wardrobe featuring violence, dirt, bad-ass boots, and a gun. The original comic artists, Jamie Hewlett and Alan Martin, describe Tank Girl as "Mad Max designed by Vivienne Westwood; Action Man designed by Jean-Paul Gaultier."[31]

Introducing gender ambiguity in the realm of fashion means pushing against the binary construct that is so epistemologically comfortable to us. This "challenges the eye with beauty that [does] not conform to society's ideals of what is attractive on a male body or what is beautiful on a female body."[32] Yet, as with the temporal tension of pink and blue as gender signifiers

Image 2.8. *Tank Girl.*

mentioned earlier, there remain deeply rooted ideologies and essentialist con-nections to the physical body, *even at the same time* we might claim that we are transcending the issue of hypermasculinity by, say, dressing a female body in boy clothes.

Because masculinity does not belong to the biological body, women can also dress in so-called masculine ways—women in pants or suits are easy examples. Designer Antonio Berardi agrees, stating "Tailoring is power. A woman in a man's suit is the embodiment of authority, of control, of strength.[33] Yet when Parnian writes that the women in her fashion illustra-tions had a "masculine edge" because they were "often sporting a mysterious bulge in their pants,"[34] masculinity is melded not only with ideology, but directly with the phallus. That means we might mess with gender constructs, but we haven't quite escaped the trap of gender essentialism. Even when the references are not directed toward the physical, sexed body, so often the associations of masculinity with power over others remains entrenched, as with the example of shoulder pads (the symbolic armor invoking contact-combat sports like football).

Wrapping It Up (in Gender)

To wrap this up, let's touch back on *Brüno*. The filmmakers explain they intended to satirize and expose homophobia in this *Borat* follow-up. Wardrobe choices feature heavily in this movie and in its marketing campaign. And, like its non-filmic fashion counterparts—Dolce & Gabbana ads, Dwayne "The Rock" Johnson's TV appearance in teen-girl drag, or the entry of mandals, man-purses, and manscaping into our slang vocabulary—*Brüno*'s contemporary fashion statements garner complicated attention and poke at our collective unfinished business. There remain compelling questions about whether it is possible to successfully transform, subvert, or transcend stereotypes and rigid expectations about masculinity, manhood, and male sexuality.

We know that visual pop culture has profound impact on constructing and reinforcing our ideas about gender. We also know that gender is not a binary category, even though it is often presumed as such, as in phrases like the "opposite" or the "Other" gender. Gender is a continuum of identities and presentations of self. As such, there is no binary, there is no Other. With deft comedic swipes, actor Cohen-as-Brüno lays bare the camp and construct of hypermasculinity. In doing so, Cohen (perhaps imperfectly) suggests the possibility of transforming our assumptions of masculinity, manhood, and male sexuality through style. Rashad Robinson, senior director of programs at GLAAD, the Gay & Lesbian Alliance Against Defamation, is unconvinced, arguing that fashion antics and outrageous over-the-top style cannot successfully expose rigid expectations of masculinity or transform homophobia. For too many, Robinson explains, these stereotypes confirm rather than expose or shift preconceived prejudice.[35]

The even larger question that remains unanswered is whether it is ever really possible that mainstream images of fashion and style can move beyond a binary of masculine and feminine in opposition to each other and in ways that get picked up by people on the street and in everyday life. Or does the coding of masculinity and femininity run so deeply through our collective psyches that any attempt to subvert this phenomenon will remain incomplete? Further, how might we imagine moving beyond this binary to expand options for all of us in regard to how we behave, whom we love, and how we do it? These questions matter because dominant ideologies about gender are related to issues of interpersonal violence, choices in caring, nurturing and domestic roles, human limitations, and human possibilities. To paraphrase Baudrillard, in the end, as restless of a conclusion as this may be, perhaps only the allegory of the masculine remains.

Notes

1. Susan Bordo, *The Male Body: A New Look at Men in Public and in Private* (New York: Farrar, Straus and Giroux, 1999), 47.

2. Shira Tarrant, *Men and Feminism* (Berkeley, CA: Seal Press, 2009), 59.

3. Ibid., 60.

4. The term "Great Masculine Renunciation" is coined by psychologist John Carl Flugel in *The Psychology of Clothes* (London: Hogarth Press, 1930). See Laura Vivanco, "Interview: Sarah on Women Constructing Men," *Teach Me Tonight,* January 31, 2010, http://teachmetonight.blogspot.com/2010/01/interview-sarah-on-women-constructing.html; and Joanna Bourke, "The Great Male Renunciation: Men's Dress Reform in Inter-war Britain," *Journal of Design History* 9, no. 1 (1996): 23–33.

5. Matthew Henry, "He Is a 'Bad Mother*$%@!#': 'Shaft' and Contemporary Black Masculinity" *African American Review* 38, no. 1 (Spring 2004): 119.

6. Susan M. Alexander, "Stylish Hard Bodies: Branded Masculinity in *Men's Health* Magazine," *Sociological Perspectives* 46, no. 4: 535.

7. Jeffrey Meikle quoted in Kenon Breazeale, "In Spite of Women: *Esquire* Magazine and the Construction of the Male Consumer," *Signs* 20, no. 1 (Autumn, 1994): 2.

8. Breazeale, "In Spite of Women: *Esquire* Magazine and the Construction of the Male Consumer."

9. Brent Shannon, "Refashioning Men: Fashion, Masculinity, and the Cultivation of the Male Consumer in Britain, 1860–1914," *Victorian Studies* 46, no. 4 (Summer, 2004): 598.

10. When Dockers launched its "Wear the Pants" ad campaign for men's khakis and the accompanying "Man-ifesto" in 2009, the company urged men to "wear the pants again," a strategy that generated heated feminist critique. These debates questioned the ways by which representations of masculinity serve as commentaries on so-called crises of masculinity and how media representations are often used to bring masculinity back (to whatever it senses it has lost). See "The Dockers Man-Ifesto: Pants, Pants, Devolution," *Jezebel,* December 6, 2009, http://jezebel.com/5420105/the-dockers-man+ifesto-pants-pants-devolution.

11. Michael Kimmel quoted in Douglas B. Holt and Craig J. Thompson, "Man-of-Action Heroes: The Pursuit of Heroic Masculinity in Everyday Consumption," *The Journal of Consumer Research* 31, no. 2 (September 2004): 426.

12. Bordo, *The Male Body,* 173.

13. Ibid.

14. Ibid., 190.

15. Ibid., 192.

16. It is worth noting that gender expression is so easily and problematically melded with assumptions about sexual orientation.

17. Danae Clark, "Commodity Lesbianism," in *The Gender and Consumer Culture Reader*, ed. Jennifer Scanlon (New York: New York University Press, 2000), 377.

18. Thanks to Andrew M. Lopas for this observation.

19. Judith Halberstam, "An Introduction to Female Masculinity: Masculinity Without Men," in *The Masculinity Studies Reader*, eds. Rachel Adams and David Savran (Malden, MA: Blackwell, 2006), 355–374.

20. Tarrant, *Men and Feminism,* 86.

21. Denise Gellene, "Men Found to Be Anorexic, Bulimic Also," *Los Angeles Times* February 1, 2007, A12.

22. Ellen Jordan and Angela Cowan, "Warrior Narratives in the Kindergarten Classroom: Renegotiating the Social Contract?" in *Men's Lives*, eds. Michael Kimmel and Michael A. Messner (San Francisco: Pearson, 2007), 81.

23. See RebelDad, "Stay-at-Home Dad Statistics," *Rebel Dad*, http://www.rebeldad.com/stats.htm.

24. Jerk crews that favor skinny jeans with color wash reject the baggy, sagging gangsta style, and mock the "old men" who wear the oversized pants. *New York Times* journalist comments that elements of jerkin' originate in gang culture, and some of the dance moves riff on "well-established gangsta steps like the Crip Walk or the Hoover Stomp. But the overall spirit of the movement is far from criminal. And its rebellious disregard for the conventions of urban style and music" are exemplified by the fact that old school hip-hop artists are referred to as "baggy daddies." Guy Trebay, "Hip-Hop's New Steps," *New York Times,* November 20, 2009, http://www.nytimes.com/2009/11/22/fashion/22jerking.html?pagewanted=all.

25. Alexander, "Stylish Hard Bodies," 536.

26. Jacques Derrida, "Structure, Sign and Play in the Discourse of the Human Sciences" in *Writing and Difference*, trans. A. Bass (Chicago: University of Chicago Press, 1966), 351–370; Jean Baudrillard, *Simulacra and Simulation*, trans. S. F. Glaser (Ann Arbor: University of Michigan Press, 1981).

27. Alexander, "Stylish Hard Bodies," 552.

28. Jean Baudrillard, *Simulations* (New York: Semiotext(e), 1983), 4.

29. Fred Davis, *Fashion, Culture, and Identity* (Chicago: The University of Chicago Press, 1992), 57.

30. Parisa Parnian, "Fashion Outlaw: How a Genderqueer Fashion Label Was Born," in *It's So You: 35 Women Write About Personal Expression Through Fashion & Style*, ed. Michelle Tea (Emeryville, CA: Seal Press, 2007), 77.

31. Dan Thompson, "Tank Girl," http://www.ihatedanthompson.com/article.php?story=20030826103939347.

32. Ibid.

33. Lisa Armstrong, "The New Suits," *Harper's Bazaar*, May 2009, 104.

34. Ibid.

35. Rashad Robinson, " 'Bruno' Doesn't Help Gays," *Los Angeles Times*, July 12, 2009, A-24.

Chapter 3

The Baby Bump Is the New Birkin

Renée Ann Cramer

Current mania for the pregnant celebrity body has created a new fashion trend: the baby bump, and clothing dedicated to accentuating it. Media coverage of sexy, powerful pregnant women highlights their bellies, and closely watches their growing bumps. The message is clear: Contemporary women no longer need to cover the visual evidence of fertility, but can instead show off in body-skimming fashions and bump-conscious designs.

As such, popular coverage of celebrity pregnancies offers the potential for self-accepting fashion, and the promise that average women can show their pregnancies in a wide variety of ways, best fitting their unique personalities. Celebrity pregnancy fashion provides welcome relief from treacly-sweet, pastel-hued, and shapeless maternity clothes of the past.

Yet no matter how fashion-forward these celebrities are, media coverage of their pregnancies stops short of its emancipatory promise. Tabloids and glossy magazines watch and judge these pregnant bodies. Given that celebrities provide models of fashion that everyday women try to emulate, the sexy new baby bump establishes standards of pregnant and post-baby female beauty that are unattainable—perhaps even undesirable—to most.

What's more, press coverage of celebrity moms predictably replicates tired tropes and existing power gaps in class, race, and gender. Splashed across popular magazines, blogs, and entertainment TV are images of Jennifer Garner portrayed as an earthy, wholesome girl-next-door, and Katie Holmes as the cultured, cloistered woman now emerging from her maternal cocoon. While Britney Spears is judged as a trashy lady and a bad mom, Angelina

Jolie has managed to shed her wild-child image to be redeemed by mother-hood. And celebrity women of color—Halle Berry, Salma Hayek, and Jennifer Lopez—are portrayed as hot, sexy mamas. These women's pregnancies gain press attention in very different ways, but for all of them, fashion plays an enormous role in the way their motherhood is constructed, both before and after the appearance of the bump.

Babies—and Bodies—Are the New Birkin

Pop culture attention to the pregnant celebrity body is obsessed with the beginnings, growth, and loss of the "baby bump"—the primary visual indi-cator of a woman's pregnancy. The check-out line of any grocery store is filled with magazine covers proclaiming:

"Angelina Jolie Debuts Her Baby Bump!"[1]

"Jennifer Garner: She's Pregnant!"[2]

"Jennifer Lopez a Radiant Mom-to-Be."[3]

Photos of celebrities clad in form-fitting, belly-revealing, and stylish cloth-ing abound. The clothes themselves, though, are seldom the issue; they are merely meant to highlight the bump.

This kind of coverage is a far cry from the uproar when Demi Moore posed provocatively, pregnant—and nude—in a series of sensual and beautiful photos for *Vanity Fair*. Moore's nude *Vanity Fair* cover was controversial. Some stores refused to carry the magazine with Moore on the cover, and readers flooded the magazine with correspondence both loving and hating it.

The Demi Moore cover was a watershed event. Since the 1980s, in large part because of celebrity openness about their pregnant physiques, some pregnant women's bodies are losing their image as repulsive, embarrassing, or considerably private. The modern, mainstream, American woman is instead encouraged to display her pregnancy quite publicly. A significant part of this display is the coveted Bump.

In her classic essay, "Motherhood Under Capitalism," feminist scholar Barbara Katz Rothman notes that under capitalism, *everything* has a price tag. She argues that mothers are not valued in American society; rather, babies, as commodities, are. Popular author Molly Jong-Fast took this analysis famously far in a 2003 essay for the *New York Times*, where she wrote, "it seems as if babies are the new Birkin bag."[4]

This quote got picked up in 2008 by Katie Lee Joel, the then-26-year-old wife of pop singer Billy Joel, who told *E!*, perhaps ill-advisedly, "I'm always thinking about cute [baby] names. I always say that babies are the new Birkin. They're the hottest accessory right now. Everybody has to have one."[5]

And it is not only the baby that has been commodified in popular culture; the pregnant body itself, with the feverish obsession paid to the baby bump, has become a product in its own right. The baby bump is the accessory of the season. Appearing on *The Daily Show* in late October 2008, CNN journalist Campbell Brown patted her belly and said with pride, "I've got the bump!" Then, in an aside to the audience remarked, "I'm pregnant." Wearing a body-skimming turquoise knit dress, Brown looked neither heavy nor pregnant—but she was quick to clarify that any additional curves on her body were the result of pregnancy, not self-indulgence.[6] Brown unwittingly confirmed what recent scholarship suggests: To a great extent, women are comfortable with their weight gain in pregnancy precisely because it is socially acceptable weight gain, undertaken in the pursuit of motherhood.[7] Even more, this weight gain is acceptable because it is *temporary.*

The Post-Baby Body

Once her pregnancy is a thing of a celebrity woman's past, tremendous ink is spilled on the shape and status of her post-baby body. J. Lo trained for and competed in a triathlon within months of giving birth to twins. Angelina Jolie publicly mourns the loss of her bump and the voluptuousness of pregnancy, but steps out stylishly svelte within months of giving birth. And then there is "yummy mummy" Gwyneth Paltrow, mother of two young children, who wowed the paparazzi at the *Ironman* movie premieres in increasingly shorter mini dresses to show off her lean physique.

At the same time that women enjoy the openings provided by the pregnant celebrity body—the chance to be pregnant and sexy, pregnant and powerful, pregnant and athletic—they are also being assaulted by images of (usually) ultra-thin celebrities with a (usually) manageable "bump." And, as they eye the celebrity bumps while measuring their own, "regular" women are told, in nearly every article on celebrity pregnancy, that each star already has a plan to get back to her post-baby body. The insinuation, of course, is that they should, too.

Paltrow has had the good sense to stress that she works out nearly four hours a day, and does so in large part because her job as a movie star requires it of her.[8] She also points out that she is supported by staff, scheduling, and money in her pursuit of the post-baby body, things to which most women have no access. The vast majority of new mothers not only don't have the necessity of making their body their business, they also don't have the time, or the requisite money, to spend those long hours in the gym. The celebrity post-baby body is far from reality for the majority of everyday moms.

Yet, unrealistic as it is, second only to the bump, the post-baby body is a coveted item. The post-baby body is a style to possess. And it is yet another physical manifestation of how we judge mothers. Did they gain enough weight (20 to 35 pounds)? In the right places (belly or boobs)? And did they lose it quickly enough?

Fantasies of Femininity

Media coverage of these sexy, powerful, and creative women as expectant mothers can offer new and positive models for parenthood, and highlight the creative potentials of corporeal femininity. Some of these images certainly appear liberatory, and many of them give sexual and relational agency to women in a way that reimagines the pregnant female. Communications scholar Angela McRobbie notes that "fragments of 'info' " provided in popular magazines about favorite films stars and TV celebrities "are now the raw material of fantasy."[9] Clearly, some of these fantasies might be transgressive, transversive, and emancipatory. They might celebrate creative power, maternal sensuality, and independence.

At least they have the potential. But tabloids, glossy magazines, and entertainment TV do not often cooperate with the goal of emancipation from limiting, constructed, and highly stylized gender norms. In fact, a close look at the coverage of celebrity pregnancies reveals three troubling trends. First, pregnant celebrities are given a limited range of roles and identities in which to perform their pregnancies. These tropes not only reinforce gender norms, they also reinforce racial and ethnic stereotypes by making pregnant women of color "exotically sexy." As well, pregnant celebrities have become tabloid fodder and magazine staples in ways that suggest their bodies—and by extension all women's bodies—are meant to be surveilled, scrutinized, and judged. The size of their bump is fair game for comment, and their slimmed down, post-baby bodies are coveted.

This obfuscates the role of wealth and access to resources in obtaining perfect "bumps," babies, and postpartum bodies; no matter their economic status, women are expected to be able to discipline their post-baby bodies. Sandra Bartky notes that the discipline of women in postmodernity is "widely dispersed, everywhere and nowhere, internalized."[10] Certainly the images fed us by tabloid and celebrity magazines are everywhere, and, even if not universally internalized, they create a norm for pregnant women. As they proliferate, these images feed fantasies about femininity, pregnancy, and power that have the potential to become disciplinary, and create expectations inscribed on the body of the mother-to-be. And, the coverage of pregnant celebrities by pop culture media constitutes and extends a surveillance of the female body that reminds women that their pregnancies are public events, which can be commented on and judged by the general public, and regulated by the state.

The Baby Bump occupies an unusual space in the world of fashion. Though it is spoken of as an accessory, like a Birkin bag, an accessory usually offsets an outfit, or completes a look. For these women, the point of the outfit is to accentuate the bump itself. On a pregnant celebrity, the bump is worn and accessorized by the clothing, all with the effect of creating an image of motherhood that so-called average women are meant to emulate. So, on the surface, mainstream media focuses on the allegedly best accessories a woman can have: the baby bump, followed by a svelte post-baby body. Media coverage has the more significant effect of showing women how to perform their pregnancies, how to dress and accessorize in ways that will show them to be "good mothers." Not surprisingly, the bodies that are dressed and fashioned as ideals of motherhood are predominantly white, wealthy, and heterosexual.

Good Girls, Bad Moms, and Sexy Women

Meet the Good Girls: Down-to-Earth Jennifer and Fashion-Plate Katie

Jennifer Garner is celebrity-styled as the girl-next-door, lauded for her pregnancy look, her parenting, and her "naturalness." Portrayed as a devoted, down-to-earth mom, Garner is most often photographed in casual clothes: jeans and T-shirts, sundresses; her long and straight hair is simply styled. One widely distributed photo shows a pregnant Garner in a long, blue-and-cream floral cotton dress, holding pigtailed daughter Violet, two years old in the picture. Garner's image is cute, traditional, and accessible. On the celebrity gossip blog *Popsugar,* this traditional appeal translates into idealized motherhood. Commenter "colormesticky" says Garner is "so cute. She could have 12 kids one right after another and I wouldn't pick on her for it."[11] "Caligirl1201" adds, "I would love for someone as nice and beautiful as Jennifer G. to have more kids."[12] On *Celebitchy,* Garner and her movie-star husband Ben Affleck receive praise for eschewing "trendy Hollywood baby names," in favor of "more traditional names."[13] It turns out that Garner's family even eats traditionally; *Celebitchy* breathlessly reports, "Garner let us get a glimpse of her shopping list, which includes organic hotdogs, wheat germ, chicken, and chocolate."[14]

From her clothing to her grocery list, Jennifer Garner's pregnancies and parenting are portrayed as traditional, homey, and cozy. This stylized contrivance is part of her allure. The girl next door, after all, is more than beautiful. She plays by the rules and follows tradition. She's safe, and as comfortable, as a cozy cable-knit sweater.

The image projected by Katie Holmes, actress and wife of mega-star Tom Cruise, is quite different from Garner's easy comfort and apple-pie appeal. Yet, Holmes is also styled as the "ideal mom" through her fashion choices, many of which replicate her daughter Suri's wardrobe. Considerably younger than her husband, and best known for her work on the television show *Dawson's Creek* where she portrayed a "typical" American teenager, her transformation through a stylized and highly publicized wardrobe has allowed Holmes to shed her youthful image and step out in a more grown-up, sophisticated, and polished role.

Few paparazzi photos of Katie Holmes were made while she was pregnant. In the absence of photos, the press began to write its own narrative—one of Katie Holmes as a cloistered, closeted young woman in need of liberation from a hovering and powerful spouse. Stories about the birth plan, allegedly influenced by the tenets of Scientology, and envisioning a drug-free, "peaceful" or "quiet" birth, were widely distributed with panicked headlines, like *Slate* magazine's, "Silent Night? Holy Crap!"[15] There was even a "Free Katie Holmes" movement spearheaded by *Salon.com*, culminating in "Free Katie!" T-shirts for sale.[16]

This effectively infantilized Holmes during her pregnancy, constructing an image of woman-as-vulnerable, in need of rescue, cosset, or care. After daughter Suri's birth, and well into her toddlerhood, she and Holmes were often photographed wearing matching outfits and with similarly styled hair. This matchy-matchy fashion continued the semiotic message of Holmes as childlike, rather than an autonomous adult. Remarkably, however, this has changed.

Famous friends to Posh Spice (Victoria Beckham), Holmes has undergone a fashion metamorphosis from childlike to sophisticated. *Glamour* magazine profiled her in April 2009; the accompanying photos featured her in svelte haute couture, mile-high Manolos, and fishnet stockings.[17] Holmes's move to a shorter, sophisticated haircut, and remarked-upon appearances at Fashion Week events have changed the way the press reports on her. She is now a cultured fashionista, a style maven, and a mom.

Though Katie Holmes doesn't quite present like wholesome Jennifer Garner, she is still marked as a good girl by virtue of a docility that is written on her material body and expressed through the evolution of her fashion sense. Holmes is marked as good precisely because she is both maternal and fashionable—a woman who mothers, while stepping out effortlessly, stylishly, and with considerable poise. She can even wear fishnets and high heels, without evoking the image of bad girls in need of redemption—like Britney Spears and Angelina Jolie.

Bad Girls Redeemed by Motherhood?

Britney Spears is one of the most famous pregnant and parenting celebrities of the last decade. Pop-sensation-turned-mother-of-two, with a troubled personal life, Spears was, for a time, vilified daily online and in magazines as a bad mom.

Where other celebrities get glowing copy about their pregnant bodies, Britney's body and fashion were mocked. As the Internet site *BumpShack* put it, "Pregnancy Not Always Pretty For Britney Spears."[18] Online comments posted to *The Superficial*, alongside a photo of Britney heading to the gym in a midriff-baring top and baggy sweatpants, are uniformly critical. "Pat" writes, "just what this world need [sic] is another trailer trash baby from a trailer trash mama. . . ."[19] Britney's bad mother persona also rested on her post-baby antics, many of which were made evident on her body. Her tattoos, shaved head, and panty-less poses were, to the press, physical manifestations of erratic behavior (and possible postpartum psychosis), and thus signaled Spears as unfit for parenthood. Her bad-mom persona is marked through her fashion specifically, her "trailer park" style featuring short-short denim skirts, midriff-baring tops, and low-cut blouses that strain buttons across her chest.

This image was so pervasive that it proved hard for Spears to shake, even when her style shifted to a more sophisticated image. *Bazaar* featured Spears in 2006, pregnant with her second child, in a striking series of photographs. Nude save for jewels, Spears takes rather modest poses. The public response was more approbation than approval; gossip Web site *Backseat Cuddler* posted one image from the magazine, adding the comment: "Oops, did she do it again? Reproduce that is."[20]

Sympathy is lacking from most conversations about Britney's body, babies, and mothering. Also missing is responsible discussion of possible mental illness, emotional distress, medication side-effects, or that Britney might have needed help instead of bad-girl blame. Instead, the media flocked to stories of Britney as a vagina-flashing, head-shaving crazy. Whether her performances of motherhood were influenced by postpartum illness and addiction, or were intentional and purposive statements against normative images of mothering, Britney Spears was either unwilling or unable to adopt a style admired by the popular press. As such, pregnancy and early motherhood did not redeem this bad girl's image; rather, she became even more vilified as a trashy girl and unfit mother. The message to the public reinforced a good-mom/bad-mom dualism and served as a clear semiotic warning to other women.

In contrast, Angelina Jolie's image has been improved by pregnancy and presentation of herself as a mother. Jolie used to be prone, as the *New York Times* reports, "to provocative statements about blood, tattoos, and bisexuality."[21] Her fashion choices once relied heavily on tight black leather and Goth-inspired creations. While pregnant, and since giving birth, she has stepped out in body- and bump-conscious, though draped and comfortable-looking gowns; Jolie wears richly hued silk, with plunging necklines and little makeup. She appears voluptuous and sexy, yet subdued.

Jolie has also been a public advocate for refugees, and has taken on humanitarian causes as pet projects. She is often photographed in gorgeous business suits, en route to hearings at the United Nations, or meetings with diplomatic staff. Those images, as well as public presentations of family life with Brad Pitt and their six children (three biological and three adopted), have rehabilitated her image. Open about her choice to breastfeed her children, Jolie told the *New York Times* that her kids are with "Mommy and Daddy every day for every meal," before telling the reporter that she might need to take a break to pump breastmilk for the twins."[22]

Some may remain unconvinced by Jolie's transformation; but by many accounts, Jolie's retooled image has been quite successful. In an *Us Weekly* magazine poll from August 2008, 64 percent of respondents said that from of a list of celebrity tots, they would most like their children to play with Shiloh Jolie-Pitt. As one reader explained, "Shiloh's family seems the most normal."[23]

Of course, they are not normal or average in any palpable way; they are extremely wealthy, and incredibly famous. Indeed, wealth and fame allow the Jolie-Pitts to achieve the image of normalcy and family life that so fascinates the media.

By contrast, though, the same poll reported that only 6 percent of respondents would want their children to play with bad-girl Britney Spears's son, Sean Federline. The transformations of Cruise and Jolie appear complete. Jolie, in particular, a former dyed-in-the-wool Hollywood bad girl seems for the most part redeemed by pregnancy and motherhood. As with Holmes, Jolie's redemption hinges on images of her pregnant and maternal body: Even some of her tattoos are maternal: Jolie wears the longitude and latitude of each child's birthplace inscribed on her back.

Sexy Salma, Hottie Halle, and Juicy J. Lo: Exoticizing Pregnant Women of Color

Jennifer Garner, Katie Holmes, and Angelina Jolie, along with so many other celebrities, are stylized as sexy women who are mothers. Their sexiness is secured and made safe by virtue of their heteronormative marriages, sophisticated fashion sense, entrepreneurial or humanitarian spirits, and displays of concern for their children. Often these celebrities are portrayed as settling comfortably, if a bit unconventionally, into domestic bliss. In their fashion choices, their sexiness regularly takes a backseat to maternity, comfort, and domesticity. Not so for the sexy women of color whose bumps and boobs are covered lasciviously by the mainstream press.

Salma Hayek and Halle Berry have received significant press attention hypersexualizing their mommy bodies. Halle Berry, who was voted "Coolest 1st Time Mom this Year," in a Hollywood poll,[24] was also named *Esquire* magazine's 2008 "Sexiest Woman Alive!"[25] *OK! Magazine* documents Berry's pregnancy in multiple photographic slides accompanying the online article, titled "Sexy Mama!"[26] The caption to a photo of Berry at a film premiere reads, "Whoa, Mama! Halle Berry Was Busting Out (in a Good Way) . . . Pregnancy Is Good for Her!"[27] The caption to another photo of a casually dressed Berry tooling around town reads, "She might look like her belly could explode any second, but that doesn't stop hot momma-to-be Halle Berry [from] hitting up the stores in Beverly Hills."[28] Accompanying a photo of Berry in a plunging V-neck dress of lavender silk, the headline on celebrity gossip blog *INFDaily* reads, "Halle Berry's got baby boobs."[29]

Salma Hayek was also often touted as a "sexy mama" during her pregnancy, a status she seemed to embrace. One much-covered photo shows Hayek in a flowing black skirt with a black cap-sleeved T-shirt covering three-fourths of a protruding belly shortly before her due date. The writing on her shirt read, "Stylish. Sexy. Pregnant." One online commenter continued in this vein by commenting on Hayek's baby's name (Valentina Paloma Pinault), "Ooh! Sexy name!"[30] Apparently, the focus on sexiness is contagious. And this hypersexualized attention also adheres by replicating—yet again—the tired trope of women of color as exotic and Other.

For Hayek, in particular, an incredible amount of media focused not only on her bump but also on her breasts. *BumpShack* posted pictures of Hayek in a spaghetti-strapped dress, and labeled her breasts, "Milk Factory #1," and "Milk Factory #2."[31] On the gossip site *CelebWarship*, "Noni" commented on a picture of Hayek, "Those boobs look pretty knocked up too. I mean, Christ . . . they're out of control!"[32] Certainly, both women possess bodies that are conventionally beautiful according to dominant aesthetic norms. But they are also bodies that are "curiously and uniquely unreliable" in their propensity to "burst" and "explode" with child. They are presented as "dangerously volatile . . . out of control." Their bodies still threaten to uncontrollably spill, leak, or seep.[33]

It is no accident that these women of color are hypersexualized in wild ways, evoking an out-of-control primal sexuality. Popular culture media has a long history of sexualizing women of color in particularly animalistic ways. Terms like "dangerous," "volatile," "out of control" follow this racist pattern. In a similar vein, *CelebWarship* commenter CocoabutteR writes that Hayek's "boobs are all filled with leche and shit."[34] Comments and captions using Spanish terms siphon out the stars' status as different from a whitewashed mainstream.

This construction of women of color as exotically sexy during pregnancy follows a dubious theme of envisioning them as available, fertile, robust vessels. The media constructs their public images as less constrained, less demure, and less docile than white women. This exoticization painfully recalls and perpetuates a particular sexual objectification and sexual use of women of color in American history. Salma Hayek and Halle Berry may be women to be admired, but in the hands of tabloid media, their admiration hinges on their status as racialized, sexy Others. Even as we are solidly in the twenty-first century, women of color can attain status and attention—but as the sexy seductress, not the good-girl next door. That (still limiting) option remains largely closed, available only to those pure and earthy, sophisticated and stylish, white girls down the street.

Surveilling the Stars

As celebrity performers or movie-star actresses, today's female stars are expected to perform their pregnancies in the public eye. Media photos of baby and mom in postpartum bliss (or breastfeeding bliss as the Angelina Jolie cover of *W*, shot by her partner Brad Pitt, shows), celebrity moms reinforce the idea that their pregnancies and babies are, to some extent, public property. The public and performative nature of these pregnancies is important. Women—and men—watch these celebrities, and learn how pregnancy ought to be performed, the risk of violating these expectations, and the fashion tools required to replicate constructed fantasy images.

While the latitude of choosing fashionable, visible pregnancy is a freedom unknown to previous generations of American women, the transformative potential is complicated by the fact that the celebrity pregnant body isn't only monitored by the public. It is stalked. Disturbingly intimate images of pregnant celebrities are routine fodder for online blogs, glossies, and television gossip. Pregnant celebrities are scrutinized, regularly caught off-guard by paparazzi. This surveillance has a dual effect. First, we come to feel entitled to voyeuristically share the private moments of total strangers. The second effect of this surveillance is more insidious. The photos and video clips remind all women, pregnant or not, that they are being watched, photographed, recorded, and judged. The message to men is that women's bodies exist as voyeuristic objects of pleasure, criticism, scrutiny, and blame. By participating in the surveillance and stalking of pregnant celebrities, we are the "hunter," but as pregnant women, women enter the realm of the hunted.

Gossip about celebrities' pregnancies, and the public and performative nature of such pregnancies, gives a green light to stepped-up surveillance of female bodies. As Robyn Longhurst puts it, "pregnant women are considered to be a public concern." Accordingly, "the everyday behaviours of pregnant women tend to be policed by strangers."[35] Witness pregnant women refused glasses of wine by well-intentioned bartenders, or advised on the dangers of tuna or other seafood by strangers in the grocery line. Note the fetal protection laws that limit women's most basic and harmless activities, the shackling of prisoners while giving birth, and court-ordered Caesareans.[36]

As women watch and judge others' pregnancies, so may they watch and judge their own. The celebrity baby bump and the svelte and sexy post-baby body have become commodities in their own right. But they are not commodities that most can realistically expect to possess. Neither are the expensive clothes that drape the pre- and post-bump bodies of these rich and famous celebrity moms.

Yes, celebrating the sexy physiques of pregnant actresses may create more options for experiencing and expressing pregnancy. Women are no longer necessarily expected to be demure, modest, covered up, and shy about their pregnancy. This once-private circumstance is losing the patina of secrecy and shame with which it was coated until the end of the twentieth century. But, this focus on celebrity pregnancy also follows a familiar script, and uses familiar tropes: bad girls aren't always redeemed by pregnancy if they violate other norms of style and propriety; women of color are still hypersexualized, even in their maternity; and the "good girls" have a limited set of identities. They are the docile bodies and the earthy, natural girls-next-door who dress stylishly, tastefully, and conservatively. None of these limiting images of women are realistic nor do they express the full range of femininity, maternity, or parenthood. They are caricatures meant to sell magazines and clothes, not, ultimately, to empower women.

For all of their accomplishments—these celebrity women are awarded Oscars, they own production companies, they testify before the United Nations, and they campaign for presidential hopefuls—pregnant and mothering celebrities are still known for, and judged by, their looks. Speculation about their pregnant bodies reinforces tropes of femininity and sells the pregnant and post-pregnant body to everyday women. Public fascination with the celebrity baby-bump markets and commodifies the female form in ways that are rather tired, and sadly predictable.

Notes

1. Queenoftab, "Angelina Jolie Debuts her Baby Bump!" *Who's Dated Who,* February 24, 2008, http://www.whosdatedwho.com/ctn_10002851/angelina-jolie-debuts-her-baby-bump/.

2. Ryan Pienciak, "Scoop. Jennifer Garner: She's Pregnant!" *People*, August 4, 2008, http://www.people.com/people/archive/article/0,,20221624,00.html.

3. "Jennifer Lopez a Radiant Mom-To-Be," *Hairstyles,* http://www.hairstyles.ws/articles/hair-styles-cat-celebrity-gossip-id-46.html.

4. Molly Jong-Fast, "View; Out of Step and Having a Baby," *New York Times*, October 5, 2003, http://query.nytimes.com/gst/fullpage.html?res=9D00E3D6143CF93 6A35753C1 A9659C8B63&sec=&spon=&pagewanted=2. Jong-Fast is referring to the famous, coveted, and insanely expensive Hermès leather bag named for Jane Birkin, a celebrity must-have item.

5. Quoted in Marc Malkin, "A Baby for Billy Joel?" *E! Online,* February 1, 2008, http://www.eonline.com/uberblog/marc_malkin/b59783_baby_billy_joel.html.

6. Campell Brown, *The Daily Show with Jon Stewart*, October 27, 2008, http://www.thedailyshow.com/watch/mon-october-27-2008/campbell-brown.

7. See Alexandra Sumner, Glenn Waller, Stephen Killick, and Max Elstein, "Body Image Distortion in Pregnancy: A Pilot Study of the Effects of Media Images," *Journal of Reproductive and Infant Psychology* 11 (1993): 203; and Sarah Earle, "Bumps and Boobs: Fatness and Women's Experiences of Pregnancy," *Women's Studies International Forum* 26, no. 3 (2003): 248–251.

8. Maureen Harrington, "Body After Baby," *People,* September 17, 2007, http://www.people.com/people/archive/article/0,,20060353,00.html.

9. Angela McRobbie, "Shut Up and Dance: Youth Culture and Changing Modes of Femininity" *Cultural Studies* 7, no. 3 (1993): 416.

10. Sandra Lee Bartky, "Foucault, Femininity, and the Modernization of Patriarchal Power," in Janet Price and Margrit Shildrick, eds., *Feminist Theory and the Body: A Reader* (New York: Routledge, 1999), 142–143.

11. Colormesticky, comment to PopSugar, "Jennifer Garner Pregnant Again?" *Popsugar,* July 13, 2006, http://www.popsugar.com/Jennifer-Garner-Pregnant-Again-11020.

12. Caligirl1201, comment to PopSugar, "Jennifer Garner Pregnant Again?"

13. MSat, "Ben Affleck and Jennifer Garner prefer traditional baby names," *Celebitchy,* October 10, 2008, http://www.celebitchy.com/14745/ben_affleck_and_ jennifer_garner_prefer_traditional_baby_names/comment-page-1/.

14. "Random Photos: Jennifer Garner, Tara Reid, Paris, Pam Anderson, Danny Devito," *Celebitchy*, July 7, 2008, http://www.celebitchy.com/12803/random_photos_jennifer_garner_tara_reid_paris_pam_anderson_danny_devito/.

15. Dana Stevens, "Silent Night? Holy Crap! Tom and Katie's scary Scientology birth plan," *Slate*, October 13, 2005, http://www.slate.com/id/2128041.

16. Lynn Harris, "Free Katie Holmes!" *Salon*, March 29, 2006, http://www.salon.com/life/broadsheet/2006/03/29/katie_silent_birth.

17. "Glamour Magazine—April 2009—Katie Holmes," *Fashionising,* http://www.fashionising.com/pictures/p--Glamour-Magazine-April-2009-Katie Holmes-2470-33934.html.

18. Joshua Holmes, "Pregnancy Not Always Pretty for Britney Spears," *Bump-Shack*, July 13, 2006, http://bumpshack.com/2006/07/13/pregnancy-not-always-pretty-for-britney-spears/.

19. Pat, comment to "Britney Spears: Pregnant or just eating a ton of her dad's cooking? You decide!" *The Superficial*, May 16, 2008, http://www.thesuperficial.com/britney_spears_stops_at_clinic-05-2008.

20. Gossipmonkey, "Is Britney Spears Pregnant?" *Backseat Cuddler*, May 18, 2008, http://backseatcuddler.com/2008/05/12/is-britney-spears-pregnant/.

21. Mark Harris, "The Mommy Track, *New York Times*, October 15, 2008, http://www.nytimes.com/2008/10/19/movies/19harr.html?_r=1&pagewanted=1.

22. Ibid.

23. Quoted in "Some thoughts on *US Weekly*'s slam," *Female First*, August 17, 2008, http://www.femalefirst.co.uk/board/viewtopic.php?f=40&t=192621.

24. "Halle Berry named Hollywood's hottest mum," April 10, 2001, *Deccan Herald*, http://deccanherald.com.

25. HerBadMother, "*Esquire*'s Sexiest Woman Alive is a Mom," *Babble*, October 8, 2008, http://www.babble.com/CS/blogs/famecrawler/archive/2008/10/08/esquire-s-sexiest-woman-alive-is-a-mom.aspx.

26. OK! Staff, "Halle Berry: Sexy Mama!" *OK!*, October 15, 2008, http://www.okmagazine.com/2008/10/halle-berry-sexy-mama-9620/.

27. "Halle Berry!" *OK!*, October 7, 2008, http://www.okmagazine.com/2008/10/halle-berry-9473/ok-image-import-17190/.

28. INF, "Halle Ain't Too Fat to Shop," *INF Daily*, January 27, 2008, http://www.infdaily.com/2008/01/halle-aint-too-fat-to-shop.html.

29. INF, "Halle Berry's Got Baby Boobs," *INF Daily*, October 24, 2007, http://www.infdaily.com/2007/10/halle-berrys-got-baby-boobs.html.

30. H.A.R., "Salma Hayek Has Baby Girl," *Waleg*, September 23, 2007, http://www.waleg.com/celebrities/archives/009406.html.

31. Joshua Holmes, "Salma Hayek With Milk Jugs," *BumpShack*, September 22, 2007, http://bumpshack.com/2007/09/22/salma-hayek-gives-birth-to-baby-girl/salma-hayek-with-milk-jugs/.

32. Nomi, comment to Alyk, "Salma Hayek is Seriously Pregnant," *Celeb Warship*, May 29, 2007, http://www.celebwarship.com/?p=2851.

33. See Robyn Longhurst, " 'Corporeographies' of Pregnancy: 'Bikini Babes,' " *Environment and Planning D: Society and Space* 18, no. 4 (2000): 453–472.

34. CocoabutteR, comment to Alyk, "Salma Hayek is Seriously Pregnant."

35. Longhurst, " 'Corporeographies' of Pregnancy," 468.

36. For important early treatments of the issues of subjectivity, law, and surveillance of pregnant bodies see Susan Bordo, "Are Mothers Persons? Reproductive Rights and the Politics of Subectivity," in *Unbearable Weight: Feminism, Western Culture, and the Body* (Berkeley: University of California Press, 1993), 71–97; Iris Marion Young, "Punishment, Treatment, Empowerment: Three Approaches to Policy for Pregnant Addicts," *Feminist Studies* 20, no. 1 (Spring 1994): 35–57; and Martha Minow and Mary Lyndon Shanley, "Relational Rights and Responsibilities: Revisioning the Family in Liberal Political Theory and Law," *Hypatia* 11, no. 1 (Winter 1996): 4–29.

Chapter 4

Fashion as Adaptation

The Case of *American Idol*

Leslie Heywood and Justin R. Garcia

One of the most glamorous idols ever . . . Look at Adam Lambert!

—Regis Philbin, *Live With Regis and Kelly*, May 27, 2009

When selecting group members, people seek those who exhibit cues suggesting they will be around in the future, such as familiarity and indices of commitment.

—Robert Kurzban and Steven Neuberg,
"Managing Ingroup and Outgroup Relations"

While fashion can be approached from a number of perspectives, including scientific ones, the genus of this particular collection is that of cultural studies, a subset of disciplines within the humanities. As such, we are accustomed to approaching topics from the perspective of culture—asking how normative cultural assumptions are expressed by particular products, acts, arts, etc., and critically considering how these affect socialization and limit human ossibilities

Image 4.1. Adam Lambert, "costly novelty" on *American Idol.*

in particular places and times. From this point of view, fashion reflects ideologies that predominate in a given location and context, as well as the
conditions of production that make it possible. An unquestioned assumption
of this kind of analysis is that because these things are cultural, they are
malleable, and can be changed for the better.

Because evolutionary psychology—the only form of evolutionary analysis that has thus far been applied to fashion—seems to suggest that basic
human characteristics, including gender differences, are not malleable, it is
often seen as antithetical to a feminist approach, and it often can be. For
instance, evolutionary behavioral scientist Gad Saad sees consumption and
fashion as a function of "conspicuous consumption choices [that are] mere
sexual signals, meant to advertise one's self to prospective mates. These
sexual signals appeal to the evolved preferences of the opposite sex."[1] Saad
states,

> [M]y goal is to demonstrate that countless consumption acts
> are specific instantiations of the four most elemental Darwinian
> modules that drive purposive behavior. Specifically, I highlight
> how many consumption phenomena can be subsumed within the
> reproductive, survival, kin selection, and reciprocation modules.[2]

In this view, consumption becomes an expression of these "elemental modules," which are the same cross-culturally and across time.

Similarly, Geoffrey Miller's book *Spent: Sex, Evolution, and Consumer
Behavior* focuses on one of those modules (the reproductive), and argues that
consumption is an expression of sexual signaling, and that human mental
traits have themselves evolved as "fitness indicators, including our capacities
for language, humor, art, music, creativity, intelligence, and kindness. Signaling theory applies equally to nature and culture. Nature produced peacock
tails . . . human culture produced luxury goods like the Hummer H1."[3] For
Miller, everything we buy is a way to advertise our "fitness," the value and
quality of our genes. Fashion, in this view, is all about sexual selection
and costly signaling in which people compete with others to advertise their
genetic quality.

Therefore, the previous research on consumption and fashion can be
summarized in the following terms: (1) fashion helps us signal group conformity, the innate, evolutionarily based need to fit in with the group; and
(2) it is about sex and status in that it increases our "mate value." On the
female side, we use products to enhance or create the illusion of youth,
beauty, and fertility, and on the male side, to display wealth and status.
We argue that this account is inadequate to explain fashion from both an
evolutionary point of view and a feminist one. It is precisely this ostensibly
"scientific" view of fashion (and other arts) that needs a feminist framework
to make it truly evolutionary, explaining the concepts of innovation and
change (known in evolutionary language as "plasticity") so vital to an accu-
rate evolutionary framework. Developing a feminist evolutionary perspective
on fashion contributes to the development of the kind of bioepistemological
model that Nancy Easterlin, a feminist cognitive literary theorist, calls for
when she formulates knowledge as the interaction between human capacities and predispositions and social values and interests. Fashion gains new
dimensions when interpreted in this light, and that interpretation is both
evolutionary and feminist. To develop this model, we will examine the concepts of innovation and creativity, and provide a broader interpretation of
sexuality and gender than that represented by the evolutionary psychology
that has been previously used to explain fashion and consumption, and
show why feminist insights have much to contribute to an evolutionary
interpretation of fashion.

To begin this examination, we talked to David Kasuga, Creative Design Director of Premiere Fabrics, who has done suiting designs for companies such as Sean Jean, Oscar de la Renta, and Brooks Brothers. In an interview, we asked him, "In fashion design, what is the relative importance of innovation versus tradition?" and he told us that

> both are equally important. Innovation and tradition are both integral parts of fashion. Fashion as a definition implies trends, newness, and often innovation. Much like in the technology sector, in fashion, there is a constant need for innovation and newness. This need is driven by the consumer's desire for performance, comfort, durability, and added-value products. Tradition plays an important part of fashion and, in fact, tradition can be a fashion trend in itself, sometimes referred to as "Retro." Oftentimes there is a fusion between tradition and innovation, traditional clothing designs using innovative fabrications and finishing applications.[4]

We can explain the tension Kasuga articulates here between tradition and innovation by reference to the importance of implementing an approach that is simultaneously cultural and biological. Although they are often seen as being at odds, together feminist cultural studies and evolutionary frameworks can provide a powerful means of interpreting the interaction between biology and culture as that interaction is expressed in fashion. Furthermore, in a parallel conceptual sense, the tension between tradition and innovation also marks a central tension in evolutionary theory between natural selection (which happens at the level of the species competing for survival) and sexual selection (which happens at the level of the individual competing for relatively more offspring than others). A third category—"group selection" (or multilevel selection)—puts an emphasis on the group-level process in navigating social interactions and the importance of group cooperation to evolution. This category has been advocated and developed in the work of David Sloan Wilson and Elliot Sober, and is the perspective we will use to integrate our analysis of the way tradition and innovation, individual and group, are negotiated in the institution of fashion.[5]

Competition and cooperation, working in tandem, help this negotiation. In *The Origin of Stories,* which argues that art can be understood evolutionarily, Brian Boyd writes, "[E]ven in bodily adornment, the closest that human arts come to sexual selection, cooperation seems also to have been present in our highly social species. Elaborate body decoration in most societies serves primarily as a mark of affiliation and group identification . . . [but also as] a display to others of prowess and judgment."[6] Fashion is simultaneously about belonging to the group *and* innovating—distinguishing oneself. It can be seen as a manifestation of particular aspects of our evolved biologies, and these aspects are linked to the expression and development of our social norms.

To the extent that it provides an outlet for creative gender expression as well as conformity, fashion is necessarily a feminist concern. It is possible to interpret the current turn to green (anti-) fashion as a sign of a politically progressive cultural moment. However, as our analysis of the 2009 finale of *American Idol* will show, the anti-fashion, "green" turn to the seemingly simple, less fabricated, more "natural" and down-to-earth ideal (that is nonetheless constructed) also marks a turn toward more traditional notions of gender, a privileging of aggregate group norms as opposed to the variations or "outliers" who might be seen as expressing something new. To the extent that evolutionary psychology has followed the tendency within the sciences to focus on norms rather than variations, its framework has been insufficient to explain fashion, whose structure necessarily incorporates both.

No Blank Slates: An Embodied Evolutionary Approach

One key aspect of evolutionary theory is the way it explains human behavior related to groups. One particular form of evolutionary psychology that is very useful for understanding fashion is concerned with theories designed to explain cooperation between people beyond kin, and the mechanisms through which we form affiliations and select partners with whom to cooperate, known in this vocabulary as our "in-group." An in-group can be any social network bound by affiliative ties—geographic origin, age, class, religion, intellectual interests, hobbies, etc. We have evolved cognitive mechanisms, the theory goes, that allow us to choose appropriate group members: "choosing from among the possibilities for social interaction represents a critical class of adaptive problems, and natural selection would, therefore, have favored cognitive mechanisms designed to make good decisions about an individual's social interactions and social interactants."[7] We tend to seek out others who have something to offer, such as prestige, status, or resources. Two aspects in particular contribute to our interaction preferences, and we unconsciously look for cues that signal trustworthiness and cooperation. The results of experiments in this area show "the particular importance of trustworthiness and cooperativeness in the context of interdependent coordination."[8]

What are these cues? We think it is arguable that fashion might be said to provide some of them, and those cues make sense if we look at fashion as a kind of evolutionary adaptation. Adaptationism is a methodology in the natural sciences that distinguishes features of an organism that are the result of an evolutionary adaptation for a particular function. These features are designed to solve a particular problem relevant to survival and reproduction. For humans, the ancestral environment of the Pleistocene epoch (from roughly 1,800,000 to 12,000 years ago) is the time frame during which many adaptations are believed to have arisen. Utilizing an adaptationist perspective, fashion can be seen as a set of signifiers that signals cognitively desirable qualities such as prestige, cultural capital, and status—something that marks an individual as different. An alliance with someone who signifies these things would ostensibly be beneficial to other individuals. On the other hand, the willingness to comply with the latest fashions could signify trustworthiness, conformity, and willingness to cooperate. To a certain extent, the very ephemerality of fashion may actually signify consistency and willingness to follow a trend, and thereby conformance to group norms. Followers of fashion may be perceived as more trustworthy and cooperative than those who don't follow, as long as the trend isn't too radical. Simultaneously, starting a new fashion signals innovation, which is also desirable for group progress if it is accepted by the group. As such, innovation is risky—you could equally be seen as a misfit who doesn't "get" the norms and is thus shunned, or you can be seen as an original and thus honored. What Boyd says of art in general applies to fashion in particular: "Unlike other species, we can imitate closely and therefore follow established forms. Crucially, we *need* to imitate in order to innovate. Building on what came before underlies all creativity, in biology and culture."[9] Boyd's analysis is reminiscent of Judith Butler's work on performativity—repetition with a difference that becomes the building blocks of cultural forms.

Social groups also require signs of commitment. Familiarity plays a part in group identification, so that if a stranger exhibits signs that are familiar, he or she is more likely to be accepted. As evolutionary theorists Robert Kurzban and Steven Neuberg explain, "people are socially attracted to those they believe are more familiar and are more likely to help them . . . when selecting group members, people seek those who exhibit cues suggesting they will be around in the future, such as familiarity and indices of commitment."[10] A principal manifestation of such cues is the exhibition of conformance to group norms through visual symbols like fashion. Conformance to norms is a key feature in the psychology that determines in-groups and out-groups, in that

> [c]ommon norms of behavior facilitate coordination and the gains from cooperation, and a signal feature of human groups is the transmission of information that enables norm sharing. This fact might partially explain why humans prefer to interact with those who share an individual's norms, to copy his or her group's norms, and, critically, to react negatively to those with different norms . . . these effects seem to be particularly pronounced, as we might expect, when those with discrepant norms have the

potential to be models for subsequent social learners within the group.[11]

This form of analysis gives us a way to understand the social transmission of information and its role in evolutionary developments throughout human history. Fashion and its normalizing capacities is a clear example of an in-group formation in which the information about what to wear is shared by members of a particular group and is used to exclude others.

An obvious contemporary example of this process is the television program *What Not to Wear*, which centers around teaching hapless women of little fashion sense (so designated by their friends and coworkers) how to create a successful new look. Each episode ends with a triumphant coming-out party for the newly fashionable subject, who twirls and turns in front of her cheering friends and family. The subject's new fashion sense is said not only to make her feel more confident, but also to gain the enthusiastic approbation of her peers. The stylists' tips are utterly norm-enforcing, as they insist that women "dress their age," and that they construct looks "appropriate" to the norms of a very particular social class and race cohort.[12] Such normalizing is group-specific and exclusionary when viewed from a humanities or political perspective that highlights how constraining norms can be. These problems are valid. Yet, from an evolutionary perspective, the made-over woman's enthusiastic embrace by her peers can be seen as *also* contributing to group cohesion. Such cohesions are extraordinarily important from an evolutionary point of view. Successful group functioning is seen by many evolutionary biologists to have facilitated the "great transition" from *homo erectus*, an earlier form of humanity, to *homo sapiens*, the current form characterized by its larger brain and capacities. While we are accustomed in the humanities to "questioning norms," and the word "norm" is used in the negative sense of coercion, manipulation, and control of the individual, in the physical sciences we tend to use "norm" to signify a positive process, the evolved in-group/out-group mechanisms that allowed groups to develop, thereby fostering—and indeed making possible—human differentiation and change. When it comes to conformity *and* innovation, fashion (and the evolutionary process) needs both.

Fashion, as an art form as well as a behavior, can be seen as a form of cognitive play that allows social interaction to flourish through elaborate systems of social signaling. This signaling inculcates fluid, plastic forms of group membership and identification that serve as ways to work through the badges of identity related to gender, ethnicity, social status, and other variables. Cultural evolutionary instantiations related to fashion, art (specifically singing), gender, and sexuality were on full display in the Spring 2009 season of *American Idol,* a phenomenon to which we now turn.

Novelty and Attention, Spring 2009:
The Case of *American Idol*

Season 8 of Spring 2009 was widely characterized as "reinvigorating" the *Idol* franchise, which had been experiencing declining ratings.[13] In his account of how art "constitutes another Darwin machine, another evolutionary subsystem effectively designed, in this case, for creativity,"[14] Boyd emphasizes how the relationship between tradition and innovation articulates itself evolutionarily through art. "In a system designed to secure attention," Boyd writes, "habituation (the loss of attention through the persistence or repetition of a stimulus) encourages innovation. Since repeating exactly the same thing over and over guarantees it will lose its impact, art faces a consistent pressure for novelty."[15] This was precisely the phenomenon that *Idol Season 8* served. It accomplished innovation through the presence of a single contestant: the glam-rock, black fingernail-polished, musically versatile Elvis/Bowie look-alike named Adam Lambert. Lambert, a twenty-seven-year-old Jewish Californian, had a musical theater background, performing in productions from the age of ten. In the innumerable Internet postings related to the show, he was often pronounced "too theatrical" even as everyone acknowledged how well he could sing. Distinguished by his charisma, tremendous vocal range, and mesmerizing performances, Lambert drew attention to himself in a way no other contestant even approximated: in spring 2009, Adam Lambert *was* fashion.

Hailed by the media as the leading contender for the *AI* title almost from the beginning of the season, the biggest question surrounding the media buzz was whether he was gay, or why—since everyone assumed he was (bolstered in part by Internet photos that showed him performing in full drag and kissing men)—he wasn't saying. This fueled speculation about whether an openly gay contestant could win the title of "American Idol," whether the show's producers wouldn't let him say, or whether he was saving it for an exclusive interview in *Rolling Stone.* When Lambert finished as the runner-up to Kris Allen, a twenty-three-year-old newlywed Christian missionary from Arkansas, whose basic singer-songwriter persona was said by many to be handsome but boring and indistinguishable from many others, there was an outcry about rigged voting, homophobia, and America "not being ready" for a gay Idol.[16]

Was Lambert's defeat the result of his "costly signaling," his vibrant use of fashion to advertise his sexuality, of his willingness, as Mark Harris put it in an *Entertainment Weekly* cover story, to sing " 'I'm gonna give you every inch of my love' while wearing skintight pants and green-glitter guyliner"?[17] Harris thought so, although he probably used a slightly different definition of "costly" than the evolutionary definition that, to reiterate, indicates a high fitness level and availability of time and resources that you can put into attracting mates because you've got the basics covered. "Maybe it's still too costly to say who you are," Harris wrote. "It's certainly costly not to. Does he feel he can't? Does the show feel he shouldn't?"[18] If one combines the evolutionary definition of "costly" with the sense of the term Harris uses here—"cost" in the sense of loss, taking something away—we arrive at a biocultural standpoint or lens through which to interpret the *Idol* goings-on of Spring 2009.

More than Lambert's sexuality contributed to the final vote. While his sexuality was at least partially expressed by signaling cues related to his fashion, those cues may have triggered unconscious in-group and out-group identifications that Kurzban and Neuberg identified, creating a sense in some viewers that his individuality and "theatricality" made him less familiar and therefore not "trustworthy" to some (and also more familiar and trustworthy to others). The independence he signaled may have made him seem more "selfish" and less likely to support and contribute to the dominant, heteronormative group. As we showed earlier, Kurzban and Neuberg note that social groups require signs of commitment to the group, and willingness to sacrifice oneself to its greater interests. Furthermore, familiarity plays a part in in-group identification, so that if a stranger exhibits signs that are familiar, he or she is more likely to be trusted and included. The outcome of the 2009 season finale of *American Idol* might be seen to exhibit this kind of inclusion bias. Top winner Kris Allen, who was portrayed in many blog comments as more self-effacing and accessible, evoked cues of familiarity for some, and boring conformity for others, while Adam Lambert, with his "theatricality" and alternative sexuality, evoked cues of difference for some groups and identification for other groups. Allen's tendency to do the nondescript, stereotypically masculine jeans-and-T-shirts thing was a marked contrast to Lambert's leather, metal wings, and platform boots, his beautiful fitted suits, and skinny ties. Self-effacement signals deference to the group, while individuality and self-assertion can be interpreted as "selfishness" and a failure to conform. Since, according to adaptationists, such adaptations evolved in a very different social context (the hunter-gatherer conditions of the Pleistocene) where group mixing and hybridity were much less common, the current context of globalization may make us prone to accept difference superficially, while the older cues related to familiarity and sameness are activated simultaneously and, perhaps ironically, create a lack of identification in viewers who see themselves as normative. In this way, the very different fashion senses of each performer might be seen to have signaled different group identifications and norms.

Furthermore, evolutionary psychologists and anthropologists Joseph Henrich and Francisco Gil-White discuss the requirement for prestigious individuals to humble themselves in relation to their followers. Perhaps Lambert's "theatricality" was seen as a refusal to do so (to others, this was a point in Lambert's favor). "Some high-status humans," they write, "display subdominant ethology (deep bows, bringing one's hands to the center of the body, lowering the head, and generally appearing bashful). . . . Self-deprecation is also common in prestige: those receiving applause and awards will publicly 'doubt' their worthiness and attribute the gesture more to client generosity than personal prowess."[19] While Lambert was consistently generous and self-deprecating in interviews, this was often read as a sign of his professionalism (and therefore not a genuine sentiment), and his performances were anything but self-deprecating. As Harris put it, "*Idol* stars are supposed to be blank slates, 'relatable' folk with extraordinary talent whom we elect in an orderly fashion and elevate to success. Meet Adam Lambert. Adam has messed that all up. Adam is nobody's idea of a blank slate. Adam is a surprise."[20]

Indeed, Lambert is a surprise that can be read in evolutionary terms, an innovative phenomenon who ran the risk of standing out, of demonstrating a gender and sexual identity different from dominant norms. Furthermore, he did so in the context of an artistic public performance that involved fashion as a central part of the performance "package." The contrast between the two post-*Idol* interviews on *Live With Regis and Kelly* (one of the top-rated syndicated daytime talk shows) with the 2009 *Idol* finalists clearly illustrates these points, as well as the point that Kris Allen was himself constructed as the "natural" masculinity that provided an alternative to Lambert. Both identities, the flamboyantly different and the "natural" conformist, were constructions defined and expressed through fashion and the stylists who defined their looks. Allen's supposed naturalness was on display when he arrived to his interview dressed in nondescript jeans, white Chuck Taylors, and a white T-shirt with an open, short-sleeved brown shirt over it, whose only embellishment was a minimal form of an epaulet on each shoulder. The audience was enthusiastic, but not wildly so. The first question Regis asked Allen was whether he was surprised when he won. Clearly constructing him as "the natural," the narrative that emerged from the questioning emphasized that Allen was a self-taught musician who learned to play guitar in his backyard, and that his *Idol* quest was largely unplanned, "a road trip [to] have fun . . . I never actually thought about winning." "You're so down to earth," Kelly gushed, a comment made repeatedly throughout the season about Allen's "modest 23-year-old Arkansas nature," another frequent descriptor.[21]

By contrast, Adam Lambert arrived to his interview dressed in polished gray boots, tight jeans, a white shirt, skinny black tie, and black jacket. The audience screamed with an enthusiasm that outflanked Allen's by many decibels. Regis introduced Lambert as "one of the most glamorous Idols ever," and the first thing he said after he walked on the stage was "Look at Adam Lambert!" When the applause died down, Regis exclaimed, "Oh, boy, this is show business you know" (gesturing toward Lambert). The interview then proceeded to chronicle Lambert's experience in musical theater, and Lambert had to forcefully turn the conversation away from the theater conversation to emphasize that he had also had a rock band. When the conversation turned to the "phenom" (Regis's word) that Lambert had become, Kelly said "I don't think anyone has ever achieved the level of stardom on that *AI* stage that you have . . . you have tapped into something that people were hungry for, looking for."

Lambert then articulated the ritual of self-deprecation that Henrich and Gil-White say is obligatory for those in status positions: "I think if you go in and just focus on performing your best and competing with yourself and not with the other competitors, it can really be a great experience." Kelly asked Lambert about his biggest style influence (note there was no parallel question for Kris Allen), to which Lambert mentioned the late British glam-inspired couture designer Alexander McQueen and his love of nice clothes and nice things. Regis responded, "But this is all part of the package, Adam, right? The way you dress, the jewelry?" Lambert, who seemed very used to handling interviewers who speak in code and utter veiled references to his sexuality, continued Regis's thought: "the nails, the eyeliner. . . ." Kelly mentioned that Lambert's fans are called "Glamberts," and then they trotted out a *Regis and Kelly* "style icon"—an older man with Adam-inspired hair, nails, and makeup, who came out flouncing and waving his nails in a parody of a drag queen. Jokingly invoking what Kurzban and Neuberg would refer to as the exclusionary mechanisms often employed for in-group dynamics—especially in the face of someone in a position of influence who evokes different norms—Kelly said, "We really should have warned the viewers at home to put your children out of the room." Lambert laughed, seeming sincerely good-natured about this quip.[22]

If Adam Lambert makes Americans want to "put their children out of the room," this surely isn't evident in the amount of interest in him. However, Kelly's comment points to the ways Lambert diverges from aggregate in-group norms, even as people, through their embrace of him also seem to be "hungry" for that divergence themselves. It is also clear in the swirl of cultural narratives surrounding the show that someone divergent like Adam Lambert is seen as constructed, artificial, "unnatural," whereas the normative Kris Allen is seen as "natural," unconstructed, and "down to earth."

The contest between Lambert and Allen represented the age-old evolutionary conflict between tradition and innovation. Boyd's evolutionary theory of art explains this dynamic through his explication of "attention": "art's effects on human minds depends on its power to compel attention."[23] Attention is crucial because "humans have a uniquely intense motivation and capacity to share attention—and this proclivity has recently been proposed as the key factor in the singular development of human intelligence and culture."[24] Those who attract attention facilitate change, and change is basic to the evolutionary process; recent work on "neuroplasticity" emphasizes how necessary new ideas and experiences are to keeping our brains alive and vital.[25] What once was seen as "style"—unique, different, and potentially threatening—can, over time, be seen as "substantial"—normative and even necessary.

This is the dynamic that a cultural evolutionary perspective gives us: Culture influences our biologies as much as our biologies constrain our cultures. As Boyd writes,

> [W]e all see the status that attention confers, [and we all have] an innate capacity for imitation. One of our main cues for social learning is 'imitate the successful.' We also have a strong disposition to conformism, which enables us to learn from what others have discovered and to operate within a cohesive group: our other heuristic is 'imitate the most common.' A new individual initiative therefore can become first a model, then a fashion, then a tradition, and eventually even a jealously enforced norm.[26]

Humans are evolutionarily marked as innovators *and* conformists, and this conflict helps explain Season 8 of *American Idol* and all the interest it precipitated—including the interest in masculine fashion and style. Our social learning was being stimulated on the one hand by the cue of "imitate the successful," and Lambert's success was noted from the beginning of the season. On the other hand, the code of "imitate the most common" was activated by the comfort of Allen's familiar-feeling, "natural" presence, even though that presence was also constructed. Lambert was innovative in ways that were clearly attractive, but also threatening, and that threat is linked to the particulars of this current historical moment, perhaps best characterized by recessionary economics and fears of scarcity.

One concern in the present context of diminished resources and declining fortunes is a swing of the cultural pendulum toward the side of "conserve resources and serve the interests of the group," and such swings tend to be associated with more traditional gender roles. James Howard Kuntzler, for instance, a "doomsday" author and blogger whose book *The Long Emergency* predicted the housing bubble, stock market crash, instability of the oil markets, and global pandemics, argues that tough economic times and periods of resource conservation are always accompanied by a return to more traditional divisions of labor and gender roles, assumptions, and practices.[27] A cultural mandate to not be flamboyant, to not stand out, and to not consume as many resources, seems to be an attitude that is in the air, linked to the current economic recession and concerns about the environment. Fashion, in this context, seems a bit profligate and selfish, and gender stand-outs in this area like Adam Lambert seem overly complex, not "simple" and "down to earth" like Kris Allen. Lambert signified to many as constructed, contrived, unnatural, the theater boy who only knows how to put on a disguise. Allen signified simplicity and authenticity, something more easily accessible and honest, less contrived. Both were constructed looks, both indicated fundamental parts of the evolutionary process, but in times of threat, we can often forget the crucial role of style and innovation play in that process.

Will fashion, and Adam Lambert as one of its icons, go the way of the Hummer H1 if we experience real grid crash? Fashion is at once an opportunity for self-expression and an expression of conformity, and the way it is interpreted has more to do with the norms it either challenges or reinforces. An evolutionary approach to fashion shows how its functions and our responses to it are the product of both biology and culture, the expression of evolved mechanisms for group behavior, artistic production, and basic neurological processes that allow us to identify with others. For better and worse, fashion relies to a certain extent on prosperity, on the ability of its practitioners to signal their biological fitness and economic health. In a recessionary and uncertain economic context, conspicuous consumption—previously seen as an individual right that exhibited power and prestige, a way of contributing to the group through promotion of economic growth—might now be seen as a threat to that same group in the context of more limited resources. Fashion choices clearly have a place in the formation of in-groups and out-groups, but these now take place in the context of a globalized consumer economy facing its own limits. Let us hope that predictions of a return to more "real" gender roles and rigid heteronormativity along with an economic collapse are greatly exaggerated, and that the positive role innovation and variation displays in our evolutionary history will not be forgotten in the context of scarcity.

Notes

1. Gad Saad, *The Evolutionary Bases of Consumption* (Mawah, NJ: Lawrence Erlbaum, 2007), 69.

2. Ibid., 59.

3. Geoffrey Miller, *Spent: Sex, Evolution, and Consumer Behavior* (New York: Viking, 2009), 92.

4. David Kasuga, personal communication, June 2, 2009.

5. David Sloan Wilson and Elliot Sober, *Unto Others: The Evolution and Psychology of Unselfish Behavior* (Cambridge, MA: Harvard University Press, 1998). The history of multilevel selection or group selection in the history of evolutionary biology is a long and complicated one. More accepted through the 1960s, it became discredited and displaced by the individualist orientation of theories that interpret human evolution and behavior through the lens of self-interest, a circumstance that is clearly amenable to ideological analysis. For concise and accessible reading that traces the history of this debate and clearly makes the argument for group selection, see David Sloan Wilson's blog on *The Huffington Post*; http://www.huffingtonpost.com/david-sloan-wilson.

6. Brian Boyd, *On the Origin of Stories: Evolution, Cognition, and Fiction* (Cambridge, MA: Belknap/Harvard University Press, 2009), 78. Boyd's is the best work we have seen to date that uses evolutionary theory to help explain phenomena in the arts. It is more effective than other approaches because it looks at biological, social, and cultural dimensions simultaneously, and values art on its own terms, not just as raw data to be interpreted through a scientific lens. On this point see 399–414.

7. Robert Kurzban and Steven Neuberg, "Managing Ingroup and Outgroup Relationships," in David Buss, ed., *The Handbook of Evolutionary Psychology* (Hoboken, NJ: Wiley, 2005), 656.

8. On the evolutionary relationship between groups and arts like singing and dancing, see Barbara Ehrenreich, *Dancing in the Streets: A History of Collective Joy* (New York: Henry Holt, 2006).

9. Boyd, *On the Origin of Stories*, 122.

10. Kurzban and Neuberg, "Managing Ingroup and Outgroup Relationships," 657.

11. Ibid., 663.

12. For further discussion, see Shira Tarrant, "New Blouse, New House, I Need a New Spouse," in *Fix Me Up: Essays on Television Dating and Makeover Shows*, ed. Judith Lancioni (Jefferson, NC: McFarland Publishing, 2010).

13. 70 percent of those polled said that this particular season had made *American Idol* seem exciting again. *Aol TV*, May 8, 2009, http://television.aol.com/american-idol/ 2009/05/08/american-idol-season-8-survey.

14. Boyd, *On the Origin of Stories*, 121.

15. Ibid., 122.

16. Some numbers that reveal a greater interest in Adam Lambert, but perhaps a greater comfort level with Kris Allen: A Google search done on June 1, 2009 turned up 16,600,000 entries for Lambert, and only 8,960,000 for Allen. Online marketer Brian Combs did an analysis of Internet data from Google Trends in May 2009 to try to predict the winner before the finale on May 20, and found a similar result, with 9,970,000 searches for Lambert compared to 3,500,00 for Allen, but also found that Lambert had only 7,937 Twitter followers compared to Allen's 14,965. Facebook fan pages showed Lambert with 172,693 fans to Allen's 61,283 fans. Twitter as the discrepant data point raised questions about the relative age of Allen's supporters (Millenials and younger) versus Lambert's (Gens X and Y). A season-end survey done by AOL before the finale again showed greater interest in Lambert when it asked what for responses to the best performance (48 percent for Lambert's rendition of "Mad World," 25 percent for Allen's "Ain't No Sunshine"); whether or not poll respondents

would vote for an openly gay contestant (59 percent yes, 29 percent "if they're good," 13 percent no), and whether, based on this season, *American Idol* was still exciting (70 percent yes). Brian Combs, "Kris Allen vs. Allen Lambert: The Numbers." *Brian Combs,* May 20, 2009, http://www.briancombs.net/2713/.

17. Mark Harris, "Adam Lambert: Shaking Up 'Idol,'" *Entertainment Weekly,* May 8, 2009, http://www.ew.com/ew/article/0,,20007164_20171835_20277643,00. html.

18. Ibid.

19. Joseph Henrich and Francisco Gil-White, "The Evolution of Prestige: Freely Conferred Deference as a Mechanism for Enhancing the Benefits of Cultural Transmission," *Evolution and Human Behavior* 22 (2001): 179.

20. Harris, "Adam Lambert."

21. See the Allen interview on *YouTube,* http://www.youtube.com/watch?v=XQrkroC5YRA. On June 1, 2009, it had 37,084 views.

22. See the Lambert interview on *YouTube,* http://www.youtube.com/watch?v=_xE62Ryl-XY. On June 1, 2009, it had 112,047 views.

23. Boyd, *On the Origin of Stories,* 362.

24. Ibid., 394.

25. See, for instance, Thomas F. Münte, Eckart Altenmüller, and Lutz Jäncke, "The Musician's brain as a model of neuroplasticity," *Nature Reviews Neuroscience* 3 (2002): 473–478.

26. Boyd, *On the Origin of Stories,* 112.

27. See James Howard Kuntsler, *The Long Emergency* (New York: Atlantic Monthly Press, 2005), especially Chapter 7.

Chapter 5

My Mannequin, Myself

Embodiment in Fashion's Mirror

Denise Witzig

How can we explain so double-edged a phenomenon as fashion?

—Elizabeth Wilson[1]

In the theatre of art and commerce that is the department store or the museum, fashion can be considered the mise-en-scène. As such, fashion is both a staging area for a discourse about aesthetics, currency, social discipline, and value, and the lens through which the dream machine of the self can be glimpsed. Fashion is the place for a discussion about both embodiment and disembodiment. We can see this from two scenes in San Francisco:

Scene 1. A lively crowd populates Union Square, the heart of urban retail, on a weekday morning. Shoppers and workers mingle on the sidewalks and in the various upscale boutiques, department stores, and chains, not pausing to consider, perhaps, the ways in which each business has worked hard to create a fantasy or dream life reflecting specific consumer identities in the midst of the carnivalesque. Macy's, Barneys, Neiman's, Saks, YSL, Betsey Johnson, Brooks Brothers, Victoria's Secret, H&M, the Gap—each conveys a particularized but dreamlike world or atmosphere competing for consumer attention, while they collaborate in the overall flow of pedestrian traffic. Carefully positioned in connection and juxtaposition, open and inviting, their huge windows display theatrical promises of entertainment and aesthetic pleasure. Once inside, the shopper believes she will be part of the spectacle and story the featured mannequins only hint at. The story is bigger than the shopper herself, but it is about her, too.

Scene 2. The tribute to the work of Yves Saint Laurent at the de Young Museum, early in 2009, featured over 120 ensembles of his best-known work. It was a popular and well-attended event. Museum-goers milled around dramatically lit mannequins wearing familiar and exotic costumes from the world of haute couture, a place the majority of those spectators had never themselves visited, most likely, but nevertheless recognized and respected. Each ensemble stood separate in its own lighting, linked as much by the featureless family of mannequins as by the aesthetic project: a parade of referents and markers of a time more refined, a sensibility more elevated. They stood in reference to each other, too, as the personal tastes and aspirations of the spectators noted a particular visual affinity that produced incremental pleasure, from one costume to the next. The spectacle produced was configured as a public tribute to the designer, recently deceased, but it was also intensely personal and interactive as the spectators were invited one by one to gaze with rapture upon the object, the idealized vision.

Each of the scenes described above is about pleasure, ritual, and spectacle, presenting fashion as a kind of *enchantment*, as Baudrillard would say.[2] Both occur in marketplaces of desire. In different but similar ways, the scenes stage the realm of fashion as a performance of aesthetics, meaning, and value, encouraging an active investment from each participant. That the shopper and the museum-goer share a purpose can be seen in the nature of the pilgrimage that is the shopping foray or the museum visit.[3] Both paths take on the quality of devotional observance in temples to commodities fetishism. Both are characterized by elements of sacred and profane in genuflections to so-called high and low culture. Most importantly, both are engaged in a discourse about embodiment and disembodiment, desire and nostalgia, the real and unreal. This paradoxical relationship, this tenuous balance between anxiety and pleasure, is the *place* where fashion happens.[4]

The shop and the museum are places closely linked by performance and temporality. Shopping, an activity that is suffused with possibility and the proliferation of selves, shares with museum-going the project of identity and the search for creative self-expression. In the mall, or at Union Square, the shopper is looking for the place that reflects and expands upon her idea of herself, or gives her a more desirable social version of that self in a ceaseless performance of self-improvement. The museum creates a larger view of self that is carefully attached to cultural value and a story about aesthetics and

meaning. The museum-goer also seeks self-improvement through the intellectual and aesthetic engagement of this story. The self reflected back to the museum-goer is a more coherent, culturally sanctioned identity, authorized by history and categorization. Shopping and museum-going are activities distinguished and linked by temporality as the scenes described above make clear. The spectacle of Union Square takes place every day, with little variation but for the ebb and flow of crowds.[5] The performance of shopping and its staged effects may perhaps be marked by store hours, seasons, and special events, but the shrines and meccas to consumer culture are always there, waiting if not actively inviting, their visual tributes to the fantasy beckoning from lit windows. The museum exhibit, on the other hand, as with the Saint Laurent exhibit described, are periodic only and subject to the interventions of special hours and crowd control. Visitors are expected to move through the spectacle in a timely manner, as they are carefully encouraged in this momentum to end their pilgrimage at the museum shop where artifacts of the invaluable (the experience of spectacle, as well as the objet d'art) can be purchased. There is a regimental or disciplinary quality to the museum visit. The spectator must observe a certain order within and, of course, must be sure to visit during that brief period the exhibit is featured. After all, Yves Saint Laurent's oeuvre, while described as "timeless" was offered for viewing at the de Young only from November 2008 to April 2009.

In subtle ways, the quality of temporality, of time and its relationship to self-expression, identity, and pleasure, has an even more complex and intrinsic relationship to performance and spectacle in the setting of the shop or museum. The experience of shopping for fashion is marked by the tenuous interaction of aspiration and anxiety. The department store and the shopper's own purpose collaborate in projecting a dream-like future self, marked by potentiality and the promise of personal transformation through consumption.[6] The narrative of advertising (a newer, better you) is the narrative of glamour in the department store, as the stage is set with color, texture, and sheer numbers of beautiful objects as the tools of transformation. But the shopper is always aware of the disjuncture between that idealized self and the reality of the mirror, the tenuous hold on embodiment. The abstract and featureless mannequin may be an imago of the shopper, but there is only a fraught symmetry between what the shopper wants and what she sees in the dressing-room mirror. And the other project of shopping, to express a unique and individualized self, is complicated by the very proliferation that offers possibility in the marketplace. Can the shopper really create an authentic future self in the machine of mass production?[7]

Alternately, the museum is a place characterized by the spectacle of the self in time, but the performance here is always about an imaginary past and a story or fantasy about collective identity. In the museum, this story achieves a kind of totemic significance or sacred quality, as do the objects engaged in the story's performance—the artifacts of cultural identity. In the fashion exhibit, the story of identity is told through a fantasy self that is nostalgic in nature. The spectacle of glamour here is not dissimilar from that of the department store, but it is determined by the pull of the past and the haunting lure of memory. The objects that perform identity and engage embodiment in the fashion exhibit—the clothing, accessories, ensembles, and sketches—convey a fantasy detached from mass culture but very much a part of it. Haute couture is, after all, about our dreams of an idealized self, an aesthetics of being. But it is also, by virtue of privileging inaccessibility, more "valuable," more precious and rare. And this character-istic is reinforced in the hierarchy of the museum as the consumable object achieves the level of art. The engagement of this vision by the spectator is orchestrated to produce envy and desire, as in the department store display, but the transaction is markedly different. The nostalgia of the fashion exhibit is, after all, for a past self, or a vision of self in culture, recovered briefly through memory, recollection, and recognition. The spectator is drawn into a dialogue about time, style, and the ephemerality of embodiment, the slippage through history of selves: I remember that dress! I wore those boots! I was younger then. That was me.[8]

The experiences of the fashion spectacle described here as marked by future and past visions of self are thus public as they are intensely personal and pleasurable. They allow the spectator to participate in the performance of *style*—the department store in a ceaseless recreation of value through the label of the "new," the museum in a similar value-driven recuperation of aesthetic cultural markers, drawn from histories of fashion. In this way, the individual's agenda of the self is engaged in a bigger project of cultural reinvention through an ongoing discourse about embodiment. With abstract and tenuous effects, the discourse is visually marked by commodity—per-haps the latest shoe or handbag, perhaps the T-shirt with a quote by Saint Laurent himself: "Fashion changes, style endures." In the fashion spectacle, in the fantasy of future and past selves projected, in the *memento mori* (the purchase, the souvenir), the individual can realize a kind of embodiment that bestows a public benediction on the personal vision. Perhaps this is the fullest evocation of Barthes' "dream of wholeness."[9]

≈

Fashion is not a drifting of signs—it is their flotation, in the sense in which monetary signs are floated today.

—Jean Baudrillard[10]

But, as discussed above, any experience or performance of embodiment in the spectacle of fashion cannot but be marked by anxiety as well, dependent as it is on the transaction between desire and commodification, individual self-expression and cultural proliferation. In the department store and the museum, participants are drawn into identification with fashion in a spectral economy, as in a hall of mirrors. This is clear in the store, where the performance of embodiment is translated through a chain of meaning from mannequin to dressing-room mirror.[11] That transaction is driven also by the association of monetary value with the commodities considered as tools of transformation. In this way, the shopper is called into a specific and disciplinary relationship with the object of purchase. That is to say, the consumer sees herself evaluated within an economy of assigned worth. Shopping at Macy's or the Gap is a much different experience than shopping in the Prada boutique. The nature of the fantasy changes to the degree that the imaginative space itself reproduces a familiar set of fashion aspirations for the shopper—as it gestures to the inchoate desires of that shopper—but the pleasure or anxiety derived therein is also a matter of identification and embodiment. Is the shopper, as suggested by who/what her body conveys, worthy of this space? This object? Does her performance of self, how she appears, mirror the carefully constructed representation of who the ideal shopper is or should be? There is a double consciousness at work here. The shopper surveills herself in her mind, judging and evaluating her representation in the theatre of the store as she does in the mirror. She is also aware of being surveilled by workers and other shoppers in her performance. The ritual of shopping is totemic in its reinforcement of social approbation and implicit hegemony in the face of individual autonomy and pleasure. It is constructed specifically as a classed experience, as it is racialized and gendered. It draws the shopper into an aesthetic economy that is idealized and offered as a communal—yet, para-doxically, exclusive—vision, but serves to commodify the shopper herself.[12] It does not just promote anxiety in the pursuit of pleasure, it is *about* that very tension. It is part of the fashion bargain, part of the discourse, part of the circular performance of specularity and the very determinance of embodi-ment. In the department store, shop or boutique, we *look* at fashion, just as we *wear* fashion, to experience an imagined pleasure in being *looked at*, while excruciatingly aware that we are bodies being *observed* and evaluated in our performance of looking.[13]

In the museum, the relationship of embodiment to specularity is autho-rized within a different economy of commodification, one that is represented within a discourse of aesthetics, history, and larger cultural meaning. The fashion exhibit engages the spectator in an idealized and sanctioned (or sanctified) relationship with fashion that is removed from the commercialism and carnivalesque of the marketplace. The theatrical darkness and silence of the museum simulate other places of worship, drawing the spectator into an atmosphere of reverence and awe.[14] The disembodied mannequins, untouchable and removed, serve as icons of an idealized world, holding each spectator in thrall to a particular moment of interaction, a particular vision of elegance and beauty. The qualities of rarity and ephemerality convey inestimable value as they assert their worth over that of the spectator. The project of the museum evokes an intimidation that differs from that of the designer boutique in that it is reinforced by the recognition of and obedience to aesthetic value. The discipline of the museum requires that the spectator perform reverence and quiet appraisal—that she shows proper reverence by subordinating herself to the object. Unlike with the shopper, the authority of the spectator is not called into question, although she operates within a similar scenario of surveillance and self-consciousness. However, a kind of commodification occurs before the spectator even sets foot inside the museum, and this is the enforcement of privilege, which also disciplines the space of purported high culture. The audience of the fashion exhibit is already selected, uniform, to some extent, and acquiescent to the rules of the spectacle.

Nevertheless, the pleasures offered in the spectacle settings of museum and department store are directly related to the engagement of fantasies of embodiment, as they are characterized by a haunting disembodiment. A spectral self is fashioned by the many possible identities offered in the mirrors between viewer and mannequin. Questions of value, worth, and authority are abstracted by what might be called a bricolage of effects suggesting subjectivity. As Baudrillard observes:

> Fashion is only a simulation of the innocence of becoming, the cycle of appearances is just its recycling. That the development of fashion is contemporary with that of the museum proves this. . . . Whereas styles mutually exclude each other, the museum is defined by the virtual co-existence of all styles, by their promiscuity within a single cultural super-institution, or, in other words, the commensurability of their values under the sign of the great gold-standard of culture. Fashion does the same thing in accordance with its cycle: it commutes all signs and causes an absolute play amongst them. The temporality of works in the museum is 'perfect,' it is perfection and the past: it is the highly specific state of what has been and is never actual. But neither is fashion ever actual. . . .[15]

Fashion changes, style endures. For the consumer-spectator, the play of signs is the site of contestation about the possibility of identity in the fashion world.

In this, shopping and museum-going become a performance of engaging the possible, despite the persistent and haunting recognition of the impossible, idealized self invoked.

~

Body becomes dress becomes body becomes dress.

—Rei Kawakubo[16]

Despite the obvious similarities of production (of pleasure, of subjectivity) between the museum and the department store in discourses about embodiment, the commercial nature of the fashion project has produced some distress among the guardians of high culture. In light of this, I shift my analysis to focus specifically on the shrine to high culture, the museum, and the growing popularity of the fashion exhibit, as it represents an emerging spectacle of the body, expanding upon the discourse of fashion, and fashion's cultural value, in a venue ostensibly removed from the marketplace. Fashion-as-art, its appropriateness to the museum blockbuster, has come under fire from purists who decry the growing mallification of a sacred aesthetic space.[17] As Valerie Steele observes, "People in the museum world complain that fashion is not art, and they think it is unworthy of being in an art museum. . . . Fashion is really seen as the bastard child of capitalism and female vanity."[18] But the critique has not impeded the path of the catwalk. After all, with its restaurant, store, live music, cocktail and mixer events, the museum has taken on many commercial aspects of entertainment, performance, and spectacle. Fashion fits the new economy of the museum.[19] And we are fascinated by the spectacle of fashion, its story, its engagement of the body, and its expression. With this centrality of the body as a performance of self (a discussion which certainly takes place on the pages of fashion magazines and in sports clubs and gyms, among many other figurative and literal places), the fashion exhibit offers the garment, uniform, or costume as a fetish of being or not being, meaning or not meaning. There are many examples of this developing discourse. One exhibit, *Superheroes: Fashion and Fantasy*, staged by the Metropolitan Museum in New York in 2008, focused specifically on the body politics of costume interpreted through couture. According to the Met, "[t]he fashionable body and the superhero body are sites upon which we can project our fantasies, offering a virtuosic transcendence beyond the moribund and utilitarian."[20] The relationship of desire and aspiration to the experience of embodiment is conveyed through an imagined super-body as it is through the super-costume, thus suggesting the metonymy between fashion and flesh.

That relationship was further interrogated in *No Body Special*, a multimedia discussion staged by the photographer Lynn Hershman Leeson at the de Young in 2008. This exhibit offered a discussion about fashion and performance and focused around a red vinyl pantsuit. The pantsuit, designed exclusively for the I. Magnin store by the house of Jean Patou in 1965, was displayed as an object in play through images of various wearers—female, male, transgendered, a Guerilla Girl—in photography, video, and on mannequins. That the garment took on dramatically different looks despite uniformity and replication dramatized the possible proliferation of identities through the mediation of clothes. In her project, Hershman Leeson invited a critique of photographic formalism, haute couture, and the museum experience as she invoked characteristics of glamour and aesthetics, as well as sexual and racial identity, theories of masquerade and subjectivity. Most crucially, she draws the viewer into a self-conscious relationship with specularity and performance in the realm of the body as commodity.

As the exhibit notes assert, Hershman Leeson's work invokes Foucault's theory of surveillance in "the nexus of private life, public space, and behavior . . . and how this intersection also shapes the notion and construction of identity."[21] It also, of course, invokes the transaction discussed above from the realm of the marketplace and the act of shopping. Whether or not the spectator is attracted to this particular red pantsuit, its plasticity and interchangeability directly attest to the paradox of fashion as a bodily practice: yes, individuality, uniqueness, self-expression *are* possible through replication, regularization, and even commodification. At least this is the promise of the fashion marketplace, where we go when we "do fashion." However, the spectacle engaged here also offers a paradigm of the central question of embodiment: how does the individual negotiate and reconcile that proliferation of ideal and real bodies? Is there a possibility for identity and creative self-expression in the fashion commodity? And how does fashion, the fashion garment itself, offer that reconciliation through a visual aesthetics?[22]

These questions were taken up by *Stylized Sculpture: Contemporary Fashion from the Kyoto Costume Institute*, an exhibit of couture by avant-garde designers Issey Miyake and Rei Kawakubo, among others, at the Asian Art Museum in San Francisco in late 2007. Here, fashion was displayed as a series of wearable sculpture that called into debate the self-representational nature of the body itself. Mannequins, as pseudo-bodies, were wrapped in form-distorting and anti-naturalistic shapes and fabrics, ripped and pulled to reveal and conceal certain body parts, which emphasized artificiality and engaged the spectator in active discourse about fashion, utility, and the body.[23] In dimly lit adjoining rooms, the exhibit matched the fashions with Hiroshi Sugimoto's black-and-white photographs of them, featuring, through the artful poses of the mannequins, a vision of bodies frozen in potentiality, representing embodiment and movement as oddly abstract. In this, the camera captured an inescapable tension of the body—its performance of subjectivity—unavailable in the actual spectacle of mannequins.[24] This may, in effect, be the property of media—photography over sculpture—but it also suggests the fluidity and facility of imagination and the organizing quality of desire within the spectator herself to create a recognizable identity in the object of the gaze.[25]

Perhaps it is not surprising that the fashion exhibit, which is formally about the body's vividness and power, can be seen as sepulchral in the museum setting. There is a crucial disembodiment in the display offered by the museum mannequin, not unlike that in the mall, but devoid of the purpose of fantasy and possibility. Robbed of movement, flesh, attitude, the fashion artifact is arrested in representation, an arrangement of cloth, thread, and design. What the museum attendee, that student of fashion-as-art, sees is a spectre of the body—at once fantastical and intentional—a projection of a self that does not look back. In a way, the fashion exhibit is a *tableau morte*, a tribute to human culture that is aesthetic, but without the living, breathing interpretations and insurrections of the corporeal beings the culture represents.[26] But there is a crucial pleasure for the spectator in the museum, in looking, in fixing the look, in arresting the wild improbabilities and superficialities of fashion and its demi-monde. Theatrically draped, on pedestal pinned by stark lighting, the mini-skirt, bustier, kilt, unitard, or shiny red pantsuit is enshrined, sanctified, and sanitized. Price tags detached, it appears to float above the marketplace to the ether of art. Meant to inspire a kind of recollection and reverence (as in other places of worship) the fashion exhibit is spectacle staged as reenactment of the event, or the performance, of the fashion object. And, as such, it allows the spectator the full measure of sensual pleasure in a relationship with fashion, without the commitment.[27]

∿

Without a body, dress lacks fullness and movement; it is incomplete.

—Joanne Entwistle[28]

In practice, fashion is a kind of performance of the body, following Foucauldean theories of the body as a process or activity marked by the implications and exigencies of history and time. As Joanne Entwistle argues, Foucault's notion of the body as a site of "force relations," imbues the individual's bodily experience as one of power and pleasure contestations.[29] For Entwistle and other cultural theorists, this notion marks a logical transition to the discourse of dress as a further elaboration on power, discipline, knowledge, and pleasure.

The performance of the body as expressed through dress thus lends itself to interrogations of aesthetics and politics. Is it possible to wear our individuality and identity? To create through mass production, interchangeable and exchangeable selves that somehow lead to authentic and faithful representations? And does this representational self convey any truth or politics about the social body, one marked by gender, race, class, age, etc.? These are questions about capital and commodity, but also about ritual, creativity, and power, particularly from the perspective of cultural capital and the body politics of self and social definition. So, we ask: Do the clothes make the woman?

To some extent, as drag (and *Sex and the City*) shows us, the answer is yes.[30] In a way, this response hinges once again on specularity: what you see is what you get. The correlative relationship, as with all cultural body practices, is the central paradox of transformation and authenticity that fashion not only offers but promises. As with plastic surgery, fashion conveys to the wearer the potential of becoming: becoming new and improved; becoming the "real you." It is a mark of reality makeover shows that the participants eventually cry through tears of joy: "now people can see who I really am," as if new wardrobe (and skin and hair) remove a veil of social misapprehension, revealing incipient beauty and, with it, power. Thus, the *reveal* becomes the *soul* of the televisual machine. Contesting dualities of self/other, inner and outer continue to drive this cultural purpose.[31]

As feminist theory makes clear, fashion can be seen as a gesture toward the reconciliation of a tension of opposites: disembodied cultural representation and the lived experience of the body. As Elizabeth Wilson notes in *Adorned in Dreams*, ". . . the thesis is that fashion is oppressive, the antithesis is that we find it pleasurable."[32] Both about bodies and ideas, fashion is a particular language, a discourse about gender, thriving on paradox and irresolute boundaries. Alternately characterized in terms of aesthetic expression and ruthless commodification, identity performance and global development, timelessness and modernity, sexual morés and resistance to them, gender oppression and liberation, fashion represents profoundly personal creativity and dangerously fascistic uniformity. Authoritarian in its attempt to control, define, and discipline the body, it nevertheless consistently and perversely gestures toward rebellion and defiant self-definition, beauty and escape. "Today is a time of freedom," observes Pierre Bergé, Saint Laurent's business and life partner. "Women have a right to do anything they want."[33] While the proclamation surely is intended to address the designer's efforts in behalf of "the equality of the sexes" by putting women in pantsuits, the emphasis on sartorial liberation is not without reason.[34] Perhaps, however, the rights and freedoms afforded by the fashion economy are most fully expressed in the female shopper's project to perform embodiment, to locate subjectivity, to experience pleasure through clothes. In the shop and the museum, the desire for transformation, the dream of symmetry between the self and its projected ideal can be realized if only briefly and imperfectly through fashion and the spectacle it generates.

~

Nostalgia is like dreaming awake. I am definitely a dreamer.

—Yves Saint Laurent[35]

While visiting the Saint Laurent exhibit for my third and last time, I drew my gaze away from the visions of exquisite detail and excess and considered the other museum-goers in the room. Under surveillance, their faces looked struck or surprised at times, but most were rapt in fantasy or some memory, transfixed by the pull of beautiful objects and the theatrical atmosphere. They walked slowly from model to model, stopping to gaze at each and read small cards offering information about fabric, year, design specification. Sometimes, the cards noted, the ensembles had been owned or worn by famous people, information that gave the garments added resonance while identifying them as singular and unique, wed to a specific story. Socialite Nan Kempner's tuxedo was more scandalous without pants (her solution upon being denied entrance to a restaurant barring women in the offending garment); Catherine Deneuve's black-and-white smock from *Belle du Jour*, seemed too small and demure for a prostitute. The sheen of celebrity and myth was all over the clothes, exultant even as it was elegiac. Saint Laurent had just died after all, despite his representation in eternal life of the demi-monde.

The spectators talked in small groups, sharing affinities and critiques of elaborate ensembles of velvet and feather and bead. Would they wear that? I wondered about some. Did they like these clothes or find them decadent? Were they impressed by glamour? Disgusted by consumption? Could they see themselves in these tableaux, these stories? Many of the spectators wore jeans and backpacks and comfortable shoes, the uniforms of tourists to entertainment venues. This was not the crowd of the demi-monde, or the near-demi-monde, or even the art-world manqué; there was no visible attempt to reflect or imitate the aesthetics of style on view, or to comment on it indirectly. The double spectacle of the event, the exhibit and its audience, bore little symmetry: there was no perceptible affinity between the mannequin and museum-goer.

And yet, the atmosphere conveyed a coherent and suffusive pleasure, in the noise of conversation and exclamation that floated above the room. There was delight on many faces, reflecting the brilliance of the spectacle and the power of the exotic Other, represented here by luxurious and dramatic costumes and clothes designed for rarified beings in rarified places. Some faces in my view looked solemn and wistful, as if recalling some thing or person, some idea, or loss. Or perhaps it was just the quality of epoch that was the very nature of the exhibit, the mannequins positioned as a parade of tastes, styles, aesthetic ideals, and social identities taken out of circulation, referring to an exalted way of being long past. Nostalgia, the flip side of desire, was part of the intended effect.

Here, it was clear, the experience of fashion was part of a correspondence as much between garment and its observer as garment and its wearer. The drama of the spectacle necessarily included the spectators as featured players in the performance of meaning. The clothes displayed in this fashion exhibit, and in any other, are not solely empty objects or commodities; they are animated by the engagement of imagination, invested with the powerful sentiments of people for their things and the qualities of being represented by those things. In this, they engage the spectators in active collaboration, calling upon the fantasy of embodiment and of possibility. The mannequin garbed in gown or suit, though vacant and disembodied, draws the gaze of each spectator, as if the viewer can see something—someone—familiar. A recognizable body is there, it seems, at least some idea or ideal of the body. The sartorial procession of the exhibit represents, after all, a vivid and ritualized performance of enchanted selves through time, through the shaping influences of memory and expectation, loss and playful subjectivity. This is what the spectator recognizes in the drape, the fold, the sweep of fabric: she sees the dream of self, in endless proliferations and possibilities, and it is an image that reflects her back to herself, although the glimpse is fleeting. The clothes are inhabited, here in the museum and in the shop, by desire and imagination, but also by the recognition of the limits of embodiment through the passage of time. That tension is the life—the past and potential—of fashion.

Notes

1. Elizabeth Wilson, "Adorned in Dreams: Introduction," in *Fashion Theory: A Reader*, ed. Malcolm Barnard (New York: Routledge, 2007), 394.

2. "Even if fashion is an enchantment, it remains the enchantment of the commodity, and, still further, the enchantment of simulation, the code and the law." Jean Baudrillard, "Fashion, or the Enchanting Spectacle of the Code," in *Fashion Theory: A Reader*, 469.

3. This analysis takes into account the major theoretical work on fashion as a discourse about the body, consumerism, and culture, particularly that of Roland Barthes, Jean Baudrillard, Fred Davis, Anne Hollander, Rachel Bowlby, Rebecca Arnold, Valerie Steele, Ted Polhemus, Elizabeth Wilson, and other theorists and historians who have elucidated the connections at play between identity, desire, cultural meaning, and com-

modification in the acts of looking at, shopping for, and wearing fashion. The fashion discourse establishes for me a starting point from which to consider the museum, particularly the fashion exhibit, in its relationship to the idea of fashion, and its many possibilities and restraints, encountered in the shopping experience.

4. Many of the following observations on shopping are based on a course I teach at Saint Mary's College, CA, "The Politics of Fashion." One of the assignments for the course includes a field trip to Union Square in San Francisco, where students are asked to evaluate distinct shopping environments and their own responses to them. In their notes, students have referred to the general atmosphere as similar to "Disneyland," "a jungle," "playland," and "a candyland." Specific venues become stages for fantasy: Betsey Johnson is a "dollhouse"; Varvatos a "bachelor pad." Student-shoppers comment on the comfortable environments of the department store or shops specifically targeted to their general demographics (Macy's, Gap, H&M), and the anxiety-producing experiences in small upscale boutiques like Prada, Gucci, and Chanel, where there are demarcated "shrines" to handbags—lit up, enclosed, out of reach. The suggestion of Foucault's Panopticon is inescapable, although the resemblance between prison and shop may seem arcane. The point, however, is that the shopper drifts between settings marked by competing fantasy scenarios of pleasure and anxiety, liberation and restraint, looking at her- or himself looking. I also would suggest an analogy to the "surveyor/surveyed" double-consciousness explored by John Berger in *Ways of Seeing*, which stipulates a relationship between spectacle and the body, particularly in the encounter with visual art. John Berger, *Ways of Seeing* (New York: Penguin, 1990).

5. I use the term "spectacle" here primarily in its relationship to theatrical dramatization and the organizing principles of visuality, as well as in reference to Baudrillard's theorization of commodities fetishism. My analysis takes into account feminist theories of the gaze (particularly in response to Laura Mulvey's more restrictive reading), which configure the female spectator as having some measure of agency in her attempt to construct meaning and subjectivity within specularity and visual culture. This analysis is further indebted to the work of Mary Ann Doane, Rosi Braidotti, Teresa DeLauretis, and Susan Bordo.

6. The narrative of transformation appears frequently in popular stories about shopping. For example, many well-known films convey the possibilities of personal and social transformation through fashion (*My Fair Lady*, *Clueless*, *Pretty Woman*, *The Devil Wears Prada*, and *Confessions of a Shopaholic*).

7. "The spectacle is money one can only look at, because in it all use has already been exchanged for the totality of abstract representation. The spectacle is not just a servant of pseudo-use, it is already in itself a pseudo-use of life." Guy Debord, *Society of the Spectacle*, trans. Ken Knabb (London: Rebel Press, 2006), 24.

8. This interactive engagement was brought home to me as I attended the Saint Laurent exhibit on one occasion with my mother, both of us relating generationally to the ensembles and specific objects as to each other, through personal sartorial histories and memories: "I remember that very hostess skirt on you!" "Remember my suede boots like those?"

9. Roland Barthes, *The Fashion System* (Berkeley, CA: University of California Press, 1990).

10. Baudrillard, "Fashion," 467.

11. For a compelling analysis of this chain of signification that calls fantasy and transformation into play, see Iris Marion Young, "Women Recovering Our Clothes," in *On Fashion*, eds. Shari Benstock and Suzanne Ferriss (New Brunswick: Rutgers University Press, 1994), 187–210. Young theorizes the imaginative relationship between the shopper's idea of herself, a projected or possible self, and what she sees in the mirror: "So I am split. I see myself, and I see myself being seen. Might such a split express a woman's relation to clothes, to images of clothes, to images of herself in clothes, whomever she imagines herself to be?," 187.

12. "Shopping consumes you," said one student-shopper, "and this is why I love it." Politics of Fashion (university course) (January, 2010).

13. The extent to which shopping is a ritual of surveillance is explored by Malcolm Gladwell in "The Science of Shopping," *The New Yorker,* November 4, 1996, 66–75. Here, Gladwell catalogues the consumer research of Paco Underhill, an urban geographer and retail consultant, who charts, by strategically placed store cameras, the random meanderings of shoppers into predictable and exploitable patterns of commodities foraging. The idea is to engage that consumer into a relationship with the things sold and with the store itself, by appealing to an abstract idea of what the shopper is really looking for. Gladwell quotes the designer Donna Karan in one of her New York stores: " 'I want [the shoppers] to think that they are walking into an environment, that I am transforming them out of their lives and into an experience, that it's not about clothes, it's about who they are as people,' " 74. The staging of spectacle and story, which engages the participant's idea of her- or himself through the display of commodities, is also central to the nature of the museum, albeit to different purpose.

14. The carnivalesque quality of the Saint Laurent exhibit was marked by the play of influences between the visceral response to theatrical entertainment and the aesthetics of high art and tradition. The spectacle thus utilizes and redoubles both the effects of high and mass culture, as is clear in this local review: ". . . it is when visitors think they have reached the end of the exhibit that the hall of wonders is revealed. The narrow, dark halls filled with blacks and grays suddenly open up into a garden of riotous colors and sparkle. It is in this last room that the spectacular, the fantastic, and the truly outrageous designs rival the displays of a mating peacock. Blocks of bright pinks and purples are combined with lime green, turquoise, and yellow; explosions of flowers and exotic animal prints cover flattering forms; silk, sequins, leather, taffeta, velvet, raffia, feathers, glass and wooden beads are the media from which these are formed." Ann Taylor, "Yves Saint Laurent: Splendor and Spectacle," *SFStation*, January 9, 2009, http://www.sfstation.com/yves-saint-laurent-a12951.

15. Baudrillard, "Fashion," 464.

16. Rei Kawakubo, quoted in *Fashion Theory: A Reader*, 269.

17. See local criticism of the Saint Laurent exhibit: Kenneth Baker, "At S.F.'s de Young Museum, Fashion Exhibitions Upset Fine Art Fans," *SFGate.com*, September 2, 2007, http://www.sfgate.com/cgi-bin/article.cgi?f=/c/a/2007/09/02/MNSMRQ8I5.DTL.

18. Valerie Steele, quoted in Virginia Postrel, "Dress Sense: Why Fashion Deserves Its Place in Art Museums," *Atlantic Online*, May, 2007, http://www.theatlantic.com/magazine/archive/2007/05/dress-sense/5789/.

19. ". . . fashion is as much a part of the dream world of capitalism as of its economy." Wilson, "Adorned in Dreams," 397.

20. Metropolitan Museum of Art, "Superheroes: Fashion and Fantasy," *Metmuseum.org*, http://www.metmuseum.org/special/superheroes/index.asp.

21. David Cornell, *Lynn Hershman Leeson: No Body Special* (San Francisco, CA: de Young Fine Arts Museum, 2008).

22. *The Uniform Project* takes the discourse about fashion and embodiment, self-expression, individualism, and uniformity in a new direction. *Uniform* is performance art produced on a daily blog by Sheena Matheiken, who has elected to wear the same black dress every day for a year, in part to comment on the possibilities and limits of creative identity in fashion (www.theuniformproject.com). See also Rob Walker, "This Year's Model," *New York Times Magazine*, July 9, 2009, 18.

23. See Malcolm Bernard's discussion of Kawakubo's "Derridean strategies" to draw the wearer into active participation with the garment in *Fashion Theory: A Reader*, 268, 335.

24. An ironic parallel to the fashion shoot can be seen in the Old Navy ad campaign in 2009 featuring "supermodelquins": fashion-wearing mannequins presented in parodic tableaux of celebrity culture, glamour, and embodiment. The supermodelquins appear in fashion blogs and have their own Facebook pages. See, for example, Allsweetness, "Exclusive First Look into the Lives of the Old Navy Supermodelquins," *MyItThings*, March 2, 2009, http://myitthings.com/allsweetness/Post/fashion/It-Brand/Exclusive-First-Look-into-the-Lives-of-the-Old-Navy-Supermodelquins.

25. A video of the exhibit, "The Model as Muse: Embodying Fashion," at the Metropolitan Museum of Art in 2009 conveys the specular correspondence among several elements: the images of the actual models in fashion photographs; restaged tableaux of famous fashion layouts; mannequins in haute couture; and spectators at the exhibit, some of whom are taking their own photos. The continuum of specularity culminates in a scene that depicts mannequins floating high in the exhibit room above the heads of spectators, who gaze up at them like looking at stars in the sky. See Special Exhibitions, http://www.metmuseum.org/special/se_event.asp?Occurrenceld={EB2C67EF-1CCB-4EB2-9329-A955A7EDFBC2.

26. See Elizabeth Wilson on the hauntedness of the costume exhibit: "We experience a sense of the uncanny when we gaze at garments that had an intimate relationship with human beings long since gone to their graves," quoted in Joanne Entwistle, "Addressing the Body," in *Fashion Theory: A Reader*, 276. The representation of glamour (or money) reinforces the analogy of the museum to the fashion shrine configured in the high-end boutique, which, through the careful staging of space and sound, encourages a literal hush upon entry.

27. The sensual nature of fashion as an experience of the body linked to time and memory is explored in Kim Sawchuk, "A Tale of Inscription/Fashion Statements," in *Fashion Theory: A Reader*, 475–88. See also Ilene Beckerman, *Love, Loss and What I Wore* (New York: Algonquin, 1995), a memoir that explicitly links the experiences of life to fashion, time, and memory.

28. Entwistle, "Addressing the Body," 276.

29. Ibid., 281.

30. I would venture further that recent theories of transgender take this relationship between the performance of the body, social location, classification, and transformation—which is at once corporeal and spiritual—in provocative directions. There is a strategic relationship here to fashion, the "outer body" of the wearer. See, for example, Kate Bornstein, "Betsey Girls Saved My Life," in *It's So You: 35 Women Write About Personal Expression Through Fashion and Style*, ed. Michelle Tea (Emeryville, CA: Seal Press, 2007), 223–230.

31. A critique of this relationship, as well as of body aesthetics and high art, can be seen in the work of performance artist Orlan, who ironically also invokes Christian metaphors of the mortification of the flesh as fleshly discipline, *and* the path to transcendence through pain and pleasure.

32. Wilson, "Adorned in Dreams," 394.

33. Pierre Bergé, "Yves Saint Laurent," in Foundation Pierre Bergé-Yves Saint Laurent, *Yves Saint Laurent: Style* (New York: Abrams, 2008), 11. Bergé sees Saint Laurent as a powerful collaborator with women in the project of transformation: ". . . Saint Laurent wanted women to be beautiful and . . . he glorified them . . . gave them self-confidence, enabled them to confront everyday life and, above all, allowed them to see their own selves."

34. Pierre Bergé, quoted in "The Wonder of YSL," *Montreal Gazette*, May 30, 2008, http://www.canada.com/story_print.html?id=47aa02b7-3ce0-4f66-9815-2d1023cb765d&sponsor.

35. Yves Saint Laurent, quoted in Foundation Pierre Bergé-Yves Saint Laurent, *Yves Saint Laurent Style*, 16.

Chapter 6

Life's Too Short to Wear Comfortable Shoes

Femme-ininity and Sex Work

Jayne Swift

They are gold. Not a rich autumnal gold, but a glossy disco kind of gold. Six-inch heeled Ellie sandals that are more tape than rubber on the sole. One ankle strap is worn so thin that any day now it will snap. Their signs of wear have not stopped the sighs of adoration from my coworkers or the signs of arousal from clients. I also like their well-worn status. On one hand, I don't ever want to take them offstage. On the other hand, I can't wait for the day that I get the excuse to wear them outside.

The shoes I'm wearing when I arrive to work are almost as beautiful. Purple suede stiletto heels that match the carpet I dance on to earn a living. These stiletto street shoes are in mint condition, and when I put them on again after I'm done performing onstage, it reminds me that similar pleasures still await me. Heading toward my lover's arms, I am certain to soon again have my heels in the air.

I was born in the same year that Barnard College's "Scholar and the Feminist" Conference showcased the fierce feminist sex wars; it would be my generational legacy to grow up in the midst of these struggles pitting so-called sex-positive activists against their sex-cautious critics. As many have attested, the 1980s were a time of bitter conflict in feminist circles, in which feminists debated whether sexual desires and practices (such as sex work) could be interpreted as feminist or not. I write as a queer femme and a sex worker whose life, like that of many other femmes and sex workers, has been profoundly structured by the histories of the feminist sex wars and their ongoing impact on feminist imaginaries. For those of us on the new frontlines of redrawn feminist battlefields, the memory of the sex wars has far from waned.[1] In this space I explore how femmes and sex workers work through the ambiguous legacies of the sex wars in their efforts to reshape feminist thought on matters of sexual agency and style.

We now live in a world in which femmes and sex workers hold their own community conferences and build political movements. Moreover, we increasingly live in a moment in which femme and sex worker subjectivities and aesthetics are appropriated and circulate widely as cultural commodities.[2] Sex workers, or at least strippers, have gone mainstream, evidenced in the growth of such things as pole-dancing aerobics classes in local fitness centers. As Ariel Levy, in her treatise decrying the rise of what she calls "raunch" culture, puts it, "I first noticed it several years ago. I would turn on the television and find strippers in pasties explaining how best to lap dance a man to orgasm."[3] The post-feminist and third-wave cultural landscape is also rife with social and cultural efforts—such as neo-burlesque—aimed at reclaiming and revamping femininity, and femme-ininities, as explicitly feminist practices. The hyper-visibility and normalization of stripper and femme aesthetics in contemporary American cultures clearly separate this historic moment from the one in which femmes and sex workers first stormed Barnard. This normalization process poses new questions and challenges for feminist theorists concerned with styles of feminine sexual subjectivity.

Drawing from my experiences as a queer femme and a sex worker, I use auto-ethnography as a method of rendering my femme and sex worker self strange, and in doing so, situate and interpret the social and historical foundations of experience.[4] Feminist theoreticians have long sought to destabilize positivist notions of the disembodied and absent researcher, insisting that scholars take pains to represent and reflect upon their own positionalities. This emphasis on "theory in the flesh" is useful for critical scholarship that examines the intersections of embodied experience and cultural power. From this critical position, I explore how femmes and sex workers have described their relationship to "high heels," in order to better understand just what theoretical and political values are distilled in these heels. The femmes and sex workers represented in this essay use high heels to mobilize a style of embodied politics that is indicative of, and responsive to, the complex historical legacies of our post-sex-wars cultural moment. I read femmes and sex workers as allies in our complex efforts to create what I call "reconnaissance femininities" on a larger feminist battlefront.

Typically, the term "reconnaissance" is used in military contexts to describe the clandestine gathering of information about an enemy's composition and capabilities. Colloquially, "reconnaissance" implies the act of going in disguise to recover that which is "lost"—knowledge, people, memories. By reworking the term, I gesture to the ways in which both femmes and sex workers fashion themselves to cross so-called enemy lines and, in doing so, reshape what feminists think of as "enemy." The question of "enemy" is given new life in the current hullabaloo over the "pornification" of our culture—in which feminists wage new battles over the old behemoths of sex work and high femme fashion. At a moment in which we collectively tiptoe through the historical wreckage of the feminist sex wars and wander onto new cultural terrain, the recon actions undertaken by femmes and sex workers are powerful sources of inspiration for a war-weary feminism.

Sex Worker Meets Femme: Do You Want to Dance?

The 1982 Barnard conference, "The Scholar and the Feminist: Toward a Politics of Sexuality," has come to be understood as a battleground site between anti-pornography and "sex radical" feminists. It is where femmes' and sex workers' voices became undeniable presences in feminist communities, and still serves as a crucial memory point for femmes and sex workers seeking to create their subjectivities, and to theorize and organize in the new millennium. The Barnard Conference signaled a shift from the political dreams of cultural/lesbian-feminism to a more postmodernist articulation of differences among women. This move revalued individual women's sexual self-determination as a new model for constructing sexual identities and feminist alliances.

Joan Nestle's "Lesbians and Prostitutes: An Historical Sisterhood" pioneered the effort to link queer women and sex workers. Rereading Nestle's essay, I'm reminded of the first time I went shopping for new work shoes—the gold heels that are by now almost worn out. While I scoured the local fetish/sex wear shops, I couldn't help but recall the dilemma Nestle named as facing both "lesbians and prostitutes." Although I am inserting the terms "sex worker" and "femme," the battle remains the same, and that "battle" is about the reshaping of feminism so that it might include "whores and women who look like whores."[5] This battle for feminist inclusion is all the more important given the moral panics over the rise of "raunch" culture that have unleashed a cultural maelstrom over just what it means to look like a "whore." For instance, Gail Dines and other anti-raunch feminist critics specifically single out the mainstreaming of stripper style—low-cut jeans, miniskirts, and "the high heels that contort our calves"—as problematic.[6] These critics see this style as evidence of a false sense of sexual empowerment, and thus "looking like a whore" is once again trashed by some as an inauthentic way of fashioning feminism.

Shoe shopping in heels can be a treacherous task. At the end of the day you will unquestionably have calluses. But if you are lucky you will also have that moment of feeling like you've turned what some feminists would name "social prisons" (i.e., high heels) into "social freedoms."[7] Walking in the world in my purple "femme" heels—on the hunt for gold "stripper" heels—I can see how both aspects of my identity, queer femme and sex worker, are bound together in their reclamation of footwear that takes them out of women's traditional "erotic, and therefore social territory."[8] Shopping for stripper heels in my femme ones drives home how whores and queers use clothing and style to inhabit their differences and claim the virtue of their existence.

When I set off to go shopping for work shoes in my purple pumps, my roommate looked at me as if I'm insane to wear heels to buy other heels. When I come home with a pair of six-inch gold stripper heels, I am greeted with a chuckle—a dismissive assumption that my lust for heels means I'm unable to see around the patriarchal corner. Backed into a corner, I want to click my heels and float away to another home, removed from the embattled feelings that my roommate's dismissal of heels elicits. I wonder how my apartment suddenly became a battleground in which my roommate—a burlesque performer—and I are placed on opposing sides. This relatively common skirmish is important because it points to the unresolved tensions over what heels signify—pleasure or danger. Putting my feet on her coffee table, it occurs to me that our differing approach to heels may have something to do with her location in burlesque communities and mine in sex work. Perhaps my roommate views my heels as a sign that my work enslaves me to normative styles of femininity, while she fashions herself as a transgressor of normative femininity. For me, these heels symbolize an aesthetic and ethical commitment to a feminist politics that can be mounted from within, or "inside" governing social norms of femininity.

As a young feminist and femme I consumed many histories about the sex worker as a woman consciously manipulating her status as sexual object for her own economic and pleasurable gain. This (problematic) fantasy spoke to my sense of myself as a femme, of existing in the world as a sexual outlaw. On visits to the city in which I now live, I would meander past the business where I now work, and spy women outside, smoking cigarettes, wearing robes in the middle of the day, clad in intimidating high heels. The heels said it all: *I am on the street, in the middle of a downtown workday, nearly naked outside of a sex business, and you cannot make me hide my face.* I was enraptured; I wanted to learn how to wear these heels, and something told me that this desire came from a sense of affinity with these women. As a wide-eyed femme encountering "working" women, I slowed my own stride in the hope that my heels might be noticed by them, recognized as symbols of a shared desire and a mutual ability to wield our sexuality for our gain.

I recognized a similar mission between my future coworkers and myself, crystallized in how our heels occupied this suddenly overlapping cultural space. Lounging in heels and little else, they dared passersby to look, and in looking to potentially brand them as whores.[9] Entering their cloud of cigarette smoke, I inhaled the attitude of subtle, almost imperceptible defiance. I saw their heels for what they were: a tactic for manipulating the gaze of others. The sex-working women were camouflaged by the sheer flamboyance and spectacle of their heels—delighting in the havoc they wreaked on this city street, prompting pedestrians to stumble over their own feet as they stared at these women. The heels called me to bear witness—however imperfectly and momentarily—to other women's existence.

The love for high heels I nurtured as a young femme eased the process of learning how to move in six-inch stiletto *stripper* heels. By this I mean that the practices central to femme-ininity—stylizing and costuming my body for public display, and the desire to perform my pleasure in the hopes of eliciting the pleasure of others—are all necessary components of my success in sex work. My time, and rewards, in gold heels would not be nearly as *en pointe* if I hadn't trained in some pretty, purple, femme ones.

Yet, it is this *en pointe* quality, the very performance of femme-ininity by sex workers that renders us as suspect for many feminists. For instance, Take Back the Night marches tend to lack women clad in high heels and feminine apparel and this lack permits that "costume to signify rape-ability, the constant vulnerability of feminine sexuality."[10] Anti-porn contingents of feminism read the whore's performance of hyper-femininity as sign, and implicitly cause, of her victimization. In my own life I have been scrutinized for marching in heels and have struggled to make others see that the *en pointe* work that femmes/sex workers specialize in is a gendered expression worthy of respect.

We spend many meaningful hours, and much effort, cultivating practices and performances of feminine self-stylization. We spend many more hours explaining how these practices allow us to claim sexual agency and pleasure—a feminist prerogative. Debates about this feminist prerogative over just *how women could, and should*, claim sexual agency and pleasure, and the role of style in doing so, were at the heart of the feminist "sex wars," of the 1980s and 1990s. Ironically, de-politicized visions of sex-positivity are now commonly used to sell such things as "porno chic" style as *the* route to female sexual agency.[11] This opens up a whole new Pandora's box for femmes and sex workers—as images of us are appropriated to sell "porno chic" styles, while we remain marginalized within both popular and feminist cultures. Thus, looking like a "whore" can render one intelligible as a post-feminist subject, while high-heeled women, including actual whores and femmes, hoping to join feminist marches remain suspect, as their heels have yet to be incorporated as intelligible under a feminist sign.

The high-heeled femme sex worker may cross the social lines that delineate the Madonnas from the whores, and trigger the ongoing skirmishes among feminists over what heels signify: Stockholm syndrome, stilettoed spy, or feminist free agent. These heels take on the uniquely feminist tasks of inspiring acts of witnessing across lines of difference and challenging dress codes that conflate femininity with a cause of violence against women. Femmes and sex workers have shown that the meanings of high heels are shifting and open-ended, not over-determined. Moreover, these heels point to the problem, and possibilities, of being misread in a world that does not see the worth of feminine stylization, precisely due to the very indeterminacy of high heels. Femme/sex worker high heels do not promise what Ruth Holliday has posited as an easy "harmony of self-explanations and self-presentations—the degree of fit between one's *explanation* of/for oneself and one's *expression* of that self—matching the inside and outside of one's body."[12] Rather, these heels articulate a uniquely femme- and sex-worker inspired approach to fashion—in which the presumed "harmony" between self-explanation and self-presentation is productively destabilized. These heels create a reconnaissance style of feminist embodiment, a style that foregrounds the political possibilities of disguise and discomfort.

Life's Too Short to Wear Comfortable Shoes: Femmes, Sex Workers, and Reconnaissance Work

If I could post one sign up at work and at home to announce what I bring into both spaces, of how I ache to complicate the divide between femme and sex worker heels, to my ongoing and simultaneous fashioning of "reconnaissance femininity," it would be:

> *I do not wear high heels because I am a feminist/*
> *I am a feminist because I wear high heels.*
> *Life's too short to wear comfortable shoes.*

As a young femme/sex worker I was continually faced with questions from those who could not reconcile how I could be both feminist and at home in high heels. This scrutiny stems from the segments of feminism that called upon women to rid themselves of a socially imposed false consciousness, and demanded that "if our shoes pinched, we went barefoot."[13] This understanding of fashion effectively erased the experiences of femmes and sex workers who offered radically different approaches to the deployment and interpretations of high heels. In response, the guiding principle of "life's too short to wear comfortable shoes" is meant to contest the erasure of femmes and sex workers within feminist histories by turning conventional feminist logic on its head—by embracing the uncomfortable. It is not my intention to minimize the long and brutal histories of women suffering in deep discomfort because fashion dictated they do so—as with practices of foot-binding. Rather, I want to point to the under-explored feminist possibilities in discomfort. Femmes and sex workers have something to gain by explicitly embracing discomfort, symbolized in our high heels, as we are too familiar with the ways in which comfort in fashion is not simply about how one's body fits into their clothes, but how one's clothes enable their body to interact in the world, and that therefore comfort is not as self-evident a goal as it may seem.

Ruth Holliday, in "The Comfort of Identity," explains how comfort is a naturalizing discourse, in which "identity is mapped onto the body," and in doing so expresses "a desire to be self-present to both oneself and others.[14] For femmes and sex workers—whose fashion and bodily presentation at times renders them unrecognizable as femmes and sex workers to others—discomfort may be a recurring feature in the fashioning of their identities. This discomfort could be read as the disjuncture between experiencing one's self-presentation as affirming a given identity, such as femme, and a cultural context that does not adequately appreciate or account for the nuances of these presentations or identities. For instance, femmes have pointed out how in a heterosexist culture in which feminine-equals-straight, to fashion femme is to continually grapple with the problem of "being read against one's signature," and the discomfort it produces.[15] The experience of comfort is structured by power, including subcultural discourses that can open up or close down opportunities for bodies and styles to be recognized and valued. As Holliday clearly shows, queer subcultures produce their own disciplinary technologies and frameworks which serve to elevate certain fashions and bodily comportments—and disavow others.[16]

Many femmes have pointed to the difficulties they face in achieving a sense of recognition or comfort in queer cultures in which they are supposed to feel at home. Notably, Rebecca Rugg has suggested that the longtime problem of femme invisibility is exacerbated in contemporary dyke/queer social scenes because the femme is "caught between being perceived as the face of assimilation and being exorcised from a pomo dyke community" which privileges gender fluidity.[17] As such, femmes may find themselves in a (sub)cultural context in which they are again subject to being misread and vulnerable to the social discomfort this can produce. To be femme, then, is in some very real social sense to court discomfort. Claiming discomfort, and its tactile embodiment in high heels, might allow femmes (and others) to articulate a counter-discourse of fashion and identity that better accounts for our lived experiences of misrecognition and the mismatch between one's stylistic intentions and others reception.

Discomfort is a feminist political virtue because it refuses the stagnancy that can come from resting on the social gains of previous political struggles. As Holliday puts it, "perhaps comfort is to be feared since it is discomfort, displacement, disruption which moves (queer) politics (and selves) forward into a more complex and less elusive or complacent place."[18] Fashioning femme identity, crystallized in my commitment to high heels, is informed by and a response to the historical memory of the feminist sex wars. Young feminists who did not live through the sex wars may still develop affective relationships to them, picking sides and choosing with whom to identify.[19] In noting this, I am trying to point to the radical historical contingency of *any* identity. The ongoing production of knowledge about the sex wars necessitates critical explorations of how this knowledge is put to use in the production of contemporary femme subjectivities—and in particular how femmes use the historical memory of the sex wars to respond to critics that conflate "femme" with "raunch." This is all the more important given that young femmes exist in a putative post-feminist moment, which is radically different from that of our femme foremothers: a cultural milieu in which "porn stars" and queer burlesquers can be post-feminist icons.

One way I make sense of this history is by using my own experiences of gendered shame as a catalyst in the cultivation and construction of femme subjectivity. If my roommate dismisses my heels, I dig my feet in deeper; deeper into the experience and examination of the cultural denigration of femininity. Deeper into the feelings of vulnerability and shame that are the historical result of peoples being told that how they desire and create gender, that their femme-ininity, has no place in the worlds to which they hope to belong. And femmes, who have written so eloquently about the erotic power of receptivity, know that there is worth to be found in vulnerability, in shame, even.[20] In particular, femmes have explained bottoming (within the erotic system of butch-femme or BDSM) as honoring a profound desire to "give up" power and refute the once common feminist interpretation that this act is simply passive.[21] In doing so, femmes envision sexual desire through the complex machinations of power, and point to the potential for sexual vulnerability to lead to new forms of communion. Claiming feminist femme-ininity means taking on the mantle of an important feminist history that has been in many ways lost, and to argue that this erasure does real political harm to subjects, including but not limited to me, and that feminists must work to undo this. In this sense, dressing in heels is a feminist act of testimony: an effort to inscribe upon my body the memories and contributions of femmes.

Of course, the fashioning of a femme aesthetic does not guarantee that my goal of historical recovery, of paying homage to femmes such as Nestle, is readable on my body. I do not own a pair of shoes that can quiet the polysemic capacities of high heels. Femme shows that high heels have multiple significations and teases out a distinct kind of feminist power. Femme is not grounded in a sartorial "fuck you" to all that is commonly read as symbolic of women's oppression—such as high heels. Rather, femme power comes from its decision to locate itself in and rework that which is considered inimical to "what a feminist looks like." I cannot hope for a pair of heels that would do the difficult work of articulating my femme-ininity for me. I expect my heels to at times render my femme self in disguise and for this to involve the pain of misrecognition, but I didn't start wearing heels because I thought they would make the walk easier.

Femme poses significant questions about the nature of "passing" and its relationship to feminist struggles. As a femme, my particular style of femme-ininity is reconnaissance, in that I often pass as straight. I eventually got used to passing as straight and started to formulize new understandings of what passing entails and how to best use it. My work in many ways relies upon a daily performance of sexualized femininity interpreted as belonging to heterosexuality. My workplace is in many respects a queer-friendly one. However, it is still a site that is intimately shaped by the dictates of heteronormativity and populated by workers who are shaped by our homophobic culture. In commercial sex venues such as the one where I work, men often come in wearing women's underwear, or with a desire to explore fantasies in which they are female or feminized. Not every woman I work alongside is prepared or inclined to provide adequate services to transvestite, transgendered, or gender-bending clients, which ends up marginalizing queerness in our workspace. I have found that my femme status enables me to start some difficult conversations in these moments—conversations that have the potential to be transformative for me as well as others.

By this I mean that our shared—albeit differently situated—ground of femininity tilts my coworkers and me on our toes, inclines us toward each other. My femme-ininity works in a reconnaissance fashion, enabling me to delicately tiptoe through what may have been hostile ground. My heels allow me entry into a space animated by what might appear to be the enemy—the homo/transphobia of some coworkers—thereby creating an opening for exchange and possibly, mutual transformation. In these moments I am reminded of how Bernice Johnson Reagon characterized the work of coalition-building: a profound discomfort that feels like you're going to 'keel over any minute and die.' "[22] Dialoguing with my coworkers while *en pointe* drives home that the work of feminist coalition building is at times an uncomfortable experience; and that it is precisely the discomfort that makes this shared time and space worthwhile. As Holliday reminds us, the experience of discomfort holds possibilities for feminist politics and fashion as it redirects us back to the ever-present social, the painful and messy necessity of making meaning in relation to, and sometimes with, others.

I create myself as sex worker in a somewhat similar fashion to how I came to create myself as femme, through a development of feminist "counter-memory."[23] I began working in the sex industry in the same decade that saw the rise of contemporary moral panics over the perceived pornification of our culture. These moral panics are fanned by cultural commentators, including anti-porn feminist activists and scholars, who argue that our society is in the midst of an epidemic of hyper-sexualization that endangers all people, but especially women and children. These commentators, including feminists, cite phenomena such as "sexting" and *Girls Gone Wild* videos as proof that mainstream culture looks more and more like the inside of your local adult store, and that this has a direct negative impact on a wide array of social life. Thus commercial pornography itself—and by implication those that produce and labor in it—is conscripted as a mass-cultural metaphor for social danger and destruction.[24] Discourses of porn culture mobilize sexual fear into politi-cal and cultural campaigns to "cleanse" the public sphere, and in doing so promulgate cultural narratives about sex workers as sites of social disease and danger. The rhetoric of porn culture vilifies the fashions and embodied style of actual sex workers—who might have something to say about the ways in which our bodies are continually used by others (who are not paying!) and who are looking to play out their fears.

I see my decision to enter into and experience sex work as, in part, another way that I name and create myself as a feminist in high heels. My sex worker heels lead me to a greater pleasure in my erotic life as femme than I knew possible.[25] And although pleasure is certainly not synonymous with agency, my stripper heels inculcate joy in my body and in that sense they lay the groundwork for feminist agency.

My stripper heels transform where and how I might find or create femme erotic power by pulling in my lover—a butch trans man who enjoys watching me dance.[26] This allows me to pair stripper and femme: in stripper heels I quite literally take femme eroticism to a whole new level. Sex worker transforms femme, and butch-femme, because when I'm onstage "the female body, the male gaze, and the structures of realism," as Sue-Ellen Case has noted, become "sex toys for the butch-femme couple."[27] My time in stripper heels hones my pleasures in femme masquerade and allows me to stage queer femme sexuality in commercial sexual venues where I labor.

My "whore" heels enact butch-femme desires on a stage in which those desires are supposedly not allowed—the stage of heterosexual sexual commerce. In the process, they reveal how it is the sex worker/femme's task to not "impale themselves on the poles of sexual difference . . . but constantly seduce the sign system, through flirtation and inconstancy into the light fondle of artifice."[28] In other words, sex worker challenges femme to find a way to work that pole, to manipulate cultural signifiers for her own gain, and in the process create pleasure on the stage on which she is located. My "round-heels" increase my erotic pleasure as femme by challenging femme to create pleasure and agency in avenues where it is not supposed to thrive.

Coming off stage, I pause putting my gold heels away. It's sobering, the fact that I can't wear these heels out with me, that my stripper shoes are prohibited from entering into my life as femme. And I know it's not ultimately because of the bylaws of my workplace that I cannot wear them into the communities and spaces I inhabit as a femme. It's because these heels, which I spend so much of my life in, would almost without question be greeted by those communities as some form of hipster kitsch or with uncomfortable silence. Both would be mistaken and I would be left feeling exposed in that ugly, raw way. My stripper shoes have to stay in these doors, and on this stage, and so I exchange them for (my also beloved and yet muted) purple stilettos, say my goodnights, and head into femme territory.

Keeping the Enemy Closer:
Femme Burlesque and Sex Workers

The closeting of stripper heels in contemporary femme communities and social spaces is transparent in the current queer love affair with neo-burlesque. Many have detailed the massive revival of burlesque as an artistic practice and noted how burlesque bills itself as a feminist entertainment dedicated to playing with and deconstructing the codes of gender.[29] I take it as a given that burlesque is an over-determined feature of urban, queer sociality and that it enables a celebration of the trappings of femininity. In doing so, it offers tantalizing opportunities for queer femme social congregation and cultural validation.

Indeed, burlesque might be read as part of a larger historical tradition of "pro-sex" cultural activism, itself a response to the feminist sex wars, in which the signifiers of femininity are celebrated as feminist ground. Burlesque's popularity among queer subcultures is partly due to the ways in which it is used to challenge feminist readings of femininity as damaged, a symptom of patriarchy. Instead, in burlesque performances, queer femininity is actively resignified to mean sexually desirable and desiring, politically engaged, and inclusive of a wide range of body types and sizes.[30] Burlesque creates a social space for play with queer femme-ininity, a space where femme heels are celebrated, and in doing so it inaugurates a host of femme fashions that exist in tension with sex workers. As such, burlesque is an important site to examine the ongoing relevance of the feminist sex wars in a "porn culture" moment, particularly as it enshrines certain fashions and forms of femininity.

Burlesque operates on a social level—distinct from any individual performers' actual relation to sex work—to silence sex workers and closet stripper heels. Quite simply, in order to exist, burlesque must separate itself from contemporary sex work; it must define itself as *not sex work.* This is evident in the sheer fact that in my city if you want to see semi-nude girls performing raunchy acts and enjoy an alcoholic beverage while doing so, you must go to a burlesque show, not a strip club.[31] Moreover, the distinction between burlesque and sex work is not neutral, but a deeply political one that serves to elevate burlesque. It does so through a discursive reiteration that stripping is about economics and labor, while burlesque is about art and a feminist eroticism.[32] This discourse of sex work portrays strippers as simply "humpers. Yes they take their clothes off, but they hump poles, they hump laps, they're not burlesque. To me, both are about fantasy, but one, humping, is more transaction oriented and less about self expression."[33]

Even when less overtly anti-sex work, burlesque draws upon and consolidates a hierarchical boundary—in which burlesque is figured as high culture and stripping is low culture. Of course, burlesque scenes are constantly haunted by the specter of its historical association with sex work and selectively draw upon this association in fashioning itself as socially transgressive and titillating. Indeed, the popularity of burlesque epitomizes how the sex worker has been problematically conceived as "a femme bad girl role model." [34]

Let me be clear: burlesque is not sex work. Rather, I am pointing out how this distinction is used to denigrate sex work and socially elevate burlesque. In doing so, it's worth continuing to ask for whom burlesque is an empowering cultural product or arena. In particular, how does the fusion of burlesque and queer femme cultural projects serve to mobilize certain fashions of femme-ininity that curiously disempower sex workers? In order to gesture toward the import of this question I show how (queer) burlesque scenes simultaneously enable a celebration of my purple *femme* stilettos and an almost censorious suppression of my gold *stripper* heels. In doing so, I want to suggest that burlesque and the femme fashions it articulates function to police sex-worker ontologies and fashions.

Queer burlesque scenes create catwalks: prior to and during the show people mingle and cruise, during the show performers' strut their stuff and audiences scream their approval, and after-parties tear down the house with music and dance. Burlesque shows become a vehicle for staging queer community; they offer a place akin to the pre-Stonewall working-class lesbian bars, described by folks such as Joan Nestle, to dress up in one's femme best. Every week, when a friend or my partner invites me to a burlesque performance, I imagine the catwalk and panic about what I would wear, which heels to select. I envision myself standing awkwardly in my purple high heels, along a wall—hearing laughter echoing my roommate's dismissive chuckle, the burlesque performer judging my penchant for certain high heels. My anxiety stems from the knowledge that my particular femme style, embodied in these purple heels, might render me a foreign, (heteronormative) outsider. Queer burlesque/femme scenes elevate a style of femininity that revolves around the playful subversion or exaggeration of feminine codes— a hipster, "radical chic" style that attempts to resist the passing effects of femme identification.

Burlesque is a space in which femininity is parodied. It uses high camp, humor, and exaggerated costuming and bodily gestures as a way to make the performance of femininity a transparent, social act. In some sense, burlesque's appeal is that it simultaneously mocks the production of femininity, while also remaining committed to doing it. This mocking approach echoes the "something's wrong with the picture" stylistic strategy that Rugg and others have described as a method for signifying a femme identity.[35] In this approach, femme is signified by disrupting the requirement to present a seamless femininity, by signalling to others that there is *something queer* about this performance of femininity.

Femme thus becomes visible through the use of hipster fashions that have the jarring effect of referencing different historical eras (1980s sunglasses and 1940s dresses) and thrift store chic, which is meant to convey downward mobility (regardless of the wearer's actual class status). Burlesque-femme-ininity displays a "love of specific retro or vintage femininities which reference precisely those feminine images that have been extensively parodied by feminist artists as emblematic of a pre- or protofeminist period. This feminine look constitutes a shared set of cultural belongings through which a community emerges. . . ."[36] Of course, this community also functions to determine what is capable of being recognized as femme. It does so by naming certain styles or looks, as arbiters of what is politically radical or retrograde—thus potentially creating a "radical chic" femme uniform.[37] In this way, "femme style" runs the risk of becoming an immobilized pattern to be mimicked and achieved, and not a matter of self-reflexive, dynamic and generative processes of styling oneself or collective fashion-making. For those who cannot or do not succeed as a hipster, "something's-wrong-with-the-picture" style, our heels fail to render us as femme.

This matters because style is not neutral. As Rugg explains, "styles signify politically and sometimes the significations are based on exclusions of groups of people . . . the problem is that certain people can't be whatever is in style. Being stylish and hip can come at someone else's expense, by inappropriate appropriation."[38] My femme-ininity is informed by my life as a sex worker, and my choice of high heels reflects multiple style commitments and social positionalities. Having rejected my purple heels at the risk of being read as a straight intruder, I consider wearing my newly retired stripper heels to the burlesque show, as a sign that I too enjoy the performative dimensions of femininity. Yet I worry about what I may invite by wearing such blatantly stripper heels in burlesque/femme space. I hear the sounds of my six-inch heels clacking their way into the theatre and see the turning of heads at this intrusion. Some might admire their excessive nature; their "trashy" gold hue and absurdly high heel. Some might even want to know where they might get a pair, and I would find myself faced with giving out names of sex worker apparel lines to non-sex workers (femmes) looking to fashion a more "authentic" porn star look. In this way, my gold heels crystallize the cultural use of the figure of sex worker as a model for femme subjectivity and style, and point to the pitfalls of this fetish for stripper heels. The accoutrements of my life as sex worker are fashionable and worth appropriating, but such fashionable appropriations strip me of both the playful and the political import of my time in these heels.

Or my stripper heels might be seen as tacky, and taken as evidence that I do not "do" femme in a thoughtful way. Some might see my style as solely imposed upon me by the need to make a living by appealing to the supposedly tasteless masses. Burlesque femme style seeks to trouble mainstream or commercial femininity precisely by becoming a "writerly" text—in which resistance to hegemonic beauty ideals is foregrounded and queerness is written onto the body. In contrast, sex worker femme styles, become "readerly" texts, in the sense that the object is not necessarily to match the inside to one's outside, but rather than to create a canvas upon which various audiences can paint their particular desires or impressions.[39] The fact that stripper style crafts itself so that it may be read as a source of sexual pleasure for consumers is interpreted in burlesque-femme scenes as a lack of queerness and a sign that we do not possess agency in our stylish endeavors. One can almost see, flashing through the minds of others, the caricature of a dictatorial pimp dressing me as he saw fit.

My gold heels, then, are politically impure because sex worker femmes, by definition, cross into so-called enemy territory. According to this logic, I wear my six-inch heels into enemy territory that invokes heteronormative, primarily (non-trans) male worlds. There is a long history of feminist renderings of sex worker as "captive," and these interpretations are modified—but not extinct—in queer communities. But I value my time in "enemy" territory, and seek to smuggle the pleasure and agency I derive from it into my femme heels. This means that my embodied identity, my style as femme, is profoundly shaped by my time working with (homogenized) straight audiences. This could produce discomfort for those who are invested in maintaining a queer safe space—protected from those deemed outsiders.

It is the sincerity of my stripper heels—that I actually labor and love in them—that makes them suspect within burlesque-femme scenes. The taboo against commercialism in style only furthers the elevation of burlesque as "high" culture, and endows burlesque-femme style with cultural capital, at the expense of sex workers. Ironically, this ends up replicating the same classist sentiments that led lesbian-feminists to misjudge femme style and dismiss femme women. The fierce battles over fashion, and high heels, that the sex wars originally showcased thus come full circle with burlesque-femme producing its own normalizing regimes and class-based dismissals of stripper styles.

Ultimately, the "reconnaissance femininity" I craft as a sex worker within burlesque-femme spaces leads me to remap my understanding of enemy territory. I am supposed to experience my work as taking me into enemy territory, and although I have certainly felt the pain and risk that can come with working in this industry, it does not mean that I see my clientele primarily as enemies. Rather, I have found the marginalization I experience as a sex worker within femme/burlesque scenes to be a more routine threat. The unstated ban on my flamboyant stripper heels and the mess they raise in these spaces shifts my understanding of what constitutes a feminist "enemy." A feminist threat, or enemy, is any constituency that appropriates or patronizes my stylization as sex worker. The "recon" work I do as a sex worker in femme communities leads me to see that there are no guaranteed alliances to be found between femme and sex worker, that there is work still to be done. Just because one has walked a mile in heels, does not mean that they have done so in stripper heels.

As a sex worker and femme, I have seen how living one's life in uncomfortable high heels leads to the development of valuable "reconnaissance femininities" that allow for remaking or remapping what we perceive as a threat to our survival. As a femme in sex work I use my time perched in heels to challenge the homophobia I find among my coworkers. As a sex-working femme, I deepen my erotic power and mark with my heels the exclusion of sex workers by femme communities and demand our worth.

I grew up in the aftermath of something feminists commonly refer to as a "war," an intellectual, political, and cultural war over sexual meanings and possibilities. The legacies and impact of this war are still being accounted for and will most assuredly look different for all involved. In living after the war, I find value in reconnaissance work that has the potential to unravel my knowledge of the enemy—and therefore alter my knowledge of myself and for what, and for whom, I am fighting. Sometimes high heels should be used as a battle cry—a method for counterattack against misogyny, heteronormativity, and cultural hatred of sex workers. Sometimes, though, they might be better worn as a flag of armistice—a sign that we wish to talk across deeply entrenched lines of difference, with others who value those who live in high heels. I wear these high heels as a testament to the historical memory of femmes and sex workers who have done brave things for feminism, and beautiful things with fashion.

Notes

1. See Alice Echols, *Daring to be Bad: Radical Feminism in America, 1967–1975*, (Minneapolis: University of Minnesota Press, 1989) and Jane Gerhard, *Desiring Revolution: Second-Wave Feminism and the Rewriting of American Sexual Thought, 1920–1982* (New York: Columbia University Press, 2001).

2. For discussions of this see Allison Fensterstock, "Stripper Chic: A Review Essay," in *Flesh for Fantasy: Producing and Consuming Exotic Dance,* eds. R. Danielle Egan, Katherine Frank, and Merri Lisa Johnson (New York: Thunder's Mouth Press, 2006), 63–84; and Angela McRobbie, "The Rise and Rise of Porno Chic," *The Times Higher Education Supplement*, January 2, 2004.

3. Ariel Levy, *Female Chauvinist Pigs: Women and the Rise of Raunch Culture* (New York: Free Press, 2005).

4. For discussions of auto-ethnographic methods, see Carolyn Ellis, *The Ethnographic I: A Methodological Novel about Autoethnography* (Lanham, MD: AltaMira Press, 2004).

5. Joan Nestle, "Lesbians and Prostitutes: An Historical Sisterhood," in *A Restricted Country* (San Francisco: Cleis Press, 1987), 155.

6. Gail Dines, *Pornland: How Porn Has Hijacked Our Sexuality* (Boston: Beacon Press, 2010), 103. See also Levy, *Female Chauvinist Pigs,* and Pamela Paul, *Pornified: How Pornography is Transforming Our Lives, Our Relationships and Our Families* (New York: Times Books, 2005.)

7. Nestle, "Lesbians and Prostitutes," 160.

8. Ibid., 159.

9. Of course, it could be argued that the ability to invite in the assignation of "whore" is uniquely enabled by, and perhaps privileged as a result of, these workers' ability to turn a corner into a business which protects them from the open assaults that structure many sex workers' experience of being publicly labelled as whore.

10. Kathryn Payne, "Whores and Bitches Who Sleep with Women" in *Brazen Femme: Queering Femininity*, eds. Chloe Rose and Anna Camilleri (Vancouver, BC: Arsenal Pulp Press, 2002), 50.

11. McRobbie, "The Rise and Rise of Porno Chic."

12. Ruth Holliday, "The Comfort of Identity," *Sexualities* 2, no. 4 (1999): 488.

13. Shari Benstock and Suzanne Ferriss, "Introduction," in *On Fashion*, eds. Shari Benstock and Suzanne Ferriss (New Brunswick, NJ: Rutgers University Press, 1994), 4.

14. Holliday, "The Comfort of Identity," 481.

15. Ibid., 488.

16. Ibid., 483.

17. Rebecca Rugg, "How Does She Look?" in *Femme: Feminists, Lesbians and Bad Girls*, eds. Laura Harris and Elizabeth Crocker (New York: Routledge, 1997), 176.

18. Holliday, "The Comfort of Identity," 489.

19. For excellent discussions of historical affect and memory that are outside the range of my chapter see Ann Cvetkovich, *An Archive of Feelings: Trauma, Sexuality and Lesbian Public Cultures* (Durham, NC: Duke University Press, 2003), and Carolyn Dinshaw, *Getting Medieval: Sexualities and Communities, Pre-and PostModern* (Durham, NC: Duke University Press, 1999). For a discussion of identification with the sex wars see Barbra Brent, "Sexual Politics from Barnard to Las Vegas," *The Communication Review* 11 (2008): 237–246.

20. See Amber Hollibaugh and Cherrie Moraga, "What We're Rollin' Around in Bed With," in Amber Hollibaugh, *My Dangerous Desires: A Queer Girl Dreaming Her Way Home* (Durham, NC: Duke University Press, 2000), 62–84; and Joan Nestle, "Butch-Fem Relationships: Sexual Courage in the 1950s," in *A Restricted Country* (San Francisco: Cleis Press, 2003), 92–103.

21. Hollibaugh and Moraga, "What We're Rollin' Around in Bed With."

22. Quoted in Cricket Keating, "Building Coalitional Consciousness," *NWSA Journal* 17 no. 2 (2005): 86–103.

23. Ladelle McWhorter makes good use of Foucault's notion of counter-memory, defining it as that sustained ethical effort to "make ourselves aware of what official interpretations of the world leave out, to find where the gaps live and where, therefore, the potential lies for thinking and living differently." Ladelle McWhorter, *Bodies and Pleasures: Foucault and the Politics of Sexual Normalization* (Bloomington, IN: Indiana University Press, 1999), 199.

24. See Laura Kipnis, *Bound and Gagged: Pornography and the Politics of Fantasy in America* (Durham, NC: Duke University Press), 1999; and Lisa Henderson, "Slow Love," *The Communication Review* 11 (2008): 219–224.

25. Let me be clear; this is not to say that I have not ever felt the toll of working in this industry or that sex work can magically improve a worker's personal erotic life, or that the only significant thing to say about my labor is that it has "improved my sex life." Rather, I am explaining how this work—painted by some feminists as ongoing victimization—has given me pleasure.

26. I understand and use the term "butch-femme erotic system" to specifically include transmen/FTMs.

27. Sue-Ellen Case, "Toward a Butch-Femme Aesthetic," in *The Lesbian and Gay Studies Reader*, eds. Henry Abelove, Michele Aina Barale, and David Halperin (New York: Routledge, 1993), 305. I do not mean to suggest that somehow these things cannot be sex toys for other kinds of couples. However, I am drawing atten-

tion to ways in which butch-femme has been conceptualized as a theatrical endeavor that creates feminist agency capable of reclaiming such things as the male gaze for feminist pleasure.

28. Ibid., 295.

29. Clearly, there are burlesque performers who are also sex workers or sex worker allies. However, what I'm emphasizing is how burlesque functions as an over-determined social space for articulating femme subjectivity and silencing sex worker subjectivity.

30. The degree to which queer femme and burlesque cultures overlap is driven home in the recent documentary, *FtF: Female to Femme*, DVD, directed by Kami Chisholm and Elizabeth Stark (2006, AltCinema). This film, featured at queer femme conferences, is notable in that it advances an argument for femme as a gendered experience on par with transgendered identities and it not only includes interviews with burlesque performers, but burlesque pieces are used as a narrative device throughout the film. In Seattle, famous queer burlesque troupes are populated by femme-identified performers and shows regularly celebrate queer femininities.

31. The sale of alcohol in sex businesses is prohibited by Washington state law, but burlesque performance is a routine part of nightclub settings that profit from the sale of alcohol.

32. I am indebted to conversations with my friend Clare Lemke for clarifying my thoughts on this subject. See Maria Elena Buszek, *Pin-Up Grrrls: Feminism, Sexuality, Popular Culture* (Durham, NC: Duke University Press, 2006); Debra Ferreday, "Showing the Girl: The New Burlesque." *Feminist Theory* 9 (2008): 47–65; and Maura Ryan, " 'I Will Rock Some Glitter Like You've Never Seen': Burlesque, Femme Organizations, and the Cultural Politics of the Femme Movement," (PhD diss., University of Florida, 2009).

33. Michelle Baldwin, *Burlesque and the New Bump-n-Grind* (Denver: Speck Press, 2004).

34. Laura Harris and Liz Crocker, "Bad Girls: Sex, Class and Feminist Agency," in *Femme: Feminists, Lesbians and Bad Girls,* 99.

35. Rugg, "How Does She Look?" 184.

36. Ferreday, "Showing the Girl," 52.

37. I use the term "radical chic" in its contemporary and colloquial sense, as the impulse to appropriate marginalized subjectivity/fashion in service of hegemonic capitalist production. See Tom Wolfe, *Radical Chic & Mau-Mauing the Flak Catchers* (New York: Farrar, Strauss, & Giroux, 1970), and Kaja Silverman, "Fragments of a Fashionable Discourse" in *On Fashion*, 183–196.

38. Rugg, "How Does She Look?" 185.

39. Holliday, "The Comfort of Identity," 487.

Chapter 7

Japanese Lolita

Challenging Sexualized Style and the Little-Girl Look

Kathryn A. Hardy Bernal

"Lolita is back."[1]

In 1996, the art critic Hannah J. L. Feldman described an emerging phenomenon: the portrayal of the sexual little-girl as a subject in art and popular culture. In Japan, this trend was accompanied by a growing number of young women who dressed as children, or dolls. Known as Lolita, this fashion-based subculture gradually caught on worldwide and, from its inception, invoked controversy and contradiction.

Unlike Vladimir Nabokov's 1955 heroine, the new Lolita alleges she is not a victim of older men's prurient desires. Instead, she claims to transcend the "Lolita Complex," escaping men's fascination with young girls by staying in complete charge of a movement fraught with sexual undertones.

The question this trend poses, though, is whether it is possible, under patriarchal conditions, to successfully subvert male dominance, and invert female vulnerability and victimization, from a position that appears to adopt the very construct that is being challenged. As a collective identity, communicated through style, Lolita fashion represents a transgressive statement regarding female sexuality. Journalist David McNeill claims that "if the Lolita enthusiasts share a philosophy, it might be best understood as a reluctance to embrace the 'dirty world' of adulthood."[2] However, although this transgressive possibility exists, the tensions between autonomy and objectification remain unresolved. This essay investigates these complexities and paradoxes.

Going Gothloli

The Lolita subculture is a subgenre of a larger Japanese movement, known more generally as Gothic & Lolita (G&L). The most prominent face of G&L is the "gothloli," known in Japan as *gosurori*.[3] Gothloli merges the terms "Gothic" and "Lolita" to designate a young woman whose image is inspired by little girls' fashions of the Rococo, Romantic, and Victorian periods, and is signified by her child/doll-like appearance. Her dress is also based on historical mourning garb, and influenced by Sir John Tenniel's famous illustrations for Lewis Carroll's *Alice in Wonderland* and *Alice, Through the Looking Glass*.

The style encompasses a predilection for layers of bloomers, petticoats, panniers, aprons, pinafores, and ruffles. This is topped with bonnets, bows, miniature hats, and headdresses, and often completed with parasols, Mary-Jane shoes, or platform boots. A particular penchant in regard to footwear is Vivienne Westwood's rocking-horse ballerina style, a hybrid design that appropriates and blends the traditional Japanese raised-sole *geta* with the ribboned ballet slipper. Although there is sometimes more of an emphasis on the "sweeter" aspects of the style and other times on the "Gothic," the total look overall—a confectionary of frills, lace, broderie anglaise, ribbons, and embroidery—merges to create the gothloli's identity as a "living doll" (see Image 7.1).

The gothloli displays an intense relationship with the doll: she resembles a doll; often collects and plays with dolls; and designs and makes clothing for them. She can sometimes also be seen—especially around the streets of Harajuku and Shinjuku, the most popular hotspots for the subculture in Japan—parading with a real doll, a smaller version of herself. Contributing to this practice is a Japanese doll industry that caters to gothloli worldwide, creating limited editions marketed to young people aged 13 years and older (see Image 7.2).[4]

Cuteness, *Kawaii*, and the Style of Eternal Youth

The gothloli preoccupation with dolls, combined with a childlike countenance and what some consider outwardly childish or frivolous behavior, leads many

Image 7.1. Hinako (age 19), Sweet Lolita, Shinjuku, Tokyo, Japan, 2007. Photograph © Kathryn Adèle Hardy Bernal.

critics to dismiss the subculture as superficial and meaningless. Gothloli style is disregarded as merely another development of Japan's alleged postwar obsession with all things "cute" (*kawaii*).[5] Yet, this dismissive attitude overlooks more complex psychological and sociological issues behind the Lolita movement, especially in relation to *kawaii*.

Japan's attraction to *kawaisa* ("cuteness") runs deep in regard to the nation's history and its relationship with *youjika*, or what some call the infantilizing of Japanese culture after World War II. This phenomenon takes form in a widespread attraction to miniature and cute things, from *netsuke*, *bonsai*, *haiku*, and *sushi*, to *Hello Kitty* and *Pokémon*. According to Yuko Hasegawa, Chief Curator of the Museum of Contemporary Art (MOT) in

Image 7.2. Vivien (age 22), Auckland Lolita with Japanese Pullip Moon doll, both wearing Gothic Lolita designs by Angie Finn, AUT University, New Zealand, 2009. Photograph © James George Stratton Percy.

Tokyo, this style reflects a "postponement of maturity but also . . . a potential for transformation."[6]

The meaning of *kawaii*, itself, is complicated. According to Hasegawa, the "concept of *kawaii* includes elements such as 'cute,' 'pretty' and 'lovely.' "[7] But *kawaii* "also implies something precious: something that we are drawn towards . . . which stimulates one's feeling of wanting to protect something that is pure and innocent."[8] This is important considering the gothloli's efforts to represent herself as an innocent child. Japanese psychiatrist Rika Kayama states that "by dressing up like babies, the Lolitas are attempting to hang on to the carefree days of childhood."[9]

A reading of this phenomenon of cuteness might be that gothloli are symbolically mourning the loss of childhood and innocence. They often take on the image of the "Sweet Lolita," or frilly baby-doll look, but just as commonly adopt a "Gothic Lolita" persona, by which, in choosing to dress as Victorian children in mourning, conveys a particular feeling of bereavement in relation to nostalgia (see Image 7.3).

Engaging in the Lolita subculture is a means to drawing out the transitionary phase between childhood and adulthood, and extending that journey. In light of Kayama's observation, the need for the gothloli to replace or become the doll may exist for the sake of retaining or returning to a safer, familiar haven or a desire to find oneself or one's place in an unsettling

Image 7.3. Yuki (age 19), Gothic Lolita, Harajuku, Tokyo, Japan, 2007. Photograph © Kathryn Adèle Hardy Bernal.

world. It could also be a sign of disconnection from the real world, or as an intentional rejection of society's pressures, disillusionment, or a reaction against it. As Hasagawa posits, gothloli signals a reluctance to move into the adult world or a "postponement of maturity."

Most popularly, gothloli participants are adolescents or young adults. As such, the gothloli's stylized presentation of the self as both little girl and young woman simultaneously conveys an image of the perpetual child and the sexualized adult. However, in wanting to be seen as a child, the goth-loli are commonly recognized by society as refusing to grow up and hence declining to become sexual.

As with *kawaii*, the psychological dynamics of gothloli are complex. Journalist Sheila Burgel has highlighted an "almost pathological obsession with modesty and the minutiae of etiquette" that sits happily alongside a notion of "Queen Victoria's strict moral code."[10] There is a dichotomy: The gothloli image neither wholly represses nor completely embraces a sexualized identity; it does both. The gothloli, especially in connection with a Nabokovian undertone, is at once a sexualized child, but she is also an adult who wishes to be a child.

The association of the gothloli with Vladimir Nabokov's *Lolita* is con-founded: The fictional character is interpreted as a child with adult feelings; the "Lolita," or gothloli, represents an adult or young woman with seemingly childish sensibilities. The reasoning behind this refusal to grow up, and the desire to be seen as cute, modest, and innocent, is discussed by some critics in relation to contemporary Japanese social concerns.

Journalist Yuri Kageyama describes Japan as a nation plagued by an "infantile mentality," represented by the widely held obsession with all things miniature and cute.[11] Kageyama is concerned that, while the *kawaii* phe-nomenon is a powerhouse in the world economy, it will lead to the doom of Japanese culture.[12] Hiroto Mirusawa, professor at Osaka Shoin Women's University, controversially suggests "that cute proves the Japanese simply don't want to grow up."[13] Hasagawa believes that *kawaisa* is profoundly significant in relation to *youjika*, claiming that a strong connection exists between an infantilized postwar Japanese culture and the establishment of a controlling patriarchal system. Hanegawa suggests that this link resulted from "the psychological sense of despair and loss of confidence amongst the Japanese, particularly the male population, following the country's defeat in the Second World War."[14] This, argues Hanegawa, caused "the establishment of immature and distorted gender relations."[15] Such a theory—as contentious as it may be—holds that due to feelings of insecurity and desire for protec-tion, the Japanese male "seeks a mother figure" who is simultaneously "a girl whose sexuality is yet to emerge and who responds passively to his overtures."[16] This means that women often "find themselves forced into performing the contradictory roles of [both] mother and young girl in personal relationships."[17] Each of these roles, though, is similar in that they equally place women in a submissive position, as the virtuous, angelic nurturer, and the subordinate, obedient provider of pleasure.

As reporter Ilya Garger notes, "if you've spent a day in Japan, you've witnessed the hegemony of kawaii."[18] This is specifically expressed through representations of women in advertising and popular culture. Elise Tipton, Associate Professor in Japanese Studies at the University of Sydney, states that everyday media depictions "reinforce the image of women as cute (*kawaii*), childlike, and by extension . . . powerless."[19]

It would appear, then, that the gothloli, who presents herself as a child/woman, woman/child, is playing into the hands of this construct and resigning herself to a life of subservience. However, while true that a child lacks the authority of adulthood—often a problematic position for women, as well—in actively choosing to represent herself as a child, the gothloli can also be interpreted as actually refusing to conform to traditionally less powerful roles and responsibilities.

Shifting Demographics and the Changing Face of Female Independence

Although women in twentieth-century Japan could expect a life of second-class status, young Japanese women today are increasingly reluctant to surrender their independence.[20] In her seminal work on Japanese culture and society, *The Chrysanthemum and the Sword*, Ruth Benedict discusses women's lot from the start of the postwar period until 1967:

> Whatever one's age, one's position in the hierarchy depends on whether one is male or female. The Japanese woman walks behind her husband and has a lower status. . . .[21] A woman . . . wants children not only for her emotional satisfaction . . . but because it is only as a mother that she gains status. A childless wife has a most insecure position in the family. . . . Japanese mothers [therefore] . . . begin their childbearing early, and girls of nineteen bear more children than women of any age. . . . [As it is considered their honorable duty] women may not cry out in labor.[22]

As recently as 1996, Ritsuku Matsumura, writing for *Japanese Women Now II* (published by the English Discussion Society for the purpose of giving "readers a glimpse of women's life" in Japan[23]), maintained that "Japanese parents raise sons and daughters differently."[24] However, there has been a shift in demographic trends since this period, which can be identified as a resistance by society's youth to follow traditional expectations. This is reflected, particularly, in the growing rejection by many to move into adulthood and take on adult responsibilities.

Anthropologists Gordon Mathews and Bruce White note that "many Japanese young people are choosing not to enter the adult social order, not to hold stable jobs . . . or to marry and have families . . . but to follow paths of their own."[25] The authors go on to describe the reasoning behind this: "Socialization into adulthood in Japan has been a grueling process: from the demands in secondary school for constant study for examinations, to the . . . demands that mothers [should] abandon their own pursuits to devote themselves to their children. Young people have long chafed at the demands of the adult social order."[26]

For young women, resistance to conform to these demands are confirmed by statistics that highlight the rising age of marriage, as well as the average age for giving birth to a first child. According to Tipton, Japanese girls have been socialized, historically, for marriage and childbearing: "Women in their early twenties undergo intense pressure from family and friends as well as society at large to marry before they reach twenty-five. A common joke refers to them as 'Christmas cakes,' meaning that, like Christmas cakes, they will become too old and stale [to get married] after the twenty-fifth."[27]

Yet even when marriage remains their primary goal, many young women defy tradition by assertively expressing a preference "for love marriages . . . which was not the custom in earlier times."[28] Rather than being forced into an arranged and loveless marriage, many young people are electing to wait. The ways by which gothloli fashionably prolong the transition from childhood to adulthood reflects this broader demographic shift.

Pushing back against cultural pressure, the catchphrase *onna no jidai* (the era of women) has arisen, "connoting freedom, affluence and independence achieved by women."[29] In the 1990s, according to Japan's Ministry of Health, Labour and Welfare, the average age of first marriage (which had been 23 in the 1950s) rose to 26, and in 2007 this figure jumped again to 28.[30] In this context, the gothloli phenomenon indicates participation in a larger cultural rebellion. The gothloli child/doll image is not merely "cute"; it is complicated. The motivation behind this practice goes beyond playing "dress up" to also express a revolution against the institutions of society. Some psychologists go so far as to suggest that gothloli subculture is a symptom of cultural malaise, born of a reaction to social crisis, driven by global recessions and the uncertainties of financial markets.

Scholars of Japanese youth culture interpret the Lolita look as a sign of anxieties from growing up in a nation beset by economic insecurity: "Fathers are losing their jobs for the first time . . . mothers who used to be full-time homemakers now have to look for part-time jobs to supplement their house-hold income, and children find no hope in future Japan."[31] Oliviero Toscani, former Creative Director for Benetton, has described the gothloli of Harajuku in their "romper-room dresses and . . . silly shoes" as "tragic angels, living the only existence in the world that is alien to the problems of the contem-porary world, such as poverty, war . . . discrimination, or joblessness."[32]

Despite Japan's reputation "as a culture with a love of all things cute, in the face of pressing sociopolitical and economic concerns, many in main-stream Japan are [also] contemptuous of the Lolita look"; name-calling, mean looks and even "having chewing gum stuck to the backs of their dresses" is not unheard of.[33] The reason for such visceral reactions is that the gothloli's appearance often shocks and even angers critics because it is seen as disrup-tive to the social order. "Violations of the authorized codes through which the social world is organized and experienced," Dick Hebdige writes, "have considerable power to provoke and disturb."[34] And, although the gothloli image is referred to as "sweet" and "cute," it still manages to operate in the manner that Hebdige describes in regard to subcultures in general, inciting heated responses and generating fierce debate.

Personal Autonomy and Sexual Objectification: Dressing Along the Razor's Edge

This brings us to the crux of the matter: Gothloli fashion is nonconformist and antiestablishment, and, therefore, the subculture is a women's resistance movement. It is a new type of feminist statement. As Deborah Cameron puts it, the gothloli "is the baby doll face of feminism in Japan."[35] This is per-haps precisely why the phenomenon is so confrontational. Sebastian Masuda, founder of the store *6%Dokidoki*, a leading retailer of the cute aesthetic, has described the movement as "punk . . . minus the violence."[36] Lolita is a passive-aggressive rebellion. Cameron succinctly sums up this notion: "For women in Japan," Lolita is a feminist resistance simply "because it is not about *men*. Nor is it about housekeeping, children, mothers-in-law, dead-end part-time work or the national obsession with raising the birth rate."[37]

But it goes further than that: The gothloli subculture allows women to be feminine, or girly. In that it does not strive for a stereotypical womanly silhouette, it also rejects media images of often unachievable body types that accentuate breasts and a toned physique. This aspect is particularly pertinent in Japan. Leading G&L designer, Naoto Hirooka, claims that "many Japanese women feel intimidated by high fashion in the West and feel that they can never live up to the refined beauty that they feel Western women strive for. . . . So, instead, they shoot for a cute look, one that doesn't require tall, curvaceous bodies and instead emphasizes girlishness."[38]

Novala Takemoto, author of *Kamikaze Girls* (*Shimotsuma Monogatari*),[39] a cult novel in the worldwide realm of Lolita, argues that the gothloli would "rather stay girls. It's their form of resistance. . . . They don't exist to please anyone; they lean on nothing."[40] In Cameron's words, the gothloli movement "is a rebellion with frills on."[41]

In a nation—as described by Benedict—historically framed by a gendered hierarchy, where women were expected to walk behind their husbands, the gothloli subculture assists in allowing women to become visible. Journalist Ginny Parker observes that "conspicuous clothing also satisfies a craving to stand out. Japanese youth are generally less conformist than their parents and often believe it's crucial to be different."[42] In regard to gothloli, Parker cites clinical psychologist Yo Yahata, who believes that "dressing like this and having people stare at them [also] makes them feel that their existence is *worth* something."[43] That audiences stare and comment on the fashion negatively is "understandable," says reporter Jane Pinckard, since "after all, [it's] alienating to want to be someone else."[44] But, the fact that these women are noticed as a collective force can be empowering in, and of, itself.

But clearly, this isn't the end of the story. By simply embracing the gothloli as the new face of feminism, too much remains in tension, and unresolved. Participating in the gothloli subculture symbolizes several competing impulses. There is the desire to prolong childhood innocence, and thus resist entering the adult world; the yearning for a return to the preciousness and safety of the childhood state; and a declaration, through visual signs, that one is not ready to be taken, or physically used, as a married woman and or mother figure. These motivations are signified by the gothloli's obsession with the doll, in that she would rather play with dolls than take on the duty of raising a real child. On the other hand, it is, paradoxically, the presentation of the child/doll-like image that transports the gothloli endeavor into problematic territory, this can be read as hypersexualized, and is often fetishized, especially in connection with pornography.

Participants and critics alike maintain that the gothloli image is not considered to be sexually alluring. The designer Naoto Hirooka has commented that "one of the salient points about Lolita is that it is really a fashion that is not intended to attract men."[45] Similarly, Makoto Sekikawa, the founding editor of Japan's *CUTiE* magazine, states that the cute aesthetic is "the antithesis of traditional fashion," and is "not pleasing to the eye of most men."[46] On the contrary, Sekikawa claims, Japanese men generally prefer women to dress in a responsible and grown-up manner, or in clothing that emphasizes, in his words, "womanliness and common sense."[47]

However, this blanket observation ignores varieties of sexual attraction, or what may be considered sexually alluring for all genders, as well as the individual sexualities of gothloli participants. It also blatantly ignores a long cultural history of the sexualization of girls. There is no denying that the gothloli image is connected with pedophilia and the pornography industry. One of the more unavoidable and literal relationships is between the image of a doll with sex toys. In Japan, there is also a link with *lolicon* (or *rorikon*),[48] examples of *manga* and *anime* comprised of sexually explicit illustrations of very young girls. In that the gothloli style is also based on the little-girl look, the two phenomena are often confused and conflated.

As Sheila Burgel observes, "misconceptions about Gothic Lolita run rampant, [especially] in a country where words like 'Loli-Complex' . . . are embedded in the culture."[49] Burgel explains that the "demure, well-mannered Gothic Lolita [image] is ultimately a rejection of the sexual demands placed on little girls in Japanese society. Although child pornography in Japan was finally outlawed in 1999, fetishizing prepubescent schoolgirls is still common-place . . . However . . . Gothic Lolita doesn't quite carry the significance the look suggests.[50]

Burgel believes that the "prissiness and prudery" of the gothloli look is an effort "primarily intended to keep it sacred and ensure that the image is not destroyed by links to sex."[51] Journalist Francis Henville agrees, arguing that "Gothic Lolita has little or nothing to do with *roricon* or *lolicon* . . . [or] hyper-sexed *manga* or *anime* that would probably violate child porn laws in most countries."[52] Henville insists that "while Gothic Lolita certainly has sexual undertones, it's not about child porn."[53] Japanese fashion manuals such as the *Gothic & Lolita Bible*,[54] the *Gothic, Lolita & Punk Book*, and *Rococo* all claim that gothloli style is intended to represent modesty and innocence.

In virtual gothloli communities and on social networking sites and blogs, it is clear that worldwide followers of gothloli fashion are keen to preserve the purist reputation of the style and vehemently voice their oppo-sition in regard to those who suggest it is otherwise.[55] In fact, in order for "outsider" or non-Japanese members to heighten their sense of belonging to the subculture—in an endeavor to prove that they understand classic Japa-nese sensibilities—they often follow dress-code guidelines quite strictly (see Image 7.4). In his analysis of the movement, Isaac Gagné of Yale University reasons that, for gothloli,

> there is more at stake in educating each other through magazines and web forums than merely constructing a shared notion of community. Haunting the Gothic Lolita at every turn is . . . a pervasive misunderstanding of their subculture . . . and [this]

Image 7.4. Bomi and Ashleigh (both age 17), Auckland Lolita wearing their own designs, Wintergarden, Auckland Domain, New Zealand, 2007. Photograph © Bevan Ka Yan Chuang.

results in attempts . . . to distance themselves from unwanted stereotypes . . . due to its superficial similarities to bondage fashion and the fetishized Lolita of *rorikon*.[56]

Of course, as Ginny Parker highlights, the little-girl look certainly inhabits Japan's sex industry, but this particular trend of the gothloli, which she describes as "frumpy, frilly fashion" can be more intimidating than sexy.[57] And as Deborah Cameron observes, the "Japanese Lolita has a protective cordon of passion-killing petticoats."[58] According to Cameron, "the message is clear:

look but don't touch."[59] Similarly, Jane Pinckard claims that the image shouts, "we are dolls . . . but don't play with us. We bite. . . . [I]t's a 'screw you' to creepy older men who might fetishize the Lolita." [60] Understood in this light there is, therefore, rebelliousness to the gothloli style.

Furthermore, by presenting herself as a doll-like child, the gothloli is not *asking* to be seen as a man's plaything. Just as she takes on the image of the Lolita, she equally reclaims that persona as much as she claims it. She hijacks the male fantasy, takes possession of and over it, reverses and then controls it. Lolita is no longer, to the gothloli, Nabokov's "sinful" and "corruptible" child, or powerless victim. She sees herself as absolved, converted, and purified. The new Lolita reestablishes her right to be feminine.

What is unique about the gothloli, and what sets the phenomenon apart from the historical subcultural model, is that the face of this movement is female. Yuniya Kawamura, citing Hebdige, observes that "girls have been relegated to a position of secondary interest within both sociological and photographic studies of urban youth, and [that] masculine bias [has existed] . . . in the subcultures themselves," while the gothloli movement is essentially a girls' subculture.[61] Anoop Nayak and Mary Jane Kehily have also discussed this anomaly in regard to subcultures and the usual invisibility of girls, noting that "the relative absence of girls in subcultures may hinge around issues of gender and space, [with] girls being more centrally involved in the private domestic sphere of home and family life rather than the public world of the street where most subcultural activities occur."[62]

It is compelling to read the gothloli movement as representing a newly configured subcultural model, especially associated with the inclination toward "play," "display," and "parade." In dressing themselves up, going out with their dolls, and congregating with friends on the street, gothloli transfer the notion of private play to public exhibition. In taking private girls' play outside, they therefore trespass the "male" public domain, while transgressing the rule that the place for women is in the home. In doing so, they take ownership of the little-girl image and expose it, so that it is no longer secretive or mysterious, desensitizing the "naughtiness associated with privately viewing *lolicon*." Perhaps *this* is what makes the practice so confrontational, and yet so unresolved.

Notes

1. Hannah J. L. Feldman, "The Lolita Complex," *World Art* (Australia) 2, (Summer 1996): 52.

2. David McNeill, "Lolita's Bard is Sitting Pretty," *The Japan Times*, November 21, 2004.

3. Please note that "gothloli" is regularly used for both singular and plural forms of this term.

4. Vivien Masters is wearing *Evangeline*, a Gothic Lolita outfit, designed and constructed by Angie Finn for *Loli-Pop*, an exhibition that explored gothloli culture, curated by Kathryn Hardy Bernal, and held at Auckland War Memorial Museum, New Zealand, in 2007. The doll she is holding (manufactured by Jun Planning, Japan/ Cheonsng Chunha, Korea) is wearing a miniature version of *Evangeline*, also created by Angie Finn (see Image 7.2).

5. Yuri Kageyama, "Cute is King for the Youth of Japan, but It's Only Skin Deep," *The New Zealand Herald*, June 16, 2006.

6. Yuko Hasegawa, "Post-identity *Kawaii*: Commerce, Gender and Contemporary Japanese Art," in *Consuming Bodies: Sex and Contemporary Japanese Art*, ed. Fran Lloyd (London: Reaktion, 2002), 127.

7. Ibid., 128.

8. Ibid.

9. Ginny Parker, "Parasols and Pink Lace: Japan's Lolita Girls," *The Globe and Mail*, September 25, 2004; Note that the plural for Lolita is usually the same as the singular, (i.e., Lolita, not Lolitas).

10. Sheila Burgel, "Dark and Lovely," *Bust,* April/May 2007, 77.

11. Yuri Kageyama, "Cute is King."

12. Ibid.; Yuri Kageyama, "Can't Get Enough Fluff?: Infantile Japan Seen Redlining Cute Gauge," *The Japan Times*, June 21, 2006.

13. Ibid.

14. Yuko Hasegawa, "Post-identity *Kawaii*," 128.

15. Ibid.

16. Ibid.

17. Ibid.

18. Ilya Garger, "Hello Kitty: One Nation Under Cute," *Psychology Today,* March/ April 2007, 32.

19. Elise K. Tipton, "Being Women in Japan, 1970–2000," in *Women in Asia: Tradition, Modernity and Globalisation*, ed. Louise Edwards and Mina Roces (Sydney: Allen & Unwin, 2000), 222–223.

20. Ibid., 213.

21. Ruth Benedict, *The Chrysanthemum and the Sword: Patterns of Japanese Culture* (1967; repr., London and Henley: Routledge & Kegan Paul, 1977), 37.

22. Ibid., 179.

23. *Japanese Women Now II*, English Discussion Society (Kyoto: Women's Bookstore Shoukadoh, 1996), Preface, i.

24. Ritsuko Matsumura, "How to Raise Daughters," in *Japanese Women Now II*, 20.

25. Gordon Mathews and Bruce White, "Introduction: Changing Generations in Japan Today," in *Japan's Changing Generations: Are People Creating a New Society?*, ed. Gordon Mathews and Bruce White (London and New York: Routledge Curzon, 2004), 2.

26. Ibid., 4.

27. Tipton, "Being Women in Japan," 213.

28. Ibid.

29. Ibid., 208.

30. Ministry of Internal Affairs and Communications, "Statistical Handbook of Japan: Chapter 2, Population," Statistics Bureau, Director-General for Policy Planning (Statistical Standards), and Statistical Research and Training Institute, http://www.stat.go.jp/english/data/handbook/c02cont.htm.

31. Yuniya Kawamura, "Japanese Street Fashion," 343; citing John Nathan, *Japan Unbound: A Volatile Nation's Quest for Pride and Purpose* (New York: Houghton Mifflin, 2004).

32. Rebecca Mead, "Letter from Tokyo: Shopping Rebellion, What Kids Want," *The New Yorker*, March 18, 2002, http://www.newyorker.com/archive/2002/03/18/020318fa_FACT

33. Parker, "Parasols and Pink Lace."

34. Dick Hebdige, "Subculture: The Unnatural Break" (1979), in *The Fashion Reader*, eds. Linda Welters and Abby Lillethun (New York: Berg, 2007), 152.

35. Deborah Cameron, "Where There's a Frill, There's a Way to Keep Men at Bay," *The Sydney Morning Herald*, July 29, 2006.

36. Alicia Kirby, "The Fashion Victims." *6%Dokidoki* is a retail outlet promoting the cute aesthetic. For more information, go to http://www.dokidoki6.com.

37. Cameron, "Where There's a Frill."

38. Eric Talmadge, "Japan's Lolitas Seek Non-conformity through Cuteness," *Chicago Tribune*, August 18, 2008.

39. Novala Takemoto, *Kamikaze Girls* (*Shimotsuma Monogatari*, 2002), trans. Akemi Wegmüller (San Francisco: VIZ Media LLC, 2006).

40. Cameron, "Where There's a Frill."

41. Ibid.

42. Parker, "Parasols and Pink Lace."

43. Ibid.

44. Jane Pinckard, "Playing Dress Up," *Zine*, July, 2003, http://www.gamegirladvance.com/zine/200307play/playing_dress_up.html.

45. Talmadge, "Japan's Lolitas Seek Non-conformity through Cuteness."

46. Ella Mudie, "Turning Japanese: Manga Makeover," *Pulp* 58 (Winter 2008): 137.

47. Ibid.

48. Known also as *rorikon/roricon*, the term *lolicon* is a contraction of "Lolita" and "complex," or "icon."

49. Burgel, "Dark and Lovely," 77.

50. Ibid.

51. Ibid.

52. Ibid.

53. Ibid.

54. The *Gothic & Lolita Bible* was for many years solely a Japanese publication. More recently, a U.S. version has begun publication. However, the U.S. content is not based solely on an English translation of the Japanese; it contains articles and

information relevant to and appropriate for a Western audience and mindset. Therefore, an understanding of the gothloli subculture, and its rules and regulations, may differ through a reading of this material.

55. Much of my understanding in this area comes from opinions expressed by worldwide gothloli, with whom I am connected through an online MySpace community, using my alias, "Angelic Lolita (botticelliangel)": http://myspace.com/botticelliangel_nz.

56. Isaac Gagné, "SLA Prize Winning Graduate Paper 2007: Urban Princesses, Performance and 'Women's Language' in Japan's Gothic/Lolita Subculture," *Journal of Linguistic Anthropology* 18, no. 1 (2008): 139.

57. Parker, "Parasols and Pink Lace."

58. Cameron, "Where There's a Frill."

59. Ibid.

60. Pinckard, "Playing Dress Up."

61. Kawamura, "Japanese Street Fashion," 344.

62. Anoop Nayak and Mary Jane Kehily, *Gender, Youth and Culture: Young Masculinities and Femininities* (Houndmills and New York: Palgrave MacMillan, 2008), 53.

II

Fashion Choices

The Ethics of Consumption, Production, and Style

Chapter 8

Glam *Abaya*

Contemporary Emirati Couture

Jan C. Kreidler

Perhaps the most fetishized image of Middle Eastern cultures is that of the veiled female. For ages, Westerners have been enthralled by what they perceived to be the mystique of Islamic feminine garb or *hijab* (Arabic for veiling), and romanticized notions have not abated. Today, visitors to the United Arab Emirates' many lush shopping malls may be treated to impromptu fashion shows as young local women glide by in elegant, remarkably embellished, feminine Islamic fashions that express their heritage and current trends. While the regal look still holds to cultural values, at the same time, it reflects changes in women's status in progressive Islamic cultures. Islamic women's styles vary tremendously among regions and, of course, among individuals. However, in the United Arab Emirates Gulf region, specifically in Dubai and Abu Dhabi where the *abaya* (outer covering worn in public) is the national dress, young Emirati women, with the help of the most famous fashion houses, are dramatically stamping new meanings on their seemingly uniform national dress. Ironically, many wear their *haute couture abayat* in more revealing ways that deliberately draw, rather than deflect, attention to the female figure, customarily obscured by traditional Islamic garb.

While the most progressive glam fashionistas represent a small segment of society, their numbers are growing, and their presence is stimulating public dialogue about what the *abaya* represents in Gulf culture. Journalist

Tala al Ramahi observes, "From traditional wear to fashion statement, the *abaya* is undergoing a massive transformation, much like the Emirati women who wear it . . . some young women are pushing the limits of creativity while still respecting their culture."[1] This transformation represents a push in women's public self-expression that is not usually encouraged in Emirati culture. Reader letters to the regional newspaper, *Gulf News,* express various viewpoints: Rabia Akram of Dubai writes, "Nowadays, it seems as if the *abaya* is more of a fashion outfit, than what it should be used for. We wear it to cover ourselves in a decent way. However, some women wear it for who knows what reason. . . ."[2] Syed of Dubai adds, "*Abaya* [sic] represent modesty. A Muslim woman is dressed only to attract her husband and avoid strangers. . . . Donning an *abaya* looks very graceful and decent when done properly."[3] Another *Gulf News* reader asserts, "It's very sad to see some girls here who wear it more as a fashion statement in a provocative manner, which could convey a sense of mystery to attract the opposite sex. The main purpose is to guard a woman's modesty, which is not being met."[4] At this point in Emirati history, the *abaya* represents the tension of the former insular society blending with its current mushrooming multicultural atmosphere. Even Emirati women grapple with the contemporary *abaya*'s definition and the intentions of glam *abayat* wearers, and this tension represents a major cultural challenge in the United Arab Emirates today.

Material Culture in the United Arab Emirates

A vast amount of disposable income creates an unprecedented retail culture in the United Arab Emirates. Suzanne Fenton of *Gulf News* writes, "Despite the financial downturn, residents of the GCC [Gulf Cooperation Council] are maintaining their pre-crisis spending levels."[5] Dubai and Abu Dhabi specifically have emerged high on the list of the world's wealthiest countries due to the rapid development of the petroleum industry in the formerly poor, undeveloped region. In 1971 when the Emirates were first formed, the GDP was UAD 65 billion (USD 17.1 billion) compared to the reported GDP of UAE 729.73 billion dirhams (USD 198.8 billion) in 2007, a growth rate of 115 percent.[6] Further, the Emirates' GDP per capita income "surged to a record US $71,200 in 2007, the world's second highest per capita income."[7] Males were not alone in profiting from the oil boom. James Calderwood reports in *The National*, "GCC women control around US $246 billion . . . which they like to spend on shopping, beauty salons, and trendy *abayas.*"[8] Although the patriarchal social structure limits women's personal freedom in certain ways, many women do find some measures of power in the staggering amount of newly created wealth. The 2009 issue of the *United Arab Emirates Yearbook* reports that "UAE citizens spend on average the equivalent of US $27 per day, reported to be one of the highest daily per capita consumer spending rates in the world."[9] Due to this windfall, the lives of contemporary women in the United Arab Emirates have significantly changed compared to the lives of their grandmothers, and one socially acceptable form of self-expression is through fashion.

Expatriates have provided some of the technological knowledge and muscle to help create the Middle Eastern wonderlands of Dubai and Abu Dhabi; they also provide an introduction to a multitude of foreign cultures, which certainly influence each other. In Abu Dhabi, 80 percent of the population consists of expatriate workers from around the globe. The UN International Migration Report of 2002 places the United Arab Emirates as first on the "Countries with the Highest Percentage of International Migrants" list.[10] To further complicate matters, the bulk of the expatriate labor force is male, with an estimated "3.08 million males and 1.4 million females in the country at the end of 2007," which "will rise to 3.28 million males and 1.47 females in 2008 and 3.5 million males and 1.58 million females in 2009."[11] In a patriarchal society where the men outnumber the women so drastically, the issue of Muslim women covering is even more pronounced and controversial, as Emiratis strive to find balance between their traditional values and influences of outside cultures brought in to assist with the UAE's astonishing material growth.

The UAE is unique in its intersection with the West in what feminist scholar Aihwa Ong calls a "transnational network of power relations"[12] because, unlike colonized nations, the UAE is the host nation exercising power over the Westerners working in their land. As members of the dominant culture, Emiratis are not forced to adopt cultural objects and ideologies as they would were they subjugated by a colonial presence and under a threat of violence. Instead, outside ideas are woven into the cultural fabric simply by familiarization.

Refashioning a National Identity

Within such rapid expansion, UAE society is undergoing change, both subtle and dramatic, affecting all aspects of society, particularly the role of the individual. Abu Dhabi, once a sparsely, seasonally populated island with only brackish water, is now a major modern city that hosts world-class cultural events and private corporations doing business. According to scholar Ahmed Jameel'Azm, "The private sector has become a point of entry allowing individuals to participate in decision-making and has ended state control over economic decisions and wealth monopoly. This in turn means that the economic role of individuals has expanded and subsequently, their political and social roles have also been enhanced."[13] This is especially true for women who choose to participate in the public sphere. The UAE is making a conscious effort to emerge as a more progressive society; thus, there are programs in place to encourage women to further their education and participate in careers in both the public and private sectors. Many Emirati women are expanding their roles to include higher education and careers, and as they gain more autonomy and financial clout, their fashions reflect these changes. Tala al Ramahi reports in *The National* that "seven UAE civil servants in 10 are now women," citing a young, glam *abaya*-clad woman's observation that ". . . the Emirati woman is a working woman and a productive part of society, her *abaya* is reflecting that change." Al Ramahi concludes, "In part, the trend may be driven by the increasing financial independence of Emirati women."[14]

As a result of this staggering growth, Emirati culture has endured intense growing pains creating what some experience as tension between Islamic tradition and the encroachment of foreign ideas and mores some consider threatening, and this has become a source of national concern. As proud nationals, Emiratis remain loyal to the *abayat* and *shaylas* (head scarves) for women and *kandorah* (long white robe) and *ghutra* (headscarf) for men. UAE scholar Mattar Ahmed Abdullah asserts, "the imbalance in the population structure has reached a dangerous point since it has started to affect the identity and the socio-cultural character of the population, especially in the states where the nationals have become the minority, such as the UAE. . . ."[15] Clearly, UAE's national identity has been affected seriously by the influx of strangers and wealth, and this fact makes wearing national dress even more valuable as a sign of social status and wealth. However, as is the mission of all younger generations, the young have begun to challenge tradition by altering their clothing dramatically. For instance, it is not unusual to see young men wearing American-style baseball caps with their *kandorahs*. Yet, traditional male fashion remains far less dramatically changed and controversial than traditional female fashion.

Emirati women have been turning heads and raising eyebrows by making controversial changes to their *abayat*. Dramatic fashion alterations include elaborate decorative arts and trimmer, body hugging cuts of *abayat* as well as the wrap of the *shaylas*. A young woman from Dubai is quoted in the newspaper, *The National*, describing "three ways women can wear the *shaila* [sic] and *abaya*: conservative, casual, or a third way, the 'most free one.' "[16] The suggestion that a more expressive, sexualized look connotes—or enables—more freedom, reveals the ideological puzzle at the root of the glam *abaya*. These fashion statements are topics of debate in Emirati society precisely because they underscore the difficulties of working out the meanings of tradition, modernity, and freedom in a culture emerging onto the world stage so prominently and rapidly. Like most public debates, arguments vary wildly about women's use of fashion for self-expression in garments that have until now remained fairly uniform.

The *Abaya*'s Subtle Evolution

The traditional Islamic women's wear or *hijab* stems from differing, often controversial, interpretations of several Qu'ran passages; therefore, there is no clear consensus on how women should properly dress. In one ultra-conservative interpretation, Shaik Zayed bin Muhammad Haadee Al-Madkhalee argues that contemporary Muslim women are obligated to cover their entire bodies, including their faces and hands, for which he offers what he calls "clear-cut and authentic textual, logical and customary evidences."[17] These include passages such as, "O Prophet! Tell your wives and daughters and the believing women to cast their *jalaabeeb* (pl. of *jilbaab*) over themselves. That will be better, that they should be known, so as not to be bothered."[18] According to Al-Madkhalee, these passages apply to veiling women's face and hands, as well as the entire body, "to remain far away from those things that cause *fitnah*" (mischief/imbalance). He further asserts that this passage

> sends down the preventive and fortified *hijaab* so that none of the evil desires of those with diseased hearts and vile lusts, which demolish modesty and bring about bad consequences in this life and the next, can be achieved. Any fair person with common sense will not doubt that the hands and the face are the chief areas of temptation, thus it is an obligation to cover them.[19]

From another reading, Reza Aslan asserts,

> Although long seen as the most distinctive emblem of Islam, the veil is, surprisingly, not enjoined upon Muslim women anywhere in the *Qu'ran*. The tradition of veiling and seclusion (known together as *hijab*) was introduced into Arabia long before Muhammad, primarily through Arab contacts with Syria and Iran, where the *hijab* was a sign of social status.[20]

Aslan goes on to argue that there is strong textual, historical evidence—and contemporary, scholarly support for the view—that veiling was practiced primarily only by Muhammad's wives, and that this "makes perfect sense when one recalls that Muhammad's house was also the community's mosque. . . .

When delegations from other tribes came to speak with Muhammad, they would set up their tents . . . just a few feet away from the apartments in which Muhammad's wives slept."[21]

Muslimas' fashion choices range from contemporary Western styles to full coverage, and everything in between. In the end, the contemporary *Muslimas*' choice to cover or not, and to what degree, depend largely on family demands, regional traditions, and religious laws. In more politically moderate areas, such as in the UAE or in Western cultures, Muslim women might have more leeway to make personal choices according to their family's views. The *abaya* does not necessarily represent the depth of one's piety; it can also represent cultural custom, national pride, individuality, or the desire to fit in Emirati society.

Nawal El-Saadawi offers an explanation for the hyper-sexualization of females and the resulting attention to dress:

> For the Arabs, the word 'woman' invariably evokes the word *fitna*. Arab women combined the qualities of a positive personality and *fitna*, or seductiveness, to such an extent that they became an integral part of the Islamic ethos which has, as one of its cornerstones, the sexual power of women, and which maintains that their seductiveness can lead to a *fitna* within society. Here the word is used in a related but different sense to mean an uprising, rebellion, conspiracy or anarchy which would upset the existing order of things, established by Allah (and which, therefore, is not to be changed). . . .[22]

According to this concept, women are held responsible for male weakness, which creates an excuse to force females to cover. The culturally embedded fear of *fitna* also helps generate sexual connotations often projected onto veiled women. However, some contemporary fashion-conscious Gulf women are opening Islamic fashion to multiple interpretations by resignifying Emirati cultural dress, putting into question accepted cultural suppositions about female sexuality through exaggerated *abaya* features, much like the way American hip-hop artists have attempted to resignify racial slurs.

A Wide Range of Uniformity

Islamic women's fashion varies greatly worldwide. If a woman living in a strict culture is to cover her hair and face, she may be required to wear a *burqa,* which slides over the head and reveals only the eyes, except in some instances where the eye slit is covered by net. Some women wear the *kimar*, a more extreme, one-piece, flowing covering that slips overhead with an oval cutout for the face, and falls below the shoulders, like a Catholic nun's habit. It is more common to see married women wearing the *niqaab*, which is a veil worn with a *shayla* (a headscarf that is wrapped around the head or tied under the chin and draped over the shoulders). The *niqaab* is placed over the nose, tied behind the head mask-like, revealing the eyes. The rest of the ensemble includes a floor length *abaya*, often with black gloves.

In the search for modern styles that do not offend religious and cultural customs, most fashionable Muslim women wear conservative, more conventionally attractive *abayat*. A *Gulf News* reader writes, "We Emirati women wear the *abaya* because it is our cultural dress and our culture is defined by our religion, Islam. That is why it is a beautiful, conservative and traditional way to be a good Muslim and an elegant woman."[23] Even the marketing discourse of more explicitly "stylish" *abayat* reflects this effort at balancing the traditional and the elegant, the modern and the modest. One design team claims, "The EFFA '*Abaya* Couture' customer is an independent, active and modern woman that wants her *abaya* to reflect her personality whilst keeping her cultural identity. Coined by some as the 'little black dress' of the Middle East, there is an EFFA *Abaya* to take you from work to play and evening with effortless style."[24]

In the Gulf region, not all Islamic women follow specific fashion guidelines; many simply wish to cover themselves modestly. However, many others are pushing former customary boundaries with exquisitely embellished *abayat*, elaborate makeup and hair fashions, fabulously expensive designer handbags and purses, as well as enticing perfumes. The total, polished look suggests a self-conscious sexuality, with V-cut necklines, shorter lengths that reveal jeans, long flowing sleeves, *kaftans*, colors other than black, exquisite decorations, and brightly colored trim and accessories. *Abayat* are sold alongside Western fashions in the thriving shops in the Abu Dhabi and Dubai malls; one wing of the Marina Mall in Abu Dhabi offers a smorgasbord of high-end designer retail shops: Chanel, Dior, Fendi, Valentino, Calvin Klein, Coach, Tod's, Yves Saint Laurent, Gucci, Louis Vuitton, Armani Exchange, and Burberry. This mall has no less than 15 perfumeries, 12 specialty lingerie shops, 16 *abaya* and Arabic dress boutiques, and 50 jewelry and watch stores, including Tiffany & Co., attesting to the enormous cultural materialism that has sprouted in the UAE's intersection with the West.

While asserting the *abaya's* obvious links to traditional culture, designers will also often gesture to the glam *abaya's* departure from tradition. Note that the marketing language for the Spring 2007 line of EFFA's "*Abaya* Couture" boasts that it is "a modern take on the traditional black *abaya*, playing with new shapes and ideas that challenge the norms of what an *abaya* traditionally represents."[25] And challenge, designers do. Perhaps the most controversial example to date hails from British wedding-gown designer-to-the-stars Bruce Oldfield, who designed the "million dirham *abaya*" encrusted with Crosley diamonds, for an estimated Dh1.27 million (US $365,000) price tag. Such an ostentatious garment created a stir, since it seems to contradict the *abaya*'s "traditional" purpose of expressing sexual modesty. But Oldfield explains, ". . . we thought it would be a good idea to make an *abaya*. Why not? Every leading designer seems to doing this right now."[26] This is true; Abu Dhabi has begun hosting fashion shows featuring extravagant bridal gowns and *abaya* creations.[27] Such high-end garments attract attention from mainstream fashion trend watchers as well. Journalist Tala al Ramahi notes, "Global fashionistas have taken notice, too. The U.S. edition of *Marie Claire* magazine has featured *abaya*-wearing models sporting Gucci sunglasses and Hermès handbags."[28]

Accessories play a major part in glam *abaya* fashion, and they must fill three requirements: large, elaborate, and expensive. The handbags are top-end designer. *Gulf News* Reporter Suzanne Fenton cites Ian Bickley, president of Coach International, who observes that where "women wear abayas, accessories, especially handbags and shoes are really the main way women can show off their fashions and tastes in public."[29] An unwritten law seems to be the bigger and shinier the bag, the better. In Abu Dhabi, the glam *abaya* wearers prefer high stiletto heels; additionally, oversized designer sunglasses, the ubiquitous mobile phone, flawless dramatic makeup, and perfectly manicured, hennaed hands complete the glam ensemble, not to mention the head-turning, sensuous perfume wafting in their wake.

Rochelle Roxas, sales associate of Arabesque, the high-end *abaya* shop of French-trained designer Judith Duriez in Abu Dhabi, notes the changes she has witnessed in her two-and-a-half years in the business. Roxas agrees that *abaya* designs are influenced by Western culture, and that many wealthy Emirati women who travel and are educated abroad in Europe and the United States return with the latest fashion trends and designs that they want incorporated into their wardrobe, including their *abayat*. For instance, more conservative *abaya* wearers cover fully, while some more daring *abaya* wearers reveal their outfits underneath by keeping open their *abayat*.[30] Many attention-seekers wear *abayat* with long, elegant trains that drag behind them in public places such as malls (see Image 8.1).

What women wear beneath the *abaya* is also a subject of controversy. They often wear traditionally feminine colored dresses (*jalbiya*) or unremarkable Western fashions; however, the daring trendsetters consciously leave open their *abayat* to expose tight designer jeans with stiletto heels, or the latest shock, leggings with boots, in which case the female form is greatly accentuated. Some younger girls have begun to wear-knee length *abayat* with jeans and running shoes or flats. Some newer styles have cinched waists or

Image 8.1. *Abaya* haute couture from the "Arabesque" Fall/Winter 2008–2009 collection by designer Judith Duriez of Abu Dhabi, UAE.

belts. Sleeve styles are also altered for self-expression and may be full, tight from elbow to wrist, flowing or flaring at the wrist like a medieval costume. In the ongoing debate over the "true" meaning of *abaya* style, another *Gulf News* reader contends, "Nowadays, unfortunately many women are compromising [*abaya*] design by over-accessorising [sic] it and not to mention the way they wear it. Some of them wear a short skirt or some leggings beneath it. I really wonder why."[31]

  Shayla styles differ greatly. Many women are attracting attention by wearing their hair in fluffy hair clips high on the head, so the *shayla* looks like a crown. Occasionally, one sees a woman wearing an electric-colored *shayla*, such as magenta or sunshine yellow that matches the *abaya* lining, purse, and shoes. Some trendy *abaya* wearers simply drape the *shayla* around their shoulders rather than over the head exposing their hair, or the *shayla* may be made of a provocative sheer fabric. *Shaylas* and *abayat* may be trimmed in Burberry pattern, sequins, coins, handmade lace, mink fur, embroidery, fringe, ribbon, or anything else a designer can conjure. Obviously, the women wearing these flirty *abayas* turn heads, yet part of the posture is to look indifferent, so they do not make eye contact with others they glide past. Thus, the glam *abaya* gives rise to a strong tension between getting and deflecting attention, which is the central point of contention among those who are commenting on what they consider to be radical sartorial statements.

Abdullah Hussan Khunji, owner of National Ladies Fashion, has been in the textile and design business creating Islamic women's fashion for 20 years in Dubai, specializing in incorporating small stones and sequins into his trim decorations. Khunji is constantly offering new designs to his discriminating clients; normally, his company will produce no more than twelve pieces of a single design, unless he has requests for more of the same. Khunji muses that for local local women, haute couture *abayat* signify wealth and status; therefore, they demand fresh, original designs. He also notes that mature women prefer modest, elegant designs, while teens and younger women like tighter fitting and more decorated looks, perhaps even black prints as opposed to plain black fabric.[32] Popular fabrics for *abayat* are crepe, cotton/ linen mix, polyester, chiffon, Georgette, and Moroccan lace, always in black, until very recently.

The Persistence of Tradition/Modernity Logics

Western misconceptions about Islamic traditions seriously widen the chasm of understanding between cultures. The conservative Canadian-American journalist Danielle Crittenden writes, "Accepting veiling implies acceptance of a larger ideology of female subordination. And that ideology too is finding a receptive audience in our own society. . . . In the free and equal societies of North America and Europe, we are hearing of more and more cases of forced marriage, confinement of women to their homes, honour killings and female genital mutilation."[33] While it is true that many veiled women are victims of abuse, the fact that widespread violence occurs to women in *all* societies cannot be disputed. Nor can we conflate practices of veiling with practices of abuse, as if one causes, or is clear evidence of, the other. Instead, we must see the *abaya* as inherently subject to multiple meanings, heavily dependent on context. As *Gulf News* reader Sumaiya Essa states, in an explicit nod to the persistence of Western logics on this topic, "To me the *abaya* represents the dignity that Islam offers a Muslim woman, contrary to the ignorance of some cultures."[34]

Western-trained Emirati surgeon, Dr. Ali al Houlei, offers an Emirati male's perspective when he states,

As society trends and values changed with influx of western and other foreign ideas, the *abayas* evolved and modified into a more fashionable statement of identity for the Emirati women. I agree with changes in moderation that will preserve old values from the culture while allowing the modern educated and powerful Emirati women to reflect their new found position in the society as partners to men through the wearing of those fashionable *abayas*.[35]

The glam *abaya* is an artifact of cultural change involving and reflecting much more than fashion trends, as wearers of the glam *abaya* express Emirati women's role in their nation's meteoric emergence into the global economy. The larger lesson is that *hijab haute couture* defies a singular interpretation; it simultaneously conjures modesty, nationalism, globalization, tradition, and Western notions of individualism through consumerism. Aihwa Ong warns Western feminists against "using a traditional/modernity framework" to gauge women's status in non-Western societies and cites the need to "maintain a respectful distance . . . to leave open the possibilities for understanding not overly constructed by our own [Western] preoccupations."[36] Such preoccupations often include an assumption that freedom must take the form of individualism, and a love of iconoclasm for its own sake. Fashion in the UAE is a barometer indicating the flux in Emirati attitudes as their society is faced with both unprecedented outside influences *and* the pull of history. Attempting to explain the glam *abaya* in absolute, either/or terms will therefore fail to capture the more complex reality that expressive fashion, described as a departure from tradition, will also invariably entail it.

Notes

1. Tala al Ramahi, "*Abaya* Styles Evolve," *The National,* May 1, 2008, http://www.thenational.ae/article/20080501/NATIONAL/814359009/1007&profile=1007.

2. Rabia Akram, Comment to Fatma Salem, "*Abayas* Still Topping Sales in UAE Market," *Gulf News,* February 5, 2009, http://gulfnews.com/news/gulf/uae/heritage-culture/abayas-still-topping-sales-in-uae-market-1.50204.

3. Syed, comment to Salem, "*Abayas* Still Topping Sales in UAE Market."

4. Mona, comment to Salem, "*Abayas* Still Topping Sales in UAE Market."

5. Suzanne Fenton, "Gulf Consumer Spending Robust Despite Downturn," *Gulf News,* July 23, 2009, http://gulfnews.com/business/economy/gulf-consumer-spending-robust-despite-downturn-1.502378.

6. "UAE at a Glance 2009," 6–7, downloaded at http://www.uaeinteract.com/uaeint_misc/pdf_2009/UAE-at-a-Glance-2009/.

7. "Abu Dhabi GDP per Capita Hits US $71,200, Second Highest in the World," *Business Intelligence Middle East*, August 27, 2008, http://www.bi-me.com/ main. php?id=23750&t=1&cg=4.

8. James Calderwood, "Gulf Women's Wealth Can Turn Tide," *The National*, February 15, 2009, http://www.thenational.ae/article/20090215/FOREIGN/968489974/-1/NEWS.

9. "Economic Development," *United Arab Emirates Yearbook 2009*, 69, http://yearbook.uaeinteract.com/Yearbooks/2009/ENG/.

10. United Nations, Department of Economic and Social Affairs, "International Migration Report 2002," 4, downloaded at http://www.un.org/esa/population/publications/ittmig2002/2002ITTMIGTEXT22-11.pdf.

11. "Population," *United Arab Emirates Yearbook 2009*, 206–207.

12. Aihwa Ong, "Colonialism and Modernity: Feminist Re-presentations of Women in Non-Western Societies," in *Theorizing Feminism: Parallel Trends in the Humanities and Social Sciences*, eds. Anne C. Herrmann and Abigail J. Stewart (Boulder, CO: Westview Press, 1994), 373.

13. Ahmed Jameel'Azm, "Structural Transformation in Arab Countries: Growing Legitimacy of the State and the Shrinking Role of Governments," in *Current Transformations and Their Potential Role in Realizing Change in the Arab World*, ed. Jamal S. Al-Suwaidi (Abu Dhabi: The Emirates Center for Strategic Studies and Research, 2007), 148.

14. al Ramahi, "*Abaya* Styles Evolve."

15. Mattar Ahmed Abdullah, "International Migration and the Demographic Structure of the GCC States," in *Current Transformations and Their Potential Role in Realizing Change in the Arab World*, 402-409.

16. Quoted in al Ramahi, "*Abaya* Styles Evolve."

17. Shaik Zayd bin Muhammad Haadee Al-Madkhalee, "The Obligation of Veiling the Face and Hands," trans. Abu Maryam Isma'eel Alarcon (Al-Ibaanah Book Publishing, 2003), 3, downloaded at *Living Islam*, http://www.livingislam.org/n/vii_e.html. The Web site *Living Islam* provides additional arguments for women to cover based on scriptural evidence; see the section, "Obligation of Hijab as Stated in Qu'ran."

18. Ibid., 4.

19. Ibid., 6.

20. Reza Aslan, *No God but God: The Origins, Evolution, and Future of Islam* (New York: Random House, 2006), 65.

21. Ibid., 65–66.

22. Nawal El-Saadawi, "Love and Sex in the Life of the Arab," in *The Hidden Face of Eve: Women in the Arab World* (London: Zed Books Ltd., 1980), 203.

23. Khowla Farah, comment to Salem, "*Abayas* Still Topping Sales in UAE Market."

24. Dubai Fashion Festival, "Participant Designers," *Dubai Fashion Festival*, http://dubaiff.com/effadesigner.html.

25. Ibid.

26. Julia Robson, "The million dirham abaya," *Hijab Style,* July 5, 2008, http://www.hijabstyle.co.uk/2008/07/million-dirham-abaya.html.

27. "Abu Dhabi Bride Show Exhibitors Say Huge Attention from Buyers," *Gulf News,* January 24, 2009, http://gulfnews.com/news/gulf/uae/general/abu-dhabi-bride-show-exhibitors-say-huge-attention-from-buyers-1.46569.

28. al Ramahi, "*Abaya* Styles Evolve."

29. Quoted in Suzanne Fenton, "Coach Aims at 10% Market Share," *Gulf News,* February 16, 2009, http://gulfnews.com/business/economy/coach-aims-at-10-market-share-1.51925.

30. Rochelle Roxas, personal communication, February 22, 2009.

31. Shaikha Rashid, quoted in Salem, "*Abayas* Still Topping Sales in UAE Market."

32. Abdullah Hussan Khunji, personal communication, February 20, 2010.

33. Danielle Crittenden, "A Cloak of My Own—Part One of Four," *National Post,* December 7, 2007, http://network.nationalpost.com/np/blogs/fullcomment/archive/2007/12/05/danielle-crittenden-a-cloak-of-my-own-part-one-of-four.aspx.

34. Sumaiya Essa, comment to Salem, "*Abayas* Still Topping Sales in UAE Market."

35. Ali Al Houlei, personal communication, February 6, 2010.

36. Ong, "Colonialism and Modernity," 375, 377–378.

Chapter 9

Ado(red), Abhor(red), Disappea(red)

Fashioning Race, Poverty, and Morality under Product (Red)™ [1]

Evangeline M. Heiliger

Giving a new twist to neoliberal narratives on the redemptive possibilities of global capital, The Global Fund to Fight AIDS, Tuberculosis and Malaria has partnered with transnational companies to market and sell a product line called Product (Red)™, in order to raise funds for women and children affected by HIV/AIDS in Africa. Significantly, the Global Fund is eschewing notions of charity in favor of "doing business differently." This business model encourages style-savvy and socially-conscious ethical consumers to buy (Red), with the claim that "the shopper has a cool, new T-shirt and has helped save a person's life."[2] What does it mean to link social justice with shopping for fashion? A feminist analysis of (Red) that considers its marketing campaigns as commentary on consumers opens possibilities for thinking about (Red) outside its potential for poverty alleviation or caring at a distance.[3] The (Red) campaign is an example of a larger "ethical consumerism" trend, a social and economic phenomenon encouraging first-world shoppers to buy products that claim to make the world a better place for everyone by addressing issues of environmental preservation, gender equity, poverty eradication, and disease prevention in poor communities, most often located in the Third World.

I argue that (Red)'s advertising sets up a continuum of human valuation whereby certain gendered, racialized, and geographically located bodies are offered access to commodified social justice while others are ignored or left off the spectrum completely. The story being told by (Red) is a tale of virtuous style-conscious consumers who bestow life on deserving ghost-like recipients of shoppers' fashionable "good deeds." The problem is that while deploying an ostensibly well-intentioned marketing campaign, it is one that simultaneously erases from our sightline the workers who make (Red) products.

The imagined locations of consumers and recipients (as well as the now-invisible workers) are significant to the marketing of (Red), with consumers presented as living and shopping within *unnamed* geopolitical spaces that have visual and discursive linkages to the First World, while the recipients of (Red) aid, the "African women and children affected by HIV-AIDS," are conceptually part of the Third World. Consumers of (Red) occupy and exist in a space that is not-Third-World, the unnamed geopolitical space of the First World that by going unnamed, can also go unquestioned. My aim in naming this un-named space of (Red) consumers follows that of critical development scholars: to draw attention to normally invisible hierarchies of power upon which countries such as the United States or the United Kingdom depend.

The marketing emphasis on needy "African women and children affected by HIV-AIDS," combined with the erasure of workers who manufacture (Red) products, serves to reconstruct a class of North American "ethical" consumers that echoes old colonialist narratives of "the burden of the West." The (Red) campaign's take on this discourse asks consumers from industrialized nations to use their shopping power to address the devastating social and economic effects of HIV-AIDS in Africa. The distinction here is one of "hipness" in two realms: the fashion commodity itself and the act of buying a product associated with social justice. "Voting" for social justice by spending money on (Red) products is hot; boycotting companies for labor violations or unfair pricing on HIV medications is not. While it is possible for consumers of (Red) to engage both in ethical consumerism and in activism that is non-consumerist, (Red)'s practice has been to actively discourage the links between buying (Red) and the underlying causes of the HIV-AIDS pandemic. For example, (Red) has offered a (Red) Vision Film Contest at the Vail Film Festival in both 2008 and 2009. The instructions for filmmakers have consistently encouraged a "fun" and "uplifting" take on (Red). In 2008, filmmakers were given a list of instructions that included "Don't Be Sad" and "Don't Be Political."[4] In 2009, filmmakers did not receive such explicit "do" and "don't" instructions, but were guided by these words,

> We aren't looking for documentaries or pieces that highlight the crisis of AIDS in Africa, but rather, pieces that capture the spirit

of what (RED) is about: saving lives and bringing together desire
and virtue by uniting our collective power with our innate urge
to help.[5]

By guiding filmmakers away from critiques of the HIV-AIDS pandemic, and
toward a feel-good combination of desire and virtue achieved via shopping,
(Red) is influencing the ways consumers (and non-consumers) relate to and
understand the crisis of AIDS in Africa. So while purchasing (Red) is not
mutually exclusive from being an engaged activist, I suspect that this happens despite (Red)'s marketing and not because of it. (Red) T-shirts, bags,
shoes, iPods, and computers are a visual representation of one's style and
class; (Red) consumers sport an awareness of HIV-AIDS in Africa as a social
and economic injustice and flash the ability and willingness to spend money
to change it. In this way, both the (Red) product and its attendant practices
of ethical consumerism are fashionable.

The emphasis on the moral goodness of consumers in (Red) advertising
serves not only to make specters of the African women and children who
receive aid from the Global Fund, but also highlights differences between
shoppers who buy (Red) and shoppers who do not. (Red) as fashion trend
reinforces notions that differences in material and social benefits can be
conflated with differences in moral reasoning, effectively erasing histories of
racialized and gendered discrimination in which people of color and women
of all races have been socially and legally restricted in areas of wealth and
property ownership.[6] (Red)'s marketing serves to fashion class along lines
of race, poverty, geography, and morality.

Shopping for Change in the Twenty-First Century

There has been a steady increase in "ethical consumerism" following the
introduction of certified fair trade coffee on the world market in 1994. Some
scholars argue that the creation of fair trade labeling and certification standards has strengthened its economic components at the expense of its social
goals, a critique that has bolstered the popularity of non-certified ethical
consumerism options such as (Red).[7] Mainstream shoppers now have access
to a wide variety of "ethical" products such as hybrid vehicles, fair trade
coffee, and organic cotton T-shirts. This type of shopping differs from "typical" consumption in that consumers aren't merely buying coffee or a T-shirt;
they are also buying the message of moral goodness associated with the
coffee or T-shirt. The social marketing of such products explicitly references
the "ethical transformation" or "political agency"[8] of shopping, implying that
buying these products serves as a political act that directly improves or solves

social problems such as poverty, HIV-AIDS, worker exploitation, and cultural or environmental destruction. The advertisements make both the products and the act of buying them seem infused with an aura of moral superiority, whether the item is marketed as organic, fair trade, bird-friendly, child-labor-free, or linked to a social cause, as in the case of (Red).

What is interesting about recent trends promoting shopping as a means for social change is that they very deliberately set themselves apart from notions of charity and, in the case of (Red), use celebrity endorsements to infuse an element of cool.[9] An early 2007 (Red) plug by the Gap claimed, "This isn't charity; it's a new way of doing business. Gap Product (Red)™ takes what we do best—creating great products that people love—and channels it into positive change. In addition to sharing profits from Gap Product (Red)™ with the Global Fund, we're also investing in Africa by making some of our products there."[10]

This statement is remarkably similar to promotional claims made by fair trade companies about the value of fair trade products for creating social justice, not as charity projects, but as legitimate business ventures. Penny Newman, chief executive of Cafédirect coffee in the UK, highlighted the importance of businesses in creating social change when she said that fair trade coffee is "not just about giving a fair price . . . it is also about being a business, not about being a charity. You've got to be a business to be able to change the rules."[11] Although Newman represents certified fair trade products, which differ in production mechanisms from (Red) items, these two statements are a fascinating indication of how capitalist business practices have absorbed elements of charity, while verbally distancing these practices from the term "charity." Fair trade has a long history of setting itself apart from the kinds of labor, environmental, and other business practices associated with large multinational companies such as Gap, yet these statements indicate that those promoting fair trade and those promoting (Red) agree that social justice is important and capitalist markets are the venue through which to make social change.

The triangulated connections between consumerism, citizenship, and social change are complicated and contested in this neoliberal moment. Justin Lewis, et al. demonstrate that mass media in the United States and the UK encourage passive consumerism rather than active, engaged citizenry.[12] In a slightly different take on the relationship between consumerism and political engagement, Sarah Banet-Weiser suggests that consuming products marketed as having political significance acts as a substitute for political action.[13] (Red) likely falls under both rubrics. The framing of ethical consumption as both more moral than other forms of economic exchange and a worthy political act is deliberate; this framing is a form of "social marketing," which Kristy Golding and Ken Peattie describe as marketing that "utilizes the tools, techniques and concepts derived from commercial marketing" in order to "change behavior to increase the well being of individuals and/or society."[14] Michael Goodman critiques social marketing for openly fetishizing the location and lives of producers (e.g., "poor Third World women") in order to sell an idea.[15] I propose that the (Red) campaign's focus on consumers as fashionable heroes shifts the tone of ethical consumerism by encouraging consumers to think of themselves as "better" global and national citizens through advertising that uses visual and discursive cues of race, gender, poverty, and geographic location. (Red)'s advertising explicitly emphasizes differences between the gender-neutral ethical consumer and the feminine/feminized (Red) African beneficiary, while implying ethical consumers are superior to nonparticipants in ethical consumerism.

Who Are the Needy Ones?

(Red)'s marketing campaigns encourage new understandings of "worthy" and "unworthy" citizens by building on shifts in discourse over the last 70 years that have linked particular human valuations to Western scripts of economic development. Arturo Escobar notes that discourses build upon each other in layers,[16] in that (Red)'s promotion of a particular brand of "ethical" consumption emerges from neoliberal discourses concerning economic and social power, which in turn arose from development discourses following post-World War II global political and economic restructuring. Just as fashion trends might contradict themselves from season to season (one season short sleeves are "in," the next season long sleeves are the rage), so too do economic discourses appear to have contradictions over time. Economic discourse favors particular economic players—consumers, producers, or businesses, for example—depending on the hegemonic ideologies and political landscapes of the era. We might consider that trends in economic discourse reflect their own social appeal, changing when it becomes fashionable to think about economic relationships differently.

(Red) seductively suggests that it is possible and desirable for fashion-conscious first-world consumers to save the lives of HIV-positive women and children living in sub-Saharan Africa. A chart called "How Red Works" starts with: "1. Shopper notices that GAP (Product) Red™ Ts are cooler than any other Ts" and finishes with: "5. The result? The shopper has a cool new T and has helped save a person's life."[17] The first indication of the potential ethical consumer is his or her eye for style; this good fashion sense is heightened by choosing to purchase the T-shirt that also helps save the lives of African women and children affected by HIV.

The (Red) campaign draws upon layered understandings of "Africa," "women," "children," and "HIV" as verbal and visual signifiers of Third

World need for First World consumers. Arturo Escobar has linked this sense of responsibility to development discourse, which created the idea of the First and Third Worlds, marking the Third World as "backward" with regard to technology, medicine, agriculture, and cultural practices. In this narrative, women, the environment, peasants, and indigenous people were the origins of such supposed backwardness, and therefore "problems" to be "fixed" by a benevolent West. Post-World War II first-world political and economic leaders invoked this "backwardness" as the cause of overwhelming levels of poverty and disease in Asia, Africa, and Latin America—grouped together as "the Third World."[18] (Red) shifts the consumer's gaze from a colonialist understanding of women/indigenous people as the *cause* of illness to one of seeing this group of people *in need of rescue* from illness (in this case, HIV) by socially aware first-world shoppers. These themes run through most social marketing of ethical products, and reinforce the ethical consumer's sense of a self who is different from, though empathic with, those whom she or he sees in the social marketing of ethical products.

The idea that first-world citizens have a responsibility as consumers of goods made by poor women and children in the Third World is not new. Frank Trentmann has traced the ways women homemakers in Britain participated in the 1925 "Buy Empire Goods" campaign, which linked the well-being of citizens in Britain to economic exchange with persons living and working in British colonies.[19] What makes contemporary ethical consumption different from that of earlier eras is the sense of responsibility toward third-world Others who are not understood in terms of productivity. Western development discourse promoted the transformation of third-world men, women, and children, understood in this discourse as lazy, backward, and hopelessly mired in pre-capitalist modes of social and economic exchange, into presumably "superior" rational, democratic, capitalist producer-citizens. This totalizing discourse mocked the political, cultural, and economic processes that contradicted its free-trade prescription for addressing perceived poverty and illness.[20] The ideal producer demonstrated a sense of the profit motive, while traditional social safety nets for the poor, practiced through "economies of affection," were denigrated as culturally backward, inherently feminine, and dangerously incompatible with modern development.[21] Catharine Scott links the gendering of development discourse to the ways different types of states and economies are viewed. The "soft" African state is juxtaposed to "hard" U.S. economic policy, with the latter upheld as "universal, integrationist and rational."[22] Scott argues that the gendered language of development "is more than just a stylistic quirk. Metaphorical language uses gender subtly to establish the superiority of capitalist modernity to pre-capitalist traditions. The repeated metaphorical gendered pairings produce a powerful definition of modernity that is purportedly 'value-free' but which consistently treats pre-capitalist/ tradition as inferior."[23] The neoliberal structural adjustment programs of the late 1970s, many of which eliminated government-sponsored programs for charitable assistance, further bolstered these values.[24] Ethical consumerism represents the latest trend in economic discourse, which weaves elements of charity and care into a discourse of "rational" economic behavior.

Where (Red) Comes In . . .

(Red) was founded by Bono, the lead singer of U2, and Bobby Shriver, a Democratic politician sitting on the Santa Monica, CA City Council, and launched at the World Economic Forum in January, 2006.[25] (Red) is being hailed as a "sustainable" fundraising and marketing campaign in which nine "iconic brands known the world over" (Gap, Armani, Converse, Dell, Apple, American Express, Starbucks, Hallmark, and Motorola) donate a certain percentage of their profits from specific (Red) product lines to The Global Fund to Fight AIDS, Tuberculosis, and Malaria.[26] North American and European consumers can buy Red T-shirts, purses, cell phones, tennis shoes, bracelets, computers, and iPods, as well as use an American Express (Red) credit card that donates money to the Global Fund regardless of what the shopper purchases. (Red) products have been in stores in Britain since February 2006, and in the United States since October 2006. The share of profits raised for the Global Fund to date is more than $100 million, which has gone toward financing testing and treatment of HIV-positive women and children in Rwanda, Swaziland, Lesotho, and Ghana.[27]

The marketing of (Red) items echoes the language of marketing used by alternative trade organizations for more than 50 years; in short, that social and economic justice for the world's poor can be achieved via carefully constructed capitalist economic trade, and that mindful first-world consumers have a critical role to play in redressing social and economic disparities. However, (Red) isn't new in terms of promoting consumption for social justice causes. Feminist geographer Joni Seager has noted the trend of a "green consumer" movement for environmentally sound products that began in Europe in the 1980s, and moved into North America during the 1990s. Fair trade products from the global South were first introduced into Northern markets in 1946.[28]

(Red) is significant to contemporary ethical consumption because it represents a cultural shift in what counts as good—and fashionable—capitalism. Whereas fair trade was once the realm of fringe consumption, and still holds a relatively small portion of the market, (Red) has made ethical consumerism mainstream, and is reaping mainstream profits.[29] Additionally, (Red) signifies an acceptance that larger, transnational companies can acceptably engage in large-scale social marketing of ethical products. Néstor García Canclini has said that "to consume is to make more sense of a world" that is otherwise unstable.[30] By linking profits with "doing good," (Red) functions as one type of response to critiques of hegemonic political and economic power, simultaneously shaping and being shaped by cultural understandings of the links between economic exchange and social justice. Canclini's work illuminates (Red)'s appeal as both a fashion garment and an ideological statement. Consumption, particularly buying objects to wear or display, contributes to the ways we integrate and communicate social order. "Ethical" fashion commodities such as (Red) create shared meanings across social classes even as they create hierarchical distinctions between the racially unspecified male, female and child bodies of economically privileged First World consumers who buy (Red), the unnamed consumers who don't buy (Red), and the African women and children who benefit from (Red).[31]

The Wheel of Ethical Consumerism

The marketing of "ethical consumerism" relies on four interrelated actors to tell a convincing story that prompts shoppers to purchase a specific item linked to a social justice project: third-world producers of goods, first-world owned businesses that sell those goods, first-world consumers, and third-world recipients of profits or material goods.[32] I think of them collectively as the "wheel of ethical consumerism," because they are connected to one another and to economic processes like spokes on a wheel. At least two—and sometimes all four—of these actors are present in the marketing of ethical products. Marketing of so-called ethical goods under social marketing involves filtering images from each category in order to present not only certain goods as being most desirable, but also particular types of consumers, businesses, producers, and recipients as well. When analyzing ethical consumerism, I find it useful to think about these relationships, because while all of these characters are potentially available for selling an ethical product, very often, one or more are deliberately left out at the expense of hyper-emphasizing another. In the case of fairly traded products, the third-world individuals who produce particular goods are the same people who receive the profits of that original labor. Whereas (Red)'s recipients of the malaria tents, HIV medications, or housing and shelter provided by the Global Fund to African women and children are rarely the producers of (Red) T-shirts, shoes, watches, and cell phones.[33]

Missing: Productive Workers

The workers who make (Red) items are missing from the story told by the marketing campaigns. The implications of this include diverting attention from issues of workers' rights, environmental destruction, and the fair distribution of resources. One key difference between (Red) and many fair trade items is that while producers who wish to attain fair trade certification for their products are required to uphold particular ethical standards in regard to wages, working conditions, and environmental preservation, the Global Fund recommends but does not require its partner companies to engage in ethical production. An example is that the Gap produces some of its (Red) T-shirts in Lesotho, employing African workers and using only African cotton, but is not required by the Global Fund to pay these workers a living wage, nor to provide safe working conditions.[34] The workers who produce (Red) items aren't included in this narrative of "ethical" first-world consumers delivering justice to "deserving" third-world recipients. This is an important distinction. Why have the workers who make (Red) goods been disappeared? Why, at this historical moment, are producers not held up as the "rational" and "deserving" recipients of the benefits of global capitalism?[35] (Red)'s particular style adds value to the "ethical" purchase, commodifying the very act of consumption. Purchasing (Red) therefore becomes a kind of consumer fetishism that boosts the standing of consumers over any other actor in the wheel of ethical consumption.[36]

Creating the Deserving Ones: African Women and Children

One could argue that the purpose of erasing producers from (Red)'s narrative is to shine a spotlight on the African women and children who are cast as the "deserving" recipients of (Red) aid, and avoid creating a conflict in the minds of consumers about which gendered and racialized bodies are most in need in this particular context. Yet it is interesting to note that for the first 15 months of the (Red) campaign (October 2006–December 2007), (Red) promoters made very little information available to consumers about the extent of the HIV pandemic in Africa. (Red) advertising invoked "African women and children," but these very people were curiously absent from the advertisements and news stories about (Red).

(Red)'s commercials have made the recipients of (Red) aid invisible through hyper-visibility of the "cool consumer," one example of which can be seen in a Superbowl commercial for a (Red) Dell computer, first aired on February 1, 2008.[37] This commercial features a white man, perhaps in his 20s or 30s, leaving a building in Buenos Aires with a red-colored computer tucked under his arm. To his astonishment, he becomes the focus of increasing attention, receiving hundreds of nonverbal affirmations from a wide spectrum of people. A traffic cop reaches to smack the man's derrière, and people with white, brown, and black skin applaud him from balconies, buses, cars, and motorcycles, smiling and pointing as he passes. This sequence is highlighted by Mick Jagger's "Charmed Life" playing in the background; the music swells as crowds swarm the young computer-holder. The climax of the commercial occurs when a beautiful woman runs up to the man and kisses him passionately. The commercial concludes with the man sliding into a café table alone, smiling as he connects the attention he just received with the (Red) Dell computer in front of him. The commercial flashes to a series of phrases: "Buy Dell," "Join (Red)™," and "Save Lives."

The commercial doesn't indicate what (Red) is, or how joining (Red) saves lives. There certainly is no reference made to Africa or to HIV. Indeed, viewers watching this commercial are given the impression that purchasing a relatively inexpensive computer could lead to being treated like a rock star, admired by men, women, and children of all ethnic backgrounds and ages, while increasing one's chances of being kissed by a beautiful woman. Not being mugged while carrying a computer in plain sight on an urban street is simply an unremarkable bonus of his white skin privilege. Who *wouldn't* want this computer?

This placement of a young white man as the protagonist of consumer consciousness is fascinating, in part because it emphasizes the absent or peripheral manner in which African women and children—the intended beneficiaries of the purchase—are displayed in the advertising of (Red) products. Other (Red) commercials—such as a thank-you commercial titled "Because You Chose (Red)"—highlights the role of the consumer in making a difference in the lives of distant others. This commercial, issued during the American Thanksgiving holiday in November 2007, tells consumers that their choice to purchase (Red) has generated over $50 million, and touched more than one million lives affected by HIV in Africa. African tribal music plays in the background as statistics flash across the screen, concluding with a request to "do even more" in the next year.[38] In this commercial, as with others, only after hearing the consumer-focused praise do viewers have the option to click away from this visually appealing feel-good screen for more information about Africa or specific African women or children recipients of aid from the Global Fund.

(Red) has had tremendous economic success selling T-shirts and other (Red) items, simply referencing Africa as a space of need. (Red)'s advertising tactic may rely heavily on consumers' existing knowledge of the extent of the HIV pandemic in Africa. Joseph Roach's concept of *effigy* is useful here for understanding how "African women and children" stand in for the role of "helpless third-world Others" in the minds of first-world consumers who have constructed the (Red) aid recipients as both feminized and racialized. Such a move reinforces consumers' sense of their own worth as non-racialized or "white" consumers.[39]

The "Ethical" Consumer

(Red) serves as a catalyst for the creation of a new type of global citizen in the contemporary ethical consumer. While there is a long history of first-world citizen-consumers making purchases based on a sense of morality and duty to selves and distant others,[40] the most recent manifestation of this "responsible first-world citizen" emerges as the fashionably "ethical" consumer, who purportedly fulfils his or her duty to uplift the Third World's poor while simultaneously stimulating economic growth and prosperity in First World nations. This image of coolness is achieved not through charity, but through shopping and self-stylization, and is reinforced in (Red)'s borrowing of the advertising tactics used in fair trade with the business practices of its affiliated multinational companies not engaged in fair trade production. The discourse of (Red) and of campaigns like it suggests that ethical consumption is an easy, painless way to "do good," while being an ethical consumer is a fantastically hip way to "be good," all while aiming to "look good."

The (Red) campaign calls for socially-aware consumers to use their dollars to "help" those people considered most in need. This echoes what feminist scholar Grace Hong has described as "liberal white male possessive individualism, demonstrated through benevolence toward racialized subjects."[41] This benevolence serves to reinforce the subjectivity of the "benevolent" individual consumer, over and against a racialized other. In the case of (Red), while these "ethical" consumers are racially unspecified and gender-non-specific, the ethical consumer category creates class distinctions based not only on income and the ability to spend on the latest fashions, but also on social class distinctions based on a sense of reason and morality—thus setting up (Red) consumers as more thoughtful, mindful, and moral than other types of consumers. What remains unacknowledged in (Red)'s narrative are the ways women and people of color have had differing degrees of access to economic resources, including expendable income.[42] This rendering of the new social elite under Product (Red)™ serves to reinforce notions of an upper echelon who not only make choices based on "superior" reasoning, but who also have the ability to make ethical choices about consumption on the basis of economic class.[43] This creates the potential for conflating those who economically cannot afford to make elite "ethical" purchases with those who morally choose not to make "ethical" purchases—aligning poverty not only with a lack of fashion sense, but also with a racialized and gendered "lack of morality." This effectively shifts focus away from those who hold hegemonic economic and political power, while highlighting multiple ways poverty "looks bad."

One Gap (Red) men's T-shirt reads: "Da(red)" on the front. The back holds a portion of the (Red) manifesto: "All things being equal, they are not. What we collectively choose 2 buy or not 2 buy can change the course of life and history on this planet."[44] This T-shirt calls on an ideology of equality and then emphatically refutes its existence, calling the consumer to a sharp awareness of her or his relative economic and political privilege as a first-world citizen vis-à-vis the African women and children whose lives will be saved by a simple T-shirt purchase. Putting this kind of moral weight on a T-shirt, literally and ideologically, marks the ethical consumer who purchases it as being within a first-world racial hierarchy, and implicitly, as having both the moral and the economic privileges of first-world consumers.

Ethical consumerism is shifting racial formations in the United States through emphasizing geographic location, economic status, and moral reasoning. The ethics of "ethical consumerism" include the idea that being marked by race is potentially to be marked as "in need," while being unmarked by race (or having one's race be unremarkable) indicates being un-needy. (Red) highlights this in focusing consumers' attention on the medical, housing, and other needs of presumably black and brown Africans affected by HIV while remaining silent on the devastating effects of HIV on black and brown Americans.[45] Despite advertising that is explicitly multiracial in its portrayal of consumers and decidedly tilted toward blackness in their portrayal of recipients, the (Red) campaign avoids frank discussions about the ways racism has perpetuated global inequities in areas of economic exchange and health, and how this is significant to the HIV-AIDS pandemic.

(Red)'s advertising would appear to expand the category of upper/middle class in the United States by emphasizing that consumers could be of (almost) any race; advertising has showcased individuals who identify and are identifiable as black, white, Latino, Asian, and multiracial. Additionally, many (Red) products are not luxury items; T-shirts, Hallmark cards, shoes, and even iPods are considered "affordable" purchases for many Americans. Clearly, expendable income is not the realm only of wealthy white people. However, in opening the possibilities for being upper/middle class in the United States through this type of ethical consumerism, (Red)™ solidifies racial and gender differences between first-world consumers and third-world recipients—in this case, ethical consumers in the United States can make distinctions between themselves and the African women and children who receive medicine or preventive care from the Global Fund, without necessarily having to confront the racial, sexual, class, and gender hierarchies still at play within the United States.

The Fashionable Morality of Ethical Consumerism

(Red) has re-popularized ethical consumption by making it fashionable to shop our way to social justice, engaging in a pleasurable activity currently so socially infused with moral goodness that many first-world consumers can avert their eyes and minds from evidence to the contrary, such as violations of workers' rights, manufacturing practices that harm the environment, or agreements ensuring that drug companies' profits take priority over affordable HIV medications. (Red)'s cool factor comes both from the desirability of the products and from the social cache attached to this fashionable act of consumption.

Ethical consumerism reflects trends in economic discourse, currently favoring those perceived as the most helpless and in need of assistance, ignoring the needs of productive workers in favor of those who are outside this particular producer-consumer loop. As long as it is considered acceptable and desirable to channel social justice through market forces, companies will utilize familiar and compelling images and ideas of race, gender, location, poverty, and morality to sell their products. (Red) strengthens global racial hierarchies by invoking a geographically gendered and racially tinged mythology of African dependence on American consumers' shopping habits; explicit (Red) images link ethical consumerism, expendable income, and morality to form the "non-racialized" ethical consumer.

At the same time, the emphasis on individual American consumer choice ignores the privileges of wealth, race, and gender needed to engage in (Red)'s form of ethical consumerism. The fashionableness of ethical consumerism compels participation, yet this phenomenon is dependent upon its very inaccessibility for so many. This risks assuming those who are economically unable to participate in ethical consumption's latest trend have failed, morally, to shop for change. The selective shifting between the extreme "worthiness" of those who purportedly benefit from (Red) and the "unworthiness" of those who fail to redeem themselves through buying (Red) highlights only the value of the ethical consumer. This marketing tactic creates a hierarchical distinction that focuses only on the power of potential consumers—both those who consume, and those who do not—and serves to further dehumanize the vaguely described "African women and children" who are relegated to the status of dark specters who haunt the landscape of charity in the imaginations of first-world "ethical" consumers.

Notes

1. This essay is one of many interdisciplinary scholarly publications on the social significance of Product (Red)™. See the special (RED) issue of *The Journal of Pan African Studies* 2, no. 6 (2008): 1–133, for its wonderfully nuanced engagement with Product (Red)™.

2. Gap, "Gap.com: Products that help women and children affected by HIV/ AIDS in Africa," http://www.gap.com/browse/division.do?cid=16591&tid=gpvan011.

3. Jo Littler, *Radical Consumption: Shopping for Change in Contemporary Culture* (New York: Open University Press, 2009); Clive Barnett et al., "Consuming Ethics: Articulating the Subjects and Spaces of Ethical Consumption," *Antipode* 37, no. 1 (2005): 23-45; Lisa Ann Richey and Stefano Ponte "Better (Red)™ Than Dead: Celebrities, Consumption and International Aid," *Third World Quarterly* 29, no. 4 (2008): 711–729.

4. Join(RED), www.joinred.com/vail.

5. *www.vailfilmfestival.org/2009_RED_Vision_Entry_Guidelines.pdf*

6. Melvin L. Oliver and Thomas M. Shapiro, *Black Wealth, White Wealth: A New Perspective on Racial Inequality* (New York: Routledge, 1995).

7. Kristy Golding and Ken Peattie, "In Search of a Golden Blend: Perspectives on the Marketing of Fair Trade Coffee," *Sustainable Development* 13 (2005): 160; William Low and Eileen Davenport, "Postcards from the Edge: Maintaining the 'Alternative' Character of Fair Trade," *Sustainable Development* 13 (2005): 143–153.

8. "Ethical consumerism" is defined as "practices that explicitly aim to reconfigure ordinary practices of commodity consumption as sites of ethical transformation and political agency." Clive Barnett et al., "Consuming Ethics," 25.

9. Lisa Ann Richey and Stefano Ponte, "Better (Red)™ Than Dead: 'Brand Aid,' Celebrities and The New Frontier Of Development Assistance," *Danish Institute for International Studies Working Paper* 2006, no. 26 (2006): 1–33.

10. Gap, Product Red, www.gap.com/red.

11. Jane Martinson, "The ethical coffee chief turning a fair profit: The head of Cafédirect has demonstrated how to lift sales while maintaining Fairtrade values," *The Guardian*, March 9, 2007, Environment section, Food section.

12. Justin Lewis, Sanna Inthorn, and Karin Wahl-Jorgensen, *Citizens or Consumers?: What the Media Tell Us About Political Participation.* (New York: Open University Press, 2005).

13. Sarah Banet-Weiser, "The Business of Representing," *American Quarterly* 58, no. 2 (2006): 496.

14. While social marketing has generally been used to promote behaviors rather than products (i.e., campaigns to stop smoking, discourage littering, or encourage voter participation), the marketing of ethical consumption weds the two concerns by suggesting that altering one behavior—shopping—can serve two purposes: obtaining a product and addressing a social concern. See Golding and Peattie, "In Search of a Golden Blend," 160.

15. Michael Goodman, "Reading fair trade: political ecological imaginary and the moral economy of fair trade foods," *Political Geography* 23 (2005): 891–915.

16. Arturo Escobar, *Encountering Development: The Making and Unmaking of the Third World* (Princeton: Princeton University Press, 1995).

17. Gap, "Gap.com: Products that help women and children affected by HIV/AIDS in Africa," http://www.gap.com/browse/division.do?cid=16591&tid=gpvan011.

18. Escobar, *Encountering Development*.

19. Frank Trentmann, "Before 'fair trade': empire, free trade, and the moral economies of food in the modern world," *Environment and Planning D: Society & Space* 25 (2007): 1079–1102.

20. Arturo Escobar, "Economics and the Space of Modernity: Tales of Market, Production and Labour," *Cultural Studies* 19 (2005): 146.

21. See Escobar, *Encountering Development*; David Harvey, *A Brief History of Neoliberalism* (New York: Oxford University Press, 2005); and Catharine V. Scott, *Gender and Development: Rethinking Modernization and Dependency Theory* (Boulder: Lynne Rienner Publishers, 1995).

22. Scott, *Gender and Development*, 16.

23. Ibid.

24. See Harvey, *A Brief History of Neoliberalism*, and Charles Gore, "The Rise and Fall of the Washington Consensus as a Paradigm for Developing Countries," *World Development* 28, no. 5 (2000): 789–804.

25. Join(RED), "Bono and Bobby Shriver Launch Product Red to Harness Power of the World's Iconic Brands to Fight AIDS in Africa," January 26, 2006, http://www.joinred.com/News/Articles/ArticleDetail/06-01-6/bono_and_bobby_shriver_launch_product_red_to_harness_power_of_the_world_s_iconic_brands_to_fight_aids_in_africa.aspx.

26. Join(RED), "JoinRED—Fight Aids," www.joinred.com.

27. Ibid.

28. Joni Seager, *Earth Follies: Coming to Terms With the Global Environmental Crisis,* (New York: Routledge, 1993).

29. Fair Trade's share of global trade is relatively small, accounting for between .05 and 5 percent of sales in its product categories in European and North American markets. Fairtrade Labelling Organizations International (2007), www.fairtrade.net.

30. Néstor García Canclini, *Consumers and Citizens: Globalization and Multicultural Conflicts, Cultural Studies of the Americas* (Minneapolis: University of Minnesota Press, 2001), 42.

31. Ibid., 41.

32. As it falls outside the scope of this paper, I won't elaborate here on the debates about which kinds of businesses have the right to redistribute resources via capitalism.

33. Each participating brand manufactures Product (Red)™ items in their regular factories, few of which are located in Africa. One exception is the Precious Garments clothing factory in Lesotho, where the Gap sources some of its (Red) T-shirts. The employees of Precious Garments receive counseling and are encouraged to be regularly tested for HIV and to seek treatment at on-site clinics. Lesotho is one of the African countries receiving funds from the sale of (Red). "(Blog) Red," http://blog.joinred.com/2008_03_01_archive.html.

34. Shriver explains the reason for this is that the partner companies of (Red) understand that the reputation of Red is at stake, and they will therefore voluntarily make ethical choices aligned with (Red)'s reputation and that of their companies branding image. Louise Story, "Want to Help Treat AIDS in Africa? Buy a Cellphone," the *New York Times*, October 4, 2006, http://www.nytimes.com/2006/10/04/business/media/04adco.html.

35. The Global Fund could insist on standards of production similar to fair trade. The Global Fund could also shift profits from (Red) back to all its producers, rather than a select few who fit the profile of racialized, gendered, "deserving" others. However, even if these were elements of (Red)™ production, this narrative still serves to recycle familiar tales of the redemptive possibilities of global capital.

36. When the labor and labor conditions of a commodity are erased and the value of a commodity is seen only as existing within the commodity itself, Marx calls this "commodity fetishism." (Red) is interesting in that the consumption act is also fetishized, such that consumption itself becomes part of the commodity's appeal, and therefore, part of the commodity fetish. See Karl Marx, "Capital, Volume One" in *The Marx-Engels Reader second edition*, ed. Robert C. Tucker (New York: W.W. Norton, 1978), 319–329.

37. Dell Product (Red) Superbowl Commercial, *YouTube*, http://www.youtube.com/watch?v=dUEzHCdWQzM.

38. "Because You Chose (Red)," *YouTube*, http://www.youtube.com/watch?v=195BT3rPE.

39. Joseph Roach, in writing about a trans-Atlantic gendered performance of whiteness, says, "To perform as protagonists of gendered whiteness, they must rely on an unnamed black antagonist, who . . . remains forgotten but not gone." Joseph Roach, *Cities of the Dead: Circum-Atlantic Performance* (New York: Columbia University Press, 1996), 31.

40. See Trentmann's arguments in "Before 'fair trade;'" and Seager, *Earth Follies,* chapters 2 and 6.

41. Grace Hong, *The Ruptures of American Capital: Women of Color Feminism and the Culture of Immigrant Labor* (Minneapolis: University of Minnesota Press, 2006), 12.

42. Melvin L. Oliver and Thomas M. Shapiro, *Black Wealth, White Wealth: A New Perspective on Racial Inequality* (New York & London: Routledge, 1995).

43. George Yudice, *The Expediency of Culture: Uses of Culture in the Global Era, Post-Contemporary Interventions* (Durham, NC: Duke University Press, 2003); and Harvey, *A Brief History of Neoliberalism.*

44. Gap, www.gap.com.

45. The silence around the impact of HIV on Americans may shift soon, as significant cuts to services for HIV-positive people are being made in many U.S. states, including a July 28, 2009 proposed $52 million cut to services for HIV prevention and treatment in California. See "Gov. Signs Calif. Budget, Makes New Cuts," *CBS News,* http://cbs5.com/politics/california.budget.signing.2.1104656.html.

Chapter 10

_____

The Lady Is a Vamp

Cruella de Vil and the Cultural Politics of Fur

Catherine Spooner

Cruella de Vil, serial dog-napper and fashion diva extraordinaire, is among the most visually spectacular villainesses of the twentieth century. First appearing in Dodie Smith's classic British children's novel *The Hundred and One Dalmatians* in 1956, her reputation was consolidated by the animated Disney adaptation from 1961, and Glenn Close's flamboyant performance in the two live-action films *101 Dalmatians* (1996) and *102 Dalmatians* (2000). These texts have, between them, achieved extraordinary levels of exposure in Western culture: Smith's novel was a worldwide bestseller before the film rights were bought by Disney; the 1961 film has the eleventh-highest box office returns of all time when ticket prices are adjusted for inflation; and the 1996 film was the sixth-highest earner in the year of its release.[1] Each is dependent on the visual impact of both the Dalmatians' celebrated coats and Cruella de Vil's outrageous personal style. Yet Cruella's image is familiar even to those who have neither read Smith's novel nor seen its screen versions. A brief search of the Web will reveal more images of people dressed up as Cruella than of the character herself. Premanufactured fancy dress costumes based on Cruella's appearance in the animated Disney film are readily available to purchase. The key to this success is her distinctive look: through all her different incarnations, Cruella remains instantly recognizable, an iconic concatenation of furs, bold black-and-white color scheme, and parti-colored hair.

Like Frankenstein's monster, or Dracula, or Jekyll and Hyde, Cruella has become a kind of modern myth: an image of the monstrosity of the extreme fashionista. In an interview in the UK broadsheet *The Guardian*, for example, Sir Paul McCartney's then-wife Heather Mills refers to Anna Wintour, the fur-wearing editor of American *Vogue*, as "Cruella de Wintour."[2] Cruella's reputation precedes her: her name has entered the language. The power of myth, as Roland Barthes argues, is that it enables images or narratives to become detached from the historical conditions that produced them, masking ideology. In the case of Cruella de Vil, her iconic image veils a complex network of associations between feminism, animal rights discourses, and the changing moral rhetoric of motherhood. Understanding Cruella is crucial to understanding how animal rights discourses have developed a vexed relationship with feminism, in which the image of power associated historically with the fur-wearing woman becomes elided with that of the modern career woman, culminating in Anna Wintour. As a result, the condemnation of the fur-wearing woman in the *101 Dalmatians* films tends to result in a promotion of maternity over other forms of femininity and a retrogressive perception of maternity and career as mutually exclusive choices. This chapter maps how the changing representations of Cruella de Vil deploy the association of femininity and fur in order to demonize the nonmaternal woman. As such they offer a revealing commentary on changing attitudes to fur as fashion and to the women who wear it (or deliberately choose not to).

From Devil to Diva: The Metamorphoses of Cruella

Dodie Smith's attitudes toward fur appear profoundly ambivalent. She wore fur herself and, according to biographical evidence, it seems she was motivated to write *The Hundred and One Dalmatians* by sentimental preoccupation with her own Dalmatian dogs rather than by any strong convictions of animal rights.[3] In her debut novel *I Capture the Castle* (1949), the heroine Cassandra Mortmain inherits three fur coats and a rug from a deceased aunt; these furs subsequently take on various roles in the plot. Cassandra's initial reaction is one of implicit resistance: " 'But Aunt Millicent never had any furs,' I said. 'She thought they were cruel to animals.' And I always thought she was right."[4] She is, however, gradually won over by the furs themselves, which are absolved of connotations of cruelty by their secondhand status, and by their distanced origin and provenance: Cassandra discovers they did not belong to Aunt Millicent after all but to her own great-grandmother. The furs are explicitly anachronistic, and subject to historical contingency: the girls are told "I don't know if you could sell [them] for much. We treat furs so differently now."[5] Stripped of economic value, the furs seem increasingly benign, as if once removed from a system of economic motivation or indeed of glamour and high fashion, their cruelty is diminished. Smith therefore presents cruelty as contingent rather than absolute.

This ambivalence persists in *The Hundred and One Dalmatians*. Although from the animals' point of view, wearing fur is abhorrent, Cruella as charismatic villain has a tendency to steal the show. In the light of subsequent representations, what most surprises about the original illustrations in the novel by Janet and Anne Grahame Johnstone is that Cruella is sleek, elegant and extraordinarily sexy—a vamp in both senses of the word. She is also suggestively demonic: in one drawing, she appears silhouetted in the moonlight with eyes blazing preternaturally from within (see Image 10.1). She is literally the "de Vil" of her name, in contrast to the evil-but-human Cruella of the films. Appropriately enough, she enjoys anything that creates outrageous heat. She has a passion for pepper, central heating, red decor, and above all, furs. She first appears in Smith's novel wearing "a tight-fitting emerald satin dress, several ropes of rubies, and an absolutely simple white mink coat, which reached to the high heels of her ruby red shoes."[6] She is never seen without this coat and simply adds more furs underneath when the whim takes her. Fur creates her signature look and is the means through which her identity is constructed. She is suggestively a fur fetishist, stating, "I worship furs, I live for furs! That's why I married a furrier."[7] Despite her

Image 10.1. Cruella de Vil of Dodie Smith's *The Hundred and One Dalmatians* (1956). Original illustration by Janet and Anne Grahame Johnstone.

sexually predatory appearance, Cruella is a predator of animals, not of men: the desire for fur replaces her sexual desires.

Cruella's predilections inevitably recall the dominatrix Wanda from Leopold von Sacher-Masoch's novel *Venus in Furs* (1870). Whereas Wanda, however, seems largely a construction of masculine desires, Cruella's fetishism appears entirely self-determined. Her own husband is, if anything, shaped by *her* desires. Not only has he taken on her family name to prevent it dying out, but he appears to have no personal identity beyond that imparted by his wife: "a small, worried-looking man who didn't seem to be anything besides a furrier."[8] Any sexual frisson provided by Cruella's identity as female despot, however, is dissipated by a shift in point of view—from willing male slave to unwilling animal victims.

In *Venus in Furs*, furs are constructed as an essential attribute of the *femme fatale*. The narrator Severin informs us that "all the women whom the great book of history has placed under the sign of beauty, lust and violence: Libussa, Lucretia Borgia, Agnes of Hungary, Queen Margot, Isabeau, the Sultana Roxelana and the Russian Tsarinas of the last century, all wore fur garments and ermine robes."[9] Wearing fur connotes both the predatory qualities of the animals themselves, and the cruelty suggested by their slaughter. The nostalgic generalizing of Wanda's historical prototypes belies fur's nineteenth-century status as commodity and the fur-wearing woman's position as representative of a rapidly accelerating system of consumption. Alison Lurie suggests that "one of the oldest sartorial messages is the wearing of animal skins. Primitive hunters dressed in the hides of the beasts they had killed in order to take on the magical nature of the bear, the wolf or the tiger."[10] Cruella's signature coat is mink, an animal renowned for its viciousness. But Lurie's essentialized evocation of the "primitive" (a condition she inevitably associates with the animal) functions only as a ground against which Cruella asserts her modernity (signified by the streamlined, "absolutely simple" cut of her coat in the novel): a means to assert her difference from the animal she exploits.

Cruella certainly does not wish to identify with the dogs whose skins she intends to wear; rather, she sees them as expendable objects, prized only for their aesthetic and commercial value. As Lurie indicates, one of the key messages conveyed by fur in modern Western society is economic: "most purchasers of fur coats are unfamiliar with the behavior of the beasts from which they come: all they want to say is 'I am a very expensive animal.'"[11] In *The Hundred and One Dalmatians*, dog fur is the ultimate commodity, as the dogs' equivalence to humans in the novel provides them with a value that transcends mere monetary exchange. Cruella is emphatically *not* made to resemble an animal through wearing fur. Rather, her willingness to turn animals into objects makes her inhuman—a monstrous, even Satanic being.

The text thus complicates conventional dichotomies: humans are not defined in opposition to animals, who are presented as sharing similar forms of social behavior and separated mainly through their inability to fully understand and/or vocalize each other's language. The human/dog division, in fact, is presented as profoundly unstable through frequent inversion, such as the dogs "only putting the Dearlys on the leash to lead them over crossings."[12] Ultimately the defining feature of the animal within the text is its vulnerability to cruelty or exploitation by humans. Cruel and exploitative humans, however, are suggestively redefined as inhuman. At one point the puppy Lucky describes Cruella's henchmen, the Badduns: "They never change their awful old clothes . . . and they never wash. I don't think they are real humans, father. Is there such thing as a half-human?" Smith remarks that "Pongo could well believe it after seeing the Badduns, but he couldn't imagine what their non-human half was. It was no animal he had ever seen."[13] Interestingly, Lucky thinks that the Badduns can't be human because they don't seem to care about their clothes, the opposite to Cruella who cares too much about them. In the dogs' world, clothing is functional (like Mr. Dearly's "dog-walker" jacket,[14] the Nannies' work uniforms, or collars and leads) and washing signifies care, for example when mothers wash their puppies or the Nannies wash off the dogs' sooty disguise. Not washing—indeed, not caring—or wearing clothes that flout social convention, is a signal that one might not be a "real human." Maternal washing of puppies—being made presentable and taught how to present oneself—constitutes a socialization process that effectively places those who do not participate in it outside the humanizing influences of the domestic. Not to be fully human, however, is not to be animal, but to be something else, whether suggestively demonic, as for Cruella, or simply inhumane.

Smith's novel comfortably accommodates a variety of sexual and gender roles in both its human and animal characters: Nanny Cook and Nanny Butler, for example, mimic the Dearlys' marriage in their performance of what is implicitly a butch-femme pairing (Nanny Butler insists, to Mrs. Dearly's consternation, on wearing trousers). Cruella's excessive glamour on her first appearance is thus contrasted both with the conventionally dressed Mrs. Dearly, "very pretty in the green going-away suit from her trousseau," and the Nannies in their respective "white overall" and "well-cut tail-coat and trousers, plus dainty apron."[15] Women are presented as using fashion in a variety of different ways here: to stand out, like Cruella; to conform, like Mrs. Dearly; to redefine gender roles, like Nanny Butler. As the "note of originality" added by Nanny Butler's apron suggests, unconventional femininities are enjoyed rather than critiqued in Smith's text. Among the animal characters, the female feline Pussy Willow plays a dual role as Sergeant Tib, again suggesting a gleeful multiplicity of gender possibilities.

In contrast, the animated Disney film *101 Dalmatians*, somewhat inevitably, streamlines the plot and proliferating animal characters. As a result, gender roles are subtly redrawn. Female animal characters tend to be elided into one or recast as male—Sergeant Tib, for example, becomes a male cat—resulting in a significant reduction of female roles, and as a consequence leaving only mother-figures (Perdita, Anita, Nanny, the cows) to contrast with Cruella. The animated film is thus much more prescriptive in its models of femininity. In the opening sequence, Pongo's attempt to find his "pet" a partner commences with his surreptitious examination of media images of women: a glamorous blonde in a ballgown on the page of a magazine, and another in a bathing suit on the cover of a trashy novel. Pongo thus educates himself as to what women should look like through media images, just one way in which the media mediates the dogs' view of humanity in the film. He then peruses a series of women walking dogs from the vantage point of his pet's window, finding each unsuitable. A bohemian in a beret with an Afghan hound is dismissed as "a very unusual breed;" a portly lady with a pug described as "a little too short-coupled;" a chic lady with a poodle is "much too fancy;" an elderly lady with a spaniel in her bicycle shopping basket and a child leading a puppy are "too old" and "too young," respectively. Finally, Dalmatian Perdita and her "pet" Anita appear as a twin spectacle of proper and desirable femininity, their embodiment of the norm emphasized through the contrast with the unsuitable candidates. The shot follows Pongo's gaze as it travels up Anita's body from her feet to her head, mimicking the sexualized gaze of a (human) male spectator. This parade of women and dogs focalized through a critical male gaze takes the place of Smith's multiple female characters in order to delineate the parameters of femininity within the text. It sets up a standard of "normal" feminine appearance (not too extreme, whether "unusual" or "fancy") of which Anita is the epitome, and, it follows, Cruella is the antithesis. Her monstrousness is not merely due to the lengths she will go to achieve her sartorial desire, but also to the very nature of that desire—for the extreme—in the first place. This excessiveness, however, is also paradoxically the source of Cruella's charisma: by being "showy" and "noticeable," dressing to stand out, she contravenes the passive feminine ideal.

The Disney Cruella is more overtly monstrous than Smith's; while the Johnstones' illustrations depict a sleek, stylish, and strikingly beautiful *femme fatale*, the Disney Cruella is ungainly and witch-like, a shrieking harridan rather than poised fashionista (see Images 10.2 and 10.3). Instead of the "absolutely simple white mink coat," she wears an enormous, heavily flounced coat that distorts her body shape. Smith's vamp is self-possessed and genuinely threatening; the film version is faintly farcical, as Roger's comic song "Cruella de Vil" suggests. Smith's Cruella is certainly "showy," as Mr.

Image 10.2. Cruella de Vil, poised fashionista. Dodie Smith, *The Hundred and One Dalmations* (1956). Original illustration by Janet and Anne Grahame Johnstone.

Dearly puts it, but she also figures within an industry and set of fashion practices.[16] Her husband's money comes from selling furs and she plans not only to wear her Dalmatian-skin coat but also to produce and sell multiple coats. This plan is not actually illegal until she makes the mistake of stealing, rather than purchasing, the Dearlys' puppies. Similarly, the way her clothing is described suggests the language of the fashion magazine (she envisions the Dalmatian coat as "for spring wear, over a black suit") and therefore situates her within a range of commercial fashion discourses. In contrast, Disney's Cruella is single (she declares, "Furs are my one true love") and therefore

Image 10.3. Cruella de Vil, harridan—as interpreted for film, 1961.

both implicitly at odds with the film's ideology of romance and motherhood, and dissociated from the more generalized fashion industry embodied in the furrier husband invented by Smith. She simply wants the Dalmatian coat for her own selfish enjoyment, not for potential profit or participation in fashion discourse. The animated film accentuates the economic gap between the de Vils and the Dearlys (in the book the Dearlys are decidedly upper-middle-class), producing Cruella as a lone agent of economic exploitation: no longer figuring in an industry, her wealth signifies merely her potential to pursue her own monstrous desires. While Cruella appears in both texts as a fur fetishist, the exclusive focus on her perversity in the animated film reduces the multiple resonances of fur as fashion practice, delineated by Smith in the novel.

The Disney live-action film of 1996 replays at a slightly more sophisticated level many of the gender anxieties exhibited by the earlier Disney film. In this film, Cruella is the head of the fashion House of DeVil, where she employs Anita as designer, restoring Smith's emphasis on Cruella's participation in the fashion industry. The reliance on animal actors, who are not provided with voiceovers, means that besides lead Dalmatians Pongo and Perdy, gendering of the animal characters is minimal. Among the humans, however, Cruella as fashion diva and powerful CEO is explicitly contrasted with Anita as wife and mother: while Cruella repeatedly expresses disgust at Anita's desire to marry and have children, Anita is happy to leave her job if her marital plans require it. While the film makes a nominal concession to contemporary modes of femininity in that Anita is presented as actively working, it nevertheless presents maternity and career as mutually exclusive options, and rigidly privileges one above the other. Thus the film effectively demonizes the woman who places her career above maternity and heteronormative romance. Cruella is definitively single—repeatedly referred to as "Miss de Vil"—and her extreme fashionability is presented as grotesque and misplaced, a substitute for "normal" (i.e., heterosexual, maternal) femininity.

Toward the beginning of the film, Cruella has a private meeting with Anita about one of her designs that has caught her eye. She praises Anita's work and suggests she may be poached by another fashion house. When Anita implies that she would only leave her job were she to marry, Cruella exclaims, "More good women have been lost to marriage than war, famine, disease and disaster! You have talent, darling—don't squander it!" In this scene, Cruella's passion for fur is explicitly pitched as a symptom of her refusal of romantic and later, reproductive femininity ("What use do I have for babies?" she asks). Moreover, her critique of marriage as a waste of women's talents suggests a crudely feminist positioning. While she is clearly represented as a bad career woman—a woman who tramples on others to get what she wants—in the absence of any female comparison besides the domesticized Anita and Nanny, she comes to stand for all career women.

Cruella's status as career woman is reiterated though Jean-Paul Gaultier's costume designs, which rework 1980s power dressing motifs such as padded shoulders within a couture context, marrying the business woman with the traditional vamp. Cruella's costumes in the live-action film characteristically have a triangular silhouette, producing the illusion of a masculinized body. They are also replete with phallic symbols such as stiletto heels, cigarette lighter, and long nails over her gloves, and tend to follow hard lines that counteract the soft curves of the so-called natural feminine body, all conspiring to present the image of a woman who is obsessed with clothes but is yet not remotely feminine in the conventional sense. What has traditionally, in Western discourse, been presented as a feminine trait is here both disassociated from the "good" feminine and reconceived as monstrous.

Thus Cruella's eventual humiliation is more than just the conventional comeuppance meted out to fictional villains: it is also on an underlying level the ritual "uncrowning" of a woman in power, and the deflating of fashionable excess. Cruella's image on the cover of French *Vogue* is urinated on by one of the puppies, suggestively disparaging not only Cruella but also the industry she stands for, and prefiguring her final appearance plastered in animal ordure on the front page of the newspapers. In this ending, the live-action film exceeds the anodyne safe arrival home with which the animated film concludes, and returns to the more radical ending of the novel. Smith shows the Dalmatians and the white Persian cat getting their ultimate revenge on Cruella by destroying her priceless fur collection. The violent destruction of the fur takes place as substitute for Cruella's body, as if the two are strangely equivalent. The destruction is, furthermore, subsequently registered on Cruella's body in that her black hair turns white and her white hair green from the shock. Violence is committed not upon the villainess herself, but on the outward, sartorial symbol of her cruelty; moreover, this is an act of commercial sabotage. Since the fur is apparently paid for on credit, Cruella's business is destroyed along with it. This revolutionary gesture is supposed to safeguard Dalmatians everywhere forever, but uncannily preempts the kind of actions anti-fur campaigners practiced in the 1980s and 1990s with the aim of destroying the fur industry altogether.

Dumb Animals: The Discourses of Animal Rights

Although the Animal Rights movement, first established at the end of the nineteenth century, was revitalized in 1959 with the organization Beauty Without Cruelty (three years after *The Hundred and One Dalmatians* was published), the book can only be said to tap into this emerging discourse obliquely. The same can be said of the Disney animated film, in which Anita says she would like a fur coat but can't afford it. In the book and the animated film, distinctions are implicitly made between animals that are suitable for making fur coats and those that are not; rather than an absolute moral judgment against wearing fur, it is the inappropriateness of wearing the skins of domestic pets that causes outrage. This distinction actually reproduces the criteria of the fur industry itself, albeit in inverted form: the fur industry constructs pets as trash, as their pelts are worthless.[17] The Disney live-action film of 1996, however, evokes the association with anti-fur discourses much more explicitly.

   101 Dalmatians was released as the fur trade—in decline during the 1980s and 1990s due to the prominence of anti-fur campaigning—was commencing a renaissance. Chantal Nadeau reads the film as "the quintessential fur revenge fantasy of the 1990s" and Cruella's appetite for fur "a burlesque, yet provocative piece of pro-fur rhetoric."[18] The concern with illegal trade in rare furs is established at the beginning of the film, during the opening credits, with a news report on the skinning of a rare white Siberian tiger at the London Zoo. We subsequently see Cruella wearing the tiger's pelt and parading before a mirror, in self-conscious allusion to an earlier Disney villainess. (The casting of Glenn Close, famous for her "bunny-boiling" role in *Fatal Attraction*, also has obvious intertextual resonance.) As such, Cruella's obsession with fur is linked directly with the kind of anti-fur discourses generated by animal rights pressure groups. During the 1980s, for example, the high profile media campaign orchestrated by Lynx virtually halted the fur industry in Britain, where it has yet to recover. This campaign was controversial at the time, when Greenpeace, an original supporter, rapidly withdrew their backing out of concern for the effects on the environment and lifestyles of indigenous peoples necessarily entailed by any significant decrease in the fur trade. The blend of vulgar environmentalism and sentiment that distinguished the Lynx campaign is reflected in the live-action *101 Dalmatians*: the specific threat to endangered species is shifted into a general one of cruelty to all animals. As the news reporter emphasizes, "We must ask ourselves if any animal in the world is safe": the incursion of the illegal fur trade into the protected space of the zoo prefigures its incursion into the apparently safe space of the domestic environment (see Image 10.4).

   The ideological differences between the slaughtering of the rare tiger and the pet Dalmatians are, furthermore, effectively erased in favor of a hierarchy of sentiment. On one level the film constructs the abducted tiger and the abducted puppies as equivalent victims, as is emphasized by the police discovery of the tiger skin while searching for the missing puppies. On another, the dogs are regarded as more valuable than the tiger due to their proximity to the human. Although in ecological terms the loss of a rare tiger is more significant than that of a few domestic pets, in the terms of the film

Image 10.4. Glenn Close as Cruella de Vil, 1996.

the dogs are rendered more significant through their anthropomorphization. They are suggestively part of a family and not only loved by their owners but also capable of feeling love (both romantic and parental) themselves. Again, this reverses the conventional value system of the fur industry, within which the skins of domestic animals have little economic value. However, it also allows the filmmakers to further a conventional ideology of domesticity while making a limited gesture to more radical politics. For while Cruella's business is destroyed in the film as it is in the book, it is through her own stupidity and selfishness rather than any politicized actions on the part of the animal (or human) characters.

Cruella as fur-wearing woman in this film fits precisely the 1980s stereotype propagated by the Lynx campaigns. This woman was presented partially in the tradition of the sadistic despot familiar from Sacher-Masoch, as Julia Emberley suggests in *Venus and Furs:* "the fur-bearing woman, as a class unto herself, collectively comes to figure as a cold and cruel monstrosity, an accessory to the crime, who would wear her capacity for terror and violence on her sleeve."[19] However, as Emberley argues, the Lynx campaign also deliberately made such women appear stupid—paradoxically, victims of fashion—in their infamous slogan: "It takes up to 40 dumb animals to make a fur coat. But only one to wear it."[20]

As Emberley indicates, the attendant image, which shows a woman cut off at the waist by the frame and trailing a bloody coat, renders the woman as speechless as the "dumb animals" it defends. This controversial advertisement not only placed the entire moral responsibility for the fur trade with the female consumer rather than with the (arguably male-dominated) industry as a whole, but also implied that female consumers in general were stupid. As Emberley argues,

> despite the implicit critique of the fashion advertisements for promoting fur coats, Lynx uses the advertisement format to promote an anti-fur morality. In theory, then, the logic of female passivity which pervades the advertising genre will condition women's consumer habits whether the fashion advertisers promote fur or Lynx's advertisers promote anti-fur morality. In either case, the construction of women as dumb—silent and stupid—is essential to the success of Lynx's media campaign.[21]

While Emberley fails to take into account how anti-fur campaigning and animal rights activism is itself gendered with a strong female component, what is interesting in terms of the live-action version of *101 Dalmatians* is the way that the stereotype of the cruel, stupid, and generally despicable fur-wearing woman is conflated with that of the successful career woman (and implicitly, therefore, the feminist). Ironically, Cruella is disempowered precisely by the medium that previously empowered her—fashion—and the material through which her power was displayed: fur.

A new generation of women, however, have begun to problematize and even reverse this process of disempowerment. Nadeau describes how the Canadian fur industry in particular has learned from anti-fur rhetoric, and presents itself in terms of empowered, environmentally harmonious female and First Nations subjects:

> If anthropomorphism was a key tactic of anti-fur groups, here, on the contrary, the humans are humanized, with names, a face, a culture of their own and no longer just a corporate logo . . . the strategy behind this humanizing campaign . . . has been less to sell fur than to sell names and faces to clearly thwart the image of fur as an economy of death. The idea was to personalize, individualize, humanize the purchase of fur.[22]

A more ironic reversal of anti-fur rhetoric occurs in *Sex and the City: The Movie* (2008), in which successful career woman and sexual adventurer Samantha is splashed with red paint by anti-fur campaigners as she leaves a New York Fashion Week runway show wearing a white fur coat. This scene suggestively replays PETA representatives' splattering of American *Vogue* editor Anna Wintour with tofu pies outside the Chanel and Chloe shows at Paris Fashion Week in 2005. Like both Cruella and Wintour, Samantha is a successful mature career woman who wears fur. Like Cruella in particular, she pursues her own pleasure over conventional notions of romance. She neatly fits the archetype of fur-wearing woman as sexual predator. Yet her sexual and financial freedom are celebrated by the series and the film—both the character and actress Kim Cattrall have become icons of a mature femininity not defined by conventional markers of domesticity. A profoundly ambivalent heroine for our times, Samantha resists the cultural script dictating proper feminine desire, but simultaneously reflects the self-preoccupation and narcissism of the "me generation."

Samantha's reaction to the campaigners' actions is one of shocked surprise quickly dissolving into a nonchalant shrug and smile, and the line, "God, I've missed New York!" Her blasé acceptance of the fur campaigners' actions as part of the excitement and texture of a New York lifestyle refuses the moral judgment meted out to the fashionable career woman. For Samantha, the controversy is all part of the thrill. The incident ironically overturns the Cruella myth: Samantha indulgently adopts a dog over the course of the film. However, in removing moral opprobrium from the figure of the career woman, the film cannot help shifting it elsewhere. Thus it is the campaigners—stereotypically plain and frumpy middle-aged women—who are presented as monstrous, rather than glamorous and successful Samantha. In the world of the film, where self-fulfillment, fashionable consumption, and female friendship are the prime virtues, the campaigners fail on all three fronts: they are presented as joyless harridans who persecute other women. This representation is scarcely any more balanced than the previous model of demonization. It seems where fur is concerned, popular culture will not consider a nuanced interpretation.

Cruella de Vil's clothes, therefore, are more than the mere costume of cruelty, a pantomime enactment of the villainous woman. In both Smith's novel and the Disney live-action film, they signify within an economic system and set of fashion practices. Smith's novel retains ambivalence, acknowledging the perverse sexuality and charisma of the fur-wearer even as it takes the part of the animals whose destruction enables her fetish. In the successive Disney versions, Cruella's perverse desire for fur becomes not an end in itself but a means of demonizing a nondomestic femininity. Smith's narrative is stripped of its ambiguities, and its inclusive range of femininities, in favor of a binary opposition between monstrous fashionista and idealized maternal figure. In conclusion, therefore, the novel and its subsequent film adaptations offer a particularly useful intervention into debate over the politics of fur in the contemporary culture, indicating the inescapably gendered nature of those politics.

Notes

1. *Box Office Mojo*, http://boxofficemojo.com/alltime/adjusted.htm, and http://boxofficemojo.com/yearly/chart/?yr=1996&p=.htm.

2. Rosanna Greenstreet, "Q&A: Heather Mills McCartney," *The Guardian*, May 20, 2006, Weekend section, 8. Mills McCartney was not the first to coin this nickname, but has used it widely and repeatedly in interviews.

3. Valerie Grove, *Dear Dodie: The Life of Dodie Smith* (London: Pimlico, 1996), 232–235.

4. Dodie Smith, *I Capture the Castle* (London: Virago, 1996), 80.

5. Ibid., 83.

6. Dodie Smith, *The Hundred and One Dalmatians* (London: Pan, 1975), 13.

7. Ibid., 14.

8. Ibid.

9. Leopold von Sacher-Masoch, *Venus in Furs and Selected Letters* (New York: Blast Books, 1989), 180.

10. Alison Lurie, *The Language of Clothes* (London: Heineman, 1981), 232.

11. Ibid., 233.

12. Smith, *The Hundred and One Dalmatians*, 13. Tess Cosslett notes that such inversions are frequent in children's fiction featuring animals, and reads them in relation to the Bakhtinian carnivalesque, while pointing out they are often not as subversive as they may first appear. Tess Cosslett, *Talking Animals in Children's Fiction, 1786–1914* (Farnham: Ashgate, 2006), 2–3.

13. Smith, *The Hundred and One Dalmatians*, 112.

14. Ibid., 12.

15. Ibid., 12–13.

16. Ibid., 13.

17. Julia Emberley, *Venus and Furs: The Cultural Politics of Fur* (London: I. B. Tauris, 1998), 33.

18. Chantal Nadeau, *Fur Nation: From the Beaver to Brigitte Bardot* (New York: Routledge, 2001), 167.

19. Emberley, *Venus and Furs*, 25.

20. Cited in Emberley, *Venus and Furs*, 29.

21. Emberley, *Venus and Furs*, 29–30.

22. Nadeau, *Fur Nation*, 172–73.

Chapter 11

Something Borrowed, Something Blue

What's an Indie Bride to Do?

Elline Lipkin

I never wore a pillowcase on my head as a little girl, pretending that its trailing white length was a veil. I never thought my One Big Day would correspond to pledging my troth, saying I do, or having everyone hail me in queen-for-a-day style. I never thought I would wield absolute fiat on the day I reigned as a bride. And I certainly never thought I would participate in the rituals and bonds (translation: restriction) of a traditional wedding ceremony, chiefly because I simply never thought I would get married.

But what happens when a feminist decides to get married? For women for whom the institution of marriage represents the apex of American Judeo-Christian patriarchal tradition—with its regretful-women-handed-off-as-property-from-father-to-groom history, never mind its vestigial father-walks-daughter down the aisle to symbolically make-the-trade-expectation, and the old name-change trick of erasing her identity through the subsuming claim of her husband's kin—it's not a decision that is made lightly. Then there's the bride's symbolic re-virginizing through the act of wearing white—a throwback to control of female sexuality to ensure her purity for the purpose of preserving the patrilineal line, or the act of veiling her face so that she is "reborn" post-ceremony in her husband's eyes. The bouquet toss ("all the single ladies!") that assumes all women want to get married, and the garter removal (with the bride's symbolic public stripping done for entertainment purposes and voyeuristic preview of the groom's assumed sexual prowess that night). For the self-declared feminist for whom the personal is always political, the decision to enter into a legally sanctioned, heterosexual union, is hardly as simple as saying "I do." Walking down the aisle, or merely standing in front of a justice of the peace means negotiating rituals and fashions that seem to celebrate a bride's stepping into the lockhold of heterosexual privilege—and one that historically is about serving male needs.

In the past several years a proliferation of articles and Web sites have explored the ambivalence of women who want to celebrate their unions, yet who eschew the literal and symbolic trappings of a wedding. Standing in this vexed position, and often squeezed on all sides by conflicting cultural pressures (e.g., families who expect a certain wedding script and are confused when they are denied it), these women move along a spectrum as they plan their weddings, often shifting their stance from traditional expectation to reappropriating meaning or inventing new rituals as they try to reinscribe more egalitarian substance within the material symbols of their unions. Often this process comes with self-avowed skepticism as to whether this can ever be achieved.

A sense of play may emerge as brides-to-be try to whimsically, stylishly, and originally uproot or de-center cultural standards that privilege patriarchal tradition in unexpected ways, such as walking down the aisle solo, or with a couple's beloved pet. Bouncing meaning from one cultural inscription into a new interpretation takes work—and many brides undertake this to mixed effect. Some who refuse the traditional elements of a ceremony suffer the disappointment of their families or worry about how their decisions might be misconstrued.

Author Lori Leibovich, founder of the Web site Indiebride.com describes the manifesto she wrote not long after becoming engaged. The "indie bride," she writes, has the urge "to break free from the tulle handcuffs that had been binding women for centuries and make sure our weddings reflected our fiery, feminist selves."[1] For Leibovich that means disregarding practices that privileged patriarchal tradition like the fatherly hand-off to her groom at the end of the aisle, and the bouquet or garter toss. Leibovich urges financial restraint, and resisting the To-Do lists that brides are told they couldn't have their "happiest day" without. Yet after buying a white dress and acquiescing to a veil of her own, Liebovich concludes, "I had to come to terms with the incontrovertible truth: There was nothing very 'indie' about me or my wedding."

Leibovich repositions her urge to move beyond patriarchal pressures by invoking the clause "It was all okay because I chose it." Her position captures the unresolved conflict of the feminist bride who capitulates, if reluctantly, in part because she sees few other options from which to choose. She attempts to justify her decision to veer back into the familiar by claiming it was, at least, an (allegedly) conscious choice.

On January 16, 2009, Jessica Valenti, founder of the popular Web site Feministing.com, announced that she was getting hitched. She decided to go public about her wedding in part as a platform to comment on the state of marriage—particularly gay rights—and, in part, to share the happy news. "I'm positive you'll be hearing more from me on the marriage front: Like how to do it while shirking patriarchal tradition. Or why I decided to participate in an institution that still (for the most part) excludes same-sex couples" she wrote, also mentioning she might ask for ideas about "subversive wedding favors . . . or something."

The blogosphere lit up, and Valenti found herself under attack from all sides. Kathryn Lopez, of the conservative *National Review*, wrote a post entitled "You've Never Met a Bridezilla Like a Feminist Bridezilla," which mocked Valenti's "attempts to subvert traditional wedding standards." Another blogger called Valenti a "ball-cutting cybersuccubus" and labeled her fiancé "beta of the month" invoking the idea that an "alpha male" would never marry a feminist. Some liberals asked how Valenti could capitulate to what they still see as a fundamentally patriarchal tradition, no matter how reinterpreted or reinscribed.

Valenti's March 11, 2009 response to "feministbridezillagate" was accompanied by the witty image of a man and woman pictured together with the caption, "I'd be honored if you would consider affixing your last name to mine with a hyphen." Valenti detailed the finer points of her plans: no name change, buying a not-quite-white dress from a shop that gives all proceeds to charity, and asking for donations to an organization fighting for same-sex marriage rights instead of homemaking-type gifts.

In an article, which ran in *The Guardian* on April 24, 2009 ("My Big Feminist Wedding"), Valenti fired back again, especially toward critics who were disappointed that Valenti seemed "to find flaws with patriarchy, but fail[ed] to find a way to bring it down."[2]

To Valenti, though, "It felt good, feminist even, to write about an institution so wrought with sexism and discuss ways to make it our own." Yet Valenti is clear that her rejection of a traditional ceremony wouldn't hew to so-called anti-ceremony cliché. "While our wedding will be politicized, it won't be a feminist caricature: I won't be sporting Birkenstocks under my dress and we won't ask the 'Goddess' for a blessing. But we will head into the wedding, and the marriage, as equals."

While critics may remain unsatisfied, Valenti's comments pinpoint the tension of negotiating tradition, subjugation, and reinvention in her reference to sartorial garb.

Rachel Fudge, former editor at *Bitch* magazine, also captures this tension in her essay "Why I Don't" in which she responds to the urging of friends and family that she and her "special peer," as she calls her male partner, tie the knot:

Sure . . . marriage is a problematic institution with a dubious
history, but you don't have to chuck out the bride with the bath-
water . . . think of all the fun you could have in reinterpreting
all those old wedding chestnuts with feminist flair: . . . Your best
friend could get a minister-for-a-day license and officiate; you
could substitute Huggy Bear's riot-grrrl anthems for Wagner's
processional. Use the textual and visual elements of the ceremony
itself to make explicit the deconstructed and reconstituted aspects
of your wedding vows.[3]

That's what most of her peers are doing, Fudge explains: "cooking up new
recipes for weddings and labeling them transgressive and unconventional."[4]

But ultimately Fudge isn't buying it. To her, entering into legal marriage—no matter how unmoored from its ceremonial roots—means nonetheless entering into a legally sanctioned institution at odds with her
beliefs. In other words, no "I-Do Feminism" allowed.[5] Sidney Eve Matrix
uses this term (attributed to Alexandra Jacobs) in describing the bride who
"expresses her freedom of choice and liberation from patriarchy and its traditions . . . by . . . eagerly embracing (what appear to be) classic heteronormative and hyperconsumerist rituals of the white wedding."[6] By skewing
"modern choice" inside retro packaging, Matrix writes, "it grants a bride
permission and freedom to selectively participate in wedding activities which
are still arguably overtly sexist, oppressive, and objectifying, while claiming
that the act of choosing is itself a demonstration of her agency."[7] Matrix
points out how clever advertisers capitalize by combining nostalgic and "fairy-
tale visions" with more modern images or "profeminist rhetoric." By Matrix's
estimation, nothing actually changes except perhaps swapping out dress color
or changing up the ceremony's words.

The Heteronormative Impulse

In *White Weddings: Romancing Heterosexuality in Popular Culture* author
Chrys Ingraham takes up these issues suggested by Matrix and others arguing
that heterosexuality "is a highly regulated, ritualized, and organized practice."
The wedding institution is the primary way that society and culture reinforces
a heteronormative impulse, she explains. Drawing from Adrienne Rich's essay
"Compulsory Heterosexuality and Lesbian Existence" in which Rich asserts
"that heterosexuality is neither natural nor inevitable" but instead is an
institution "contrived, constructed, and taken-for-granted,"[8] reveals why indie
brides are left in an untenable position. They are brides that won't subsume

themselves into the cultural White Wedding script, and yet must also follow it. How to rework its tenets without hypocrisy is the indie bride's challenge.

The indie bride dilemma straddles the problem of heteronormativity and what Ingraham calls the "heterosexual imaginary," a framework with roots in philosopher Jacques Lacan's concept of the "imaginary"—"that way of thinking that conceals the operation of heterosexuality in structuring gender (across race, class, and sexuality) and closes off any critical analysis of heterosexuality as an organizing institution."[9] By maintaining a (collective) romantic view of heterosexuality, Ingraham claims, most people won't see how weddings actually work "to organize gender while preserving racial, class, and sexual hierarchies as well."[10]

Held up alongside social practices as "just the way it is," reinforces the White Wedding's role in perpetuating ideological and political hegemony and demonstrates why the indie bride's objections to cultural traditions are marginalized: marital rape, domestic violence, pay inequity, and issues regarding parenting and unpaid domestic labor are kept well out of the rosy picture. What's more, notes Ingraham, is that weddings reinforce the precepts of heteronormativity, "the view that institutionalized heterosexuality constitutes the standard for legitimate and expected social and sexual relations."[11]

The independent bride's fraught position is often dismissed as she bumps up against the heterosexual imaginary. Never mind that the groom—indie or otherwise—is glaringly absent in mainstream provocations, if not in real-life wedding plans. The bride may be trivialized as kooky or unnecessarily frustrating by family or friends. Her deviations from cultural norms can be met with indulgent bemusement, chalked up to "bridezilla whims," the word itself giving a sense that the bride is transformed from "normalcy" to one of demanding (and temporarily indulged) irrationality. Each label is a form of curbing the independent bride's positioning. Each accusation reveals how the collective expectation of heteronormative tradition, both spoken and unspoken, serves as a force field of disapproval or invisible opprobrium the bride-to-be must cross.

Welcome to Brideland

Written over a decade prior to Valenti's screed, feminist pundit Naomi Wolf"s essay "Brideland," quickly zeros in on her own confusion about deciding to don the veil. Her initiation into Brideland, she says, was "abrupt" after announcing her engagement and then picking up one of the door-stoppingly large bridal magazines. Her initial intention was to "find out what the rules were that I was bound to be breaking," assuming that the literal and metaphorical trappings of a wedding would be out of sync with her feminist politics.

Perhaps eloping, "or a civil ceremony; or even an alternative ceremony so creatively subversive that it would be virtually unrecognizable for what it is," Wolf casually muses. "But not—never—a wedding."[12] Yet, by page 16 of that first bridal magazine, her "capacity for irony was totally paralyzed. . . . By page 32 I was hypnotized." Swept up in the vision of the American wedding, complete with accoutrements, rituals, and a Victorian-style white dress she thought she would eschew, Wolf's initial aversion to All Things Bridal, changed rapidly.

Wolf articulates the heart of the feminist conundrum by asking: "How can I endorse an institution that, in the not-too-distant past, essentially conveyed the woman over to her husband as property, denying her even the right to her own property? How can I support a system that allows me to flaunt my heterosexual relationship brazenly, but forbids deeply committed gay and lesbian friends of mine to declare their bonds in the same way?" Wolf concludes her litany with a final question that equally disturbs, "And, less profoundly, but no less urgently, if I were to do it, what on earth would I wear?"[13]

Sartorial Significance: The Dress

Riffing on Wolf's essay title, Lisa Walker's "Feminists in Brideland," is a confessional on the politics of the lesbian bridal dress. "When I came out as a lesbian," Walker writes, "the only thing I regretted was my chance to be a bride." Within months, however, she decided there was no reason to "sacrifice that fashion moment."

Upon meeting the woman she wants to commit to, a clear vision of herself "as an elegant and sophisticated bride evaporated into clouds of pink tulle," Walker rues. Walker, too, finds herself pulled into the same vaporous lull described by Wolf.

Walker confesses to this without apology. Obviously, "nothing in the editorial content of mainstream bridal magazines is addressed to the lesbian," she continues. Despite problematic aspects of the bridal industry, Walker claims that many lesbian and feminist women still "dream about transforming themselves into that most fantastic creature, the bride."[14]

The inherent tension, Walker notes, is that every version of bridal beauty invokes social hierarchies that uphold dominant ideals of female beauty. But, at the same time, she is unwilling to succumb to "fashion abstinence." Walker comments, "It is impossible to separate the pleasures and the politics of fashion,"[15] and faced with her own desire for The Dress, Walker, like so many indie brides, was unwilling to sacrifice one in order to avoid the other.

If a feminist's interest in wedding gowns indicates her devolution from a "conscious state of resistance to media brainwashing into a prefeminist urge to dress in lace and chiffon,"[16] this would imply that fashion success requires a fashion victim, she who is lulled into unreflective choices to endorse patriarchal institutions. Could this really be the case that indie brides are eternally trapped by the conundrum of marital tradition, lacking all free will and intentional decision-making about what to wear?

Most bridal magazines limit their discussions of any "feminist" issues to topics such as choosing not to change your name or to keep your own bank account. But, as Walker rightly points out, there are styles that seem to be designed for "the woman who regards traditional bridal fashion with suspicion."[17] Often termed the "modern bride" Walker classifies these into two categories: the minimalist who plays down the "(over)production of bridal beauty" by emphasizing "elegance over abundance." And the other is seemingly the opposite: a look that is "self-consciously ironic and draws attention to the production of bridal beauty; it stresses the elements of costume and masquerade in bridal fashion."[18] Both looks refuse many of the traditional details of bridal fashion of the past two decades. The minimalist look is simple, often a straight or A-line dress, featuring a sleek silhouette, "crisp lines, plain satins . . . and contemporary details such as pleats, small, tailored bows, and subtle embroidery." A minimalist style—which can be sartorial code for "feminist," suggests "an image of the bride who has broken free from the trance-like spell of the fantasy."[19]

The second popular modern-bride look "that might address the feminist reader of bridal magazines emphasizes masquerade, inviting women to read bridal fashion parodically." With "lush, glamorous, and theatrical" dresses, this look is distinguished from mere traditional bridal wear in its detailing. "Wittiness is at the core of this look," Walker notes, "which takes advantage of makeup, accessories, and settings to parody bridal wear. Models carry masks, feather bouquets, fan, and guns. They wear beaded chokers, heavy crosses, bracelet cuffs and fingerless gloves."[20] While material accessories change the outfit, the act of "costuming" still presents the indie bride with a paradigm of shift, but not escape, as she evades the traditional dress, but is hemmed into another set of sartorial dictates.

The dilemma remains: While she dodges the bridal-industrial complex, the indie bride still quite literally buys a so-called "alternative" bridal fashion, a ploy that "is merely a consumer mythology designed to keep the 'modern' bride firmly ensconced within the wedding industry."[21]

Class status and exploitation are also implicated within these choices. Cheaper dresses are often purchased (or avoided) with awareness of sweatshop labor practices. Bridal looks from a 2009 fashion week show many non-sweatshop, couturier styles—highly architectural dresses with exceptional details—but each costing a small fortune. Yet, there remain the DIY brides who eschew cookie-cutter wedding dresses as a way of rejecting precut notions about how a bride is supposed to look, ignoring perquisite fabrics and forms. Making one's own dress is a way that the indie bride can maximize an opportunity for individuality and negotiate the expectation of an otherwise predictable white dress.

Blogger Alix Sobler attempts with her fiancé to reinscribe the symbols of the wedding ceremony. Sobler's take on a feminist wedding is based on several tenets—one is that the two lived together for seven years, with combined finances and shared equity. "We truly had a marriage before a wedding," she writes, making it easier to upend social expectation with their wedding rather than have its rites serve as a crossing over to new status. Sobler concludes that "there needs to be room to reassign the meaning of marriage. . . . There is nothing 'inherently patriarchal' about my marriage, and maybe that is a new option within the last 100 years, but it's true. So if we can reassign the meaning of marriage, maybe it's not such a stretch to reassign the meaning behind weddings."[22]

Yet, Sobler's first "reassignment" comes with her white dress. She writes, "For generations it has symbolized the virginity and therefore value of the bride. . . . So here is my new meaning, at least partially. On the day of my wedding, my partner and I start anew. The white of my dress will signify a clean slate, a blank page, a new chance for us to write our story. It's not that all that has come before is forgotten, but let's say we are getting our chance for another fresh start, the next chapter." Sobler acknowledges that others won't see the reassignments of meaning that she intends; her choice of fashion, despite her projected intent, will still be interpreted through a conventional lens and will encourage those guests expecting to compliment her on the dress's details. What Sobler overlooks are the heavily hegemonic meanings that underscore the melding of whiteness with purity, freshness, or starting over.

Independent filmmaker Therese Shechter, whose marriage took place in September 2009, had no trouble articulating the sense of political conviction she felt when preparing for her wedding. "I knew I didn't want to wear a white dress," says Shechter, who adds that the idea was "repulsive" to her. She also refused to wear a veil. Engaged while working on a documentary film about virginity and its meanings, Shechter describes going with her producer to the ubiquitous wedding-supply store, David's Bridal, and filming her trying on dresses. "I felt more comfortable on a porn set than at David's Bridal," concludes Shechter.[23]

"Not only is it scripted," she says, referring to the rituals surrounding preparing for a wedding, "but the emotions are scripted . . . this is how you're supposed to feel and react."[24] Shechter recalls, "I felt like women were being told this is what they had to do—[there was a] blueprint and there weren't any options, according to [the sales women at David's Bridal]. . . . They weren't mean about it," says Shechter, "just matter of fact. To them, there wasn't any other universe other than the one in which you want to look like a poufy white princess."[25] Shechter ultimately chose a green-and-black dress, purchased at a department store.

"Let's take back our weddings. Let's take back the way weddings are viewed by our culture at large," writes Ariel Meadow Stallings on the Web site Offbeat Bride, echoing the indie bride's fundamental desire. The remaining challenge is whether an intention to subvert philosophical, ideological, and political issues can be achieved through intention alone. The pressure of heteronormative tradition is powerful, and yet, to assume that it is inescapable is also discrediting. As Stallings writes, "when you assume that anyone enthusiastically planning a wedding is automatically a victim of outside forces, you're asserting that women can't think for themselves and are powerless against the lures of taffeta and tiaras."[26] At the vanguard of urging women beyond reinscription to true reinvention, Stallings comments, "the internet is doing an excellent job of starting to allow women (and men) to grab on to the reins of wedding planning, and say, 'This. This is mine. And you can eff right off with your double edged swords of crazy gendered rhetoric.' . . . When someone asks us about our bridesmaids dresses, maybe we should sweetly say, 'Oh dear, no. I'm having a bridal brigade.' . . . Or when people ask about our beautiful white wedding dress, it's time to nicely say, 'It's so pretty and blue, you'll adore it.' "[27]

Not long after my own wedding and subsequent move, I wandered into a hipster gift shop in my new neighborhood saw a series of decorative cross-stitch samplers hanging on a wall, each inscribed with an ironic message. I pointed out the one that read "You had me at health insurance," to my now spouse and we burst out laughing. Its prescient, modern message, neatly stitched inside a frame evoking another era's handicrafts jarred our senses and thrilled us with its humorous disynchronousness. Health insurance was one of the chief reasons we had decided to get hitched, with equal parts relief and irritation at the receipt of legal benefits that would only come from our legal yoking.

The fusion (and confusion) of the old-fashioned form of the cross-stitch sampler with its pragmatic, contemporary message, conflating romance with legal benefits, and playfully offering a modern salvo to the illusion of idealized messages ("our happy home") seemed an apt metaphor for the axis of conflict on which the indie bride turns. When I think of her uncertain positioning I view a woman standing in a fundamentally untenable position—often rotating to respond to different pressures and perhaps to release different aspects of herself. As she grapples with the shades of tradition and the inflection of newness, the best she can do is construct a series of overlays—sometimes quite literally, in the remaking of a mother's wedding dress, the updating of a "traditional" look with fresh detail, or the need to custom-make a new pattern.

Participating in the formalization of a union, not to mention the desire to celebrate romance and publicly recognize partnership, will remain a constant and, from my own perspective, something to enjoy. But the divorce of marriage from its patriarchal roots requires a slow peel from a deeply sticky institutionalized expectation, one that no matter how "reinscribed" still partakes of collective hegemonic experience.

How the rituals of union are now enacted, and what force is needed to push up against tradition to create new celebrations—never mind what to wear—remains an open question. In my own case, my wedding, not unlike Leibovich's, was much less indie than I had initially hoped, in part because it was planned very quickly, in part because I knew the changes I insisted on were already disruptive enough to my immediate family, and in part because I didn't have any examples of how else to dress for the part. The indie bride, both vexed by her refusal to conform to a socially enforced script, and twisted into often diametrically opposed philosophical and sometimes literal positions, also stands at the vanguard of opportunity. With the press of tradition so squarely at her back, despite its risk, there remains the possibility to freefall into new territory, not unlike the venture of union itself.

Notes

1. Lori Leibovich, "My So-Called Indie Wedding," in *Altared: Bridezillas, Bewilderment, Big Love, Breakups, and What Women Really Think About Contemporary Weddings,* ed. Colleen Curran (New York: Vintage Books, 2007), 279.

2. Jessica Valenti, "My Big Feminist Wedding," *The Guardian,* April 24, 2009.

3. Rachel Fudge, "Why I Don't," in *Young Wives' Tales: New Adventures in Love and Partnership,* eds. Jill Corral and Lisa Miya-Jervis (Seattle, WA: Seal Press, 2001), 43.

4. Fudge, "Why I Don't," 44.

5. Sidney Eve Matrix, " 'I-Do' Feminism Courtesy of Martha Stewart Weddings and HBC's Vow To Wow Club: Inventing Modern Matrimonial Tradition with Glue Sticks and Cuisinart" *Ethnologies* 28, no. 2, (2006): 55–56.

6. Matrix, " 'I-Do' Feminism Courtesy of Martha Stewart Weddings and HBC's Vow To Wow Club," 55.

7. Ibid., 57.

8. Chrys Ingraham, *White Weddings: Romancing Heterosexuality in Popular Culture* (New York: Routledge, 1999), 11.

9. Ibid., 16.

10. Ibid.

11. Ibid., 17.

12. Naomi Wolf, "Brideland," in *To Be Real: Telling the Truth and Changing the Face of Feminism,* ed. Rebecca Walker (New York: Anchor Books, 1995), 37.

13. Ibid. See also Amy Benfer, "I Do—Kind of," *Salon,* August 15, 2001, http://dir.salon.com/story/mwt/feature/2001/08/15/i_do/print.html.

14. Lisa Walker, "Feminists in Brideland," *Tulsa Studies in Women's Literature* 19, no. 2 (Autumn 2000): 222.

15. Ibid., 229.

16. Ibid., 222.

17. Ibid., 223.

18. Ibid.

19. Ibid.

20. Ibid., 224.

21. Ibid., 226.

22. Alix Sobler, "A Feminist Wedding Has Gone Global," *A Feminist Wedding*, June 15, 2009, http://feministwedding.blogspot.com/2009/06/feminist-wedding-has-gone-global.html.

23. Therese Shechter, personal communication, August 20, 2009.

24. Ibid.

25. Ibid.

26. Ariel Meadow Stallings, "Offbeat Bride: Altar Your Thinking," *Offbeat Bride*, http://offbeatbride.com.

27. Stallings, "Offbeat Bride."

Chapter 12

Steampunk

Stylish Subversion and Colonial Chic

Diana M. Pho and Jaymee Goh

Not all fashion movements can claim to stem from literature, but steampunk has made the leap from the page to the person. The term "steampunk," originally conceived jokingly by science fiction writer K.W. Jeter in 1987 to describe the literary marriage between Victorian fiction and sci-fi technology, has now crossed over to encompass an entire aesthetic movement that has blossomed in recent years.[1] Initially a sci-fi genre, steampunk became an underground subculture in the 1980s and has gained increasing visibility since: examples in pop culture include the American film *Wild, Wild West* (2002), Japanese anime like *Steam Boy* (2004) and *Last Exile* (2003), and books like Alan Moore's graphic novel series *The League of Extraordinary Gentlemen* (1999).

The explosion of steampunk aesthetic in the media paralleled its development into a recognizable subculture during the early 2000s. A milestone in its transition from an aesthetic to a subculture is the launch of political *Steampunk Magazine*, founded by anarchist Magpie Killjoy in 2004. Later, steampunk gained further recognition with a much-admired metal and wood treehouse built at the Burning Man arts festival in 2007.[2] Around the same time, a variety of different artists and hobbyists contributed to the fluid definition of steampunk. Well-known DIY tinkerer Jake von Slatt, for instance, confessed that he wanted "to co-opt the term 'steampunk' and imbue it with this DIY component. DIY wasn't part of the definition of steampunk . . . but I wanted it to be."[3] Steampunk's burgeoning presence on the Internet also contributed to its community growth: The most popular sites include the UK-based BrassGoggles and Gatehouse Gazette, Steamfashion on LiveJournal, maintained by Evelyn Kriete, Jake von Slatt's own Steampunk Workshop blog, *Steampunk Magazine*'s Web site and its forum Gaslamp Bazaar, while the increasingly popular Steampunk Empire launched the ning.com platform.

As a science fiction genre, steampunk embraces sci-fi ideas both classic (time traveling and dirigibles) and modern (e.g., the fusion of steampunk and Star Wars[4]). Now, as a style and as a nascent subculture, steampunk has expanded to include modding (e.g., aesthetic modifications to laptops and flash drives), music (Abney Park and Vernian Process) and, of course, fashion.

Steampunk clothing imitates Victorian pulp fiction characters: The Tinker, The Inventor, The Street Urchin, The Explorer, and The Aristocrat, among others.[5] Other fashion styles that influence steampunk include the gothic romance of flowing materials and rich colors, or cyberpunk's discordant blend of the natural and the artificial. Specific steampunk styles depend on the type of persona being imitated. An aristocrat would have fastidiously neat and stream-lined clothing typical of Victorian upper class, while an "airship" pirate, taking a page from punk styles, could sport dreadlocks with aerial gear. Standard steampunk fashion accessories pay homage to the industrial age: gears, keys, goggles, and chains are typical. Classic European items such as pocketwatches, waistcoats, opera glasses, lace gloves, and frilled umbrellas are also favored. Fantastic weaponry—from brass and wood-styled ray guns to contraptions using sound waves as projectile forces—are tributes to its imaginative origins, and many steampunks construct and wield a personal arsenal. Self-conscious subversion of Victorian fashion standards is common, like wearing corsets over clothing. Conversely, replicating Victorian outfits, such as dressing as an African explorer can be equally recognized as steampunk.

Like many subculture fashion trends, steampunk outfits can vary from the extravagant to the everyday. Participants retrofit entire wardrobes to include waistcoats with sewn-on gears and newsboy hats for casual wear, or they create bustles, trains, frockcoats, and imaginary military uniforms to wear at sci-fi and anime conventions and other organized gatherings. Many participants treat steampunk as recreational costuming and create pulp-fantasy personas with exaggerated Victorian names to complement a particular outfit.

Because of its versatility, steampunk style is undeniably friendly to participants of all sizes and all ages. Evelyn Kriete, of the popular LiveJournal community, *Steamfashion*, points out:

> A major reason for the interest in steampunk and Victorian fash-
> ion is that it looks good on anyone, male or female, regardless

Image 12.1. Steampunk safari.

of build or body type. The same can't be said about most 20th century fashions, which heavily favor tall and thin women and very muscular men.[6]

This openness toward gender extends to socioeconomic status, as well: participants draw inspiration from every segment of Victorian society while also incorporating the DIY aspect of punk to break down the boundaries of both class and gender. Even racial minorities find it easy to participate in steampunk. The aesthetic is appealing not because it is new or novel, but because it recycles classic fashions with the option of modern, self-reflexive experimentation.

As all-encompassing as steampunk can be, however, deeper interpretations reveal steampunk's problematic implications: First, the trend glorifies imperialist culture by visually promoting Western styles over any other cultural dress during this time period. Second, insinuations of cultural appropriation or Orientalist stereotyping lurk when white steampunks incorporate non-Western styles into their outfits. The result is a sense of conflict for non-white participants when confronting a style that romanticizes their painful histories of oppression. In this essay about steampunk, we explore whether this fashion condones or criticizes its inspirational time period and, in the end, whether the trend is as punk as it claims to be.

We limit our observations to the steampunk movement as it manifests in North America. Steampunk owes much of its founding and development to Great Britain and Japan since its emergence as a subculture. Steampunk has now acquired an international following, so cultural and historical contexts can vary widely; a Japanese steampunk may consider the aesthetic from a different perspective than an American, a Brit, or a Haitian. Thus, though the observations made here about the cultural trends of steampunk may correlate with observations made in steampunk communities in other countries, we wish to acknowledge that this analysis occurs mostly within a North American subcultural context. Also, although we recognize that the racial term "white" is an invented construct, for the purposes of this essay, we will use the terms "white" and "steampunk(s) of color" (SoC) when speaking about participants. "White" refers to participants who identify themselves as having any combination of Western/European ancestral, historical, or cultural roots. SoC refers to participants who identify themselves outside this construct.

This essay explores two different perspectives on the relationship between steampunk's participants and its fashion. In Parts I and II, Diana M. Pho considers steampunk fashion's Orientalist and colonialist associations. In Part III, Jaymee Goh further explores ideas about cultural imperialism both within and outside North America, and other problematic issues that may prevent steampunk from being truly culturally inclusive. Between these two perspectives, we can observe the social justice challenges the steampunk aesthetic presents and the possibilities for this trend's progressive evolution.

Part I: Colonial Chic?
Imperial Possibilities and Orientalist Attitudes

Much of steampunk's appeal stems from the trend's imaginative possibilities. These fashion fantasies, however, do not exist inside a vacuum, but are based within historical contexts dominated by Western imperialism.

Fashions based on The Explorer, for example, include "tailored garments, but more military-influenced . . . Leather, silk, linen, tall boots, pith helmets, flying goggles."[7] To many, this outfit embodies a sense of adventure and discovery; the historical background for these items, however, is connected to the conquest of non-Western nations by European countries where these items were worn by the colonizers and denoted superior status in their controlled territories. In the British Raj, historian E. M. Collingham notes that British garb was part of a "colonial hierarchy of possible forms of clothing" that "placed Indian clothing at the bottom and British forms of dress at the summit." [8] The explorer outfit of "white tropical suit of shirt, waistcoat, jacket and trousers, all made of white linen"[9] fit somewhere in the middle of this hierarchy, but later signified the status of the white British "sahib"—the authority over colonized subjects. The pith helmet (a.k.a. a *topi* or *sola topi*), another visual signifier interpreted by steampunks as embodying the adventuresome spirit, was such a "powerful a symbol of Britishness that Eurasians took to wearing topis in order to assert their racial affinity to the British." As Collingham notes, this "was the ultimate signifier of Anglo-Indian membership and the prestige and authority that went with it."[10] Even the ubiquitous goggles, worn by an aristocratically dressed steampunk, can be linked to colonialists using goggles in India as eye-protection against the tropical sun.[11]

Not only can Victorian clothing convey pro-colonialist sentiments, but using non-Western influences in steampunk style also runs the risk of comparisons to historical Orientalism. Cultural critic Edward Said explains this dynamic: "In short, Orientalism [is] a Western style for dominating, restructuring, and having authority over the Orient."[12]

In addition to their affinity for pro-colonialist fashion, steampunks also freely appropriate styles from the colonized. Steampunk's most well-known musical band (and, interestingly enough, all-white) Abney Park features a female belly dancer in concerts and online videos.[13] Belly dancing may reflect the band's world music influences, but also risks promoting a familiar, hegemonic Western perception of the sexualized, Eastern female. Abney Park's impact upon the steampunk subculture is reflected in the embrace of steampunk belly dance by fellow participants.[14]

Steampunk resource Web sites, perhaps intending to promote diversity, nevertheless express Orientalist sentiments, too. *The Gatehouse* Web site, for example, describes steampunking Eastern culture (labeled "Victoriental"). By their assessment, blending Eastern culture with steampunk style is an allegedly innocent practice, where the East provides a rich fantasy realm for its style-heavy followers. A critical reading of *The Gatehouse* description, though, reveals an objectified culture readily co-opted under the guise of "enchantment":

Image 12.2. Finn Von Claret, former member of Abney Park.

With the increasing contact with the East and its ensuing colonization, people in the West became increasingly fascinated by this strange new world. For centuries adventurers, novelists and romantics had been interested in these lands beyond the horizon. Europe had all been explored and people became more and more familiar with the world they lived in. *The Orient was still a realm of mystery, inhabited by alien people, exotic and sometimes cruel, with customs that Enlightened Europeans thought of as barbaric; a place where time had apparently stood still.*

An age-long orientalist tradition of those who studied the East has in our times been criticized for its presumed bias and even racism. *In the realm of steampunk fiction however, we can safely recreate the Orient as it was described and depicted by nineteenth century authors and artists who might never have actually seen it. In steampunk all the myths and miracles of the East that enchanted the Victorians can come true.*[15]

The Gatehouse perspective on Victoriental steampunk presumes that the effects of colonialism are irrelevant to modern history and that Orientalist attitudes toward Eastern culture do not exist today. This frames European imperialism in a positive, nostalgic light from the standpoint of an awestruck British or French conqueror. Later in the text, this Web site isolates a fragment of Said's description about the European perspective, writing about "memories, suggestive ruins, forgotten secrets, hidden correspondences, and an almost virtuosic style of being."[16] This selective lifting subverts Said's complex argument about Orientalism and fails to convey his complete observations about Orientalism's manifestations in the historical aesthetic. What is left out is Said's fuller discourse about how these same Europeans viewed the Orient as a brutal, backward, and sexualized foil to European society, thus portraying the Orientals as an inferior people and justifying their colonization.

The Gatehouse chooses not to address the political implications behind their depiction of the Vicorientalist style, yet wants the reader to believe that they are coming from a revisionist standpoint by quoting a celebrated postcolonialist writer. As a result, the tone of this Web site—and much of the broader steampunk culture—superficially promotes a multicultural view of steampunk, but really only enforces an Orientalist stance that gives today's steampunks permission to retain the imperialist mindset of their Victorian inspiration.

These modern-day examples parallel nineteenth-century Victorian Orientalists who fetishized an exotic Other by co-opting non-Western fashions and cultures for vanity and personal distinction. A popular theme in Orientalist portraiture, for instance, is the Western subject donning Middle Eastern garb. By doing so, the Westerner is presented as "worldly, sophisticated, and fluent in another culture" while also being "the privileged surveyor of an exotic land."[17] This cross-cultural dressing enforced perceived stereotypes about Middle Eastern culture. Men were "despots and lustful harem lords," while women were hypersexualized in harem or slave settings, perfect for the male gaze or as figures of seduction like that of Salome or belly-dancing girls.[18]

In historical context, then, by dressing in these Oriental fashions, Victorians appropriate markers of the Other while never becoming the Other. In fact, they only communicate their distance from the Other by cheekily borrowing those markers. Their stylized expression of Orientalism is not simply conveyed through dress. Victorian-era Orientalists have reenacted "Oriental"

stereotypes as part of recreational costuming: at the London-based Divan
Club, British members play-acted Eastern stereotypes for personal amuse-
ment, while artists and explorers such as John Frederick Lewis and Richard
Burton re-fashioned themselves as Oriental gentleman in their Middle Eastern
travels.[19]

Though I have seen no evidence of racial caricatures played out in steampunk personas, white and non-white steampunks have often incorporated
cross-cultural dress into their outfits while maintaining Western steampunk
identities. The appropriation of visual and behavioral cues from the racial
Other by white counterculture has also been observed within the punk movement, a subculture whose politics some steampunks actively endorse.[20] In the
next section, I will describe the impact of punk philosophy and other political
ideas upon the subculture, and how these ideas affect an understanding of
steampunk.

Part II: Stylish Subversion?
Questioning the Punk in Steampunk

The colonialist messages of what steampunk clothing expresses and its unsettling parallels to historical Orientalism are addressed in a variety of ways by
members of the community, all stemming from their own definition of steampunk. Cory Gross, an observer of the subculture, suggests that steampunk
is a form of kitsch, as defined by aesthetic philosopher Celeste Olalquiaga:
"a failed commodity that continually speaks of all it has ceased to be—a
virtual image, existing in the impossibility of fully being."[21] As such, steampunk's "images" may be interpreted on a scale ranging from utopian to
dystopian—or, using the terms that Gross proposes, from Nostalgic Steampunk to Melancholic Steampunk. The positive extreme, Nostalgic Steampunk,
sees the genre as a romanticized optimistic belief in the glories of science
and technology that ignores the past injustices and the ripple effect of those
injustices into the present, while Melancholic's opposing stance leaves room
for a more nuanced interpretation of steampunk's historical basis, where
Gross writes that "we see the corruption, the decadence, the imperialism,
the poverty and the intrigue."[22]

Other steampunks, like communications professor Dru Pagliassotti,
define steampunk by striking a balance between Gross's Nostalgic and Melancholic extremes. On her blog *The Mark of Ashen Wings*, Pagliassotti proposes that steampunk is a postmodern aesthetic stance characterized "by
its use of irony, intertextuality, pastiche, and bricolage." She argues that
steampunk, though inspired by aspects of Victorian culture, uses this culture
in an intentionally ironic and playful manner through the loose interpretation

and subversion of "Victorian-inspired" fashion, the lighthearted imitation of Victorian speech and mannerisms, the re-creation of modern technology using nineteenth-century standards, and an overall reinterpretation of the Victorian age as it could have never existed: "It's a future created through the benign miracles of science and technology, absent poverty, pollution, inequality, and ignorance."[23] Adding to this multilayered description, Pagliassotti observes that the steampunk aesthetic, while optimistic, is highly aware of the historical and social ills of the Victorian Age: "Of course, this ideal future cannot be viewed today without a sense of irony and an awareness of the many ways in which that dream went awry, from the misuse of science and technology to the apparent ineradicability of prejudice and hatred."[24] Pagliassotti's postmodern definition gives steampunk a mutability that is distinctive because it defies strict categorization.

At the same time, this malleability of the steampunk subculture invites a variety of opinions ranging across the political spectrum. Pagliassotti's assertion that steampunk allows for a mix of influences, for instance, implies that the historical baggage of these influences is actively rejected from today's style. She suggests the "punk" suffix implies a liberal-progressive undertone, but stops short of claiming that steampunk is a radical movement.[25] Defining steampunk as a postmodern subculture connected to punk politics or philosophy, though, creates the opportunity for steampunks to reclaim dress associated with imperialist projects by subverting its original meaning.

The Catastrophone Orchestra and Arts Collective of New York City fiercely defends steampunk's progressive stance in their creative manifesto: "Steampunk rejects the myopic, nostalgia-drenched politics so common among 'alternative' cultures," and criticizes the lack of punk in this subculture.[26] In the British sci-fi magazine *Matrix Online*, contributor Martin McGarth passionately expresses steampunk's subversive politics by promoting the appropriation of Victorian aesthetic in order to criticize its past connotations. McGarth explicitly associates the rebelliousness of steampunk with punk music:

> This tendency to take the detritus of Victorian society, the leftover threads and scraps of thought discarded by geniuses and madmen and the predictions of half-forgotten prophets of the steam age and reconstruct them as grand theory is essential and is what defines steampunk as something more than just science fiction in a Victorian suit of clothes. Like the three-chord rockers of the late seventies, steampunk takes elements of the cozy and the safe—what could be more genteel and secure than the world of the Victorian gentleman—and kicks them firmly in the bollocks, upsetting our expectations, making utterly free with the impossible

and outlandish and regurgitating the trash, bile and sewage of an era that was, after all, built on slavery, exploitation and the raw force of arms.[27]

In contrast, Evelyn Kriete and her fellow moderators on *Steamfashion* argue that the term "punk" in steampunk has no political connotations at all: "There is clearly no link between the people of a steampunk setting and members of the punk subculture (simply because the environment that produced our modern 'punks' did not exist during the steam age). For all practical purposes, the 'punk' in steampunk is a cute turn of phrase used because it sounds interesting and exciting, without any deeper meaning than that."[28]

Ultra-nationalist interpretations also exist, such as that of *Stormfront*, a white supremacy forum that applauds steampunk for celebrating the glories of "white culture." One poster named Stolypin praises steampunk for maintaining a Western-dominated world: "I often imagine an alternative world in which the fashions, architecture and racial mindset (white superiority was rarely, if ever, questioned) are eternally as they were in the early Twentieth Century."[29] Fortunately, these sentiments come from a marginal group in the steampunk community.[30] Overall, as Pagliasotti and McGarth's statements reveal, the most prominent steampunks defend the aesthetic movement as a progressive one, denouncing both colonialism and its aftereffects. Yet steampunk is easily politically appropriated by various groups. Subculture researcher David Muggleton explains that this is a common characteristic of postmodern subcultures: subculture is "not (or not only) a style or fashion, but an attitude" that is both individually dynamic and ideologically ambiguous: This ambiguity "does not necessarily mean that subculturalists [reject] specific and coherent values, only that they are more likely to identify (and attribute to Others) those [values] that they do not hold."[31]

As a result, political interpretations of steampunk fashion have been mixed, even while it is evolving toward a liberal tradition that eschews the past imperialist connotations associated with Victorian clothing. However vocal the liberal-progressive faction is, this evolution remains unfinished: representation of progressive ideals are still not fully expressed. Liberal steampunks maintain that punk influences in their clothing indicate a critical questioning of the hegemonic narratives of past histories. Given the broad definition of steampunk fashion, however, a steampunk does not need to show any punk influence in his or her dress to be visually recognized as steampunk by peers. But politics can be more difficult to accurately ascertain than fashion. Perhaps that is why liberal steampunks (particularly white steampunks) are so adamant about expressing their political opinions to those outside the subculture: to prevent conservative assumptions about their political identities.

Steampunk's relationship to its problematic history and utopian ideals is neither straightforward nor all-encompassing; this may be symptomatic of the birthing pains of a subculture as participants try to sort out their ideological claims. There is, though, one crucial parallel between steampunk and Orientalism that links them in an unexpected way. Art historian Holly Edwards notes that in the evolution of Orientalism, its use by Victorians was more than just a gathering of prejudices against a foreign Other but, "in this era of transformation, the Orient is a useful construct that enabled people to both revisit the past and to envision the future. It allowed people to declare their convictions and affirm their values. It offered opportunities to imagine, vicariously experience, and ultimately incorporate new options into their lives. Thus, the Orient was both a tool for self-scrutiny and a foil to social change."[32]

Likewise, steampunk has been used as a construct that participants praise for the exact same reason. In the case of Orientalism, Victorians used it as a mirror that reflected whatever they wanted to believe about the "Other"—and that, in turn, revealed their own discriminatory beliefs, in all their romance and racism. Steampunk serves as another, postmodern reflector, a two-way mirror that allows the modern viewer to gaze at an unassuming Victorian past while seeing the flaws in themselves. The modern steampunks embrace both nostalgia and revisionism in their art—perhaps transforming this cultural trend into a form of Occidentalism. Nevertheless, in the same way that all good interpretations of science fiction are more than just the images and props of the genre, steampunk is likewise a tool used to express a message, but does not serve as the message itself. What exactly that message will be and how it will progress over time is debatable, but questions about its political status and its historical expression are certainly ones not being easily ignored or dismissed.

Part III: De-Centering Steampunk— From Hegemony to Diversity

While Diana has explored the historical context and political impulse of steampunk, this analysis has thus far centered around a specific experience: that of the colonizer. This is no surprise. Steampunk harks back to a time when the Industrial Revolution had just opened up worlds of possibility. Trade and exploration was at its zenith, and the bourgeoisie was on the rise, toppling the traditional aristocracy in a sort of social revolution. Nostalgia, though, is not the only reason for steampunk's popularity. The neo-Victorian aesthetic gives men more sartorial possibilities and women rediscover a joy in dressing up in full skirts and blouses, countering today's North American culture that exhorts men to limit their fashions and women to "dress less in more places."[33]

It is, however, disingenuous to say that steampunk proponents are only dressing up for the sake of personal adornment. Though the aesthetic is variously described as "the modern world through the lens of the Victorian,"[34] in fashion, the reverse is true: we reproduce the Victorian aesthetic through the lens of our postmodern world, aware that we are pulling from the past, working with what we have learnt of possibilities today. White steampunks, while loudly denouncing racism, still center the colonizer's experience through their affinity for the fashions of conquest.

The elements missing from the conversation are the varied voices of the colonized. In mostly-white settings, SoC who are cognizant of their minority status are reminded of the current Western hegemony. Though white steampunks may protest by claiming inclusivity, SoC may not feel the same way.[35] We must ask ourselves then, what our fashion choices signify, particularly as SoC adopting a reinterpretation of Western historical dress.

As Ella Shohat and Robert Stam point out with numerous examples in *Unthinking Eurocentrism* that colonialism and imperialism can manifest in subtle—yet powerful—ways, particularly through media imperialism.[36] Barbara Bush, in examining the effects of imperialism, notes that it evokes a "psychology of inferiority and dependency, a problematic internalization of Western superiority."[37] Thus, steampunk may present another example of assimilation into Western hegemonic culture. Colonial clothing, drawn from the era of Empire, which propagated the White Man's Burden as a social good for colonized countries, can prove that even a visible minority can integrate into a white-dominant subculture, simply by adopting the appropriate costuming.[38]

When we do this, we may efface any ethnic or cultural baggage that comes with our racial markers. North American minorities may dismiss racial anxiety ("I've never thought about it that way; I was brought up to think of myself as [North American]"), sometimes ignoring very real ramifications of internalized racism. In a steampunk context, the claim that race doesn't matter—that the clothes make the person—makes it easy to avoid racial baggage. One can give up being Asian for a while, in favor of clockwork and the straight lines of Victorian fashion, and no one is going to ask why an Asian is dressed up as a European aristocrat. This may be especially true for minorities who do not grow up relating to their ethnic origins, but still feel alienated by the mainstream culture on account of their race or geographic heritage. Steampunk gives its participants that niche to efface their anxieties and fit in somewhere, especially with other cool, creative types who have the gumption to eschew current fashions in exchange for old ones. Trend analysts Annette Lynch and Mitchell Strauss put it best: "If the culture you live in doesn't provide a place for you in its system of recognition, find a cultural system that does!"[39]

However, just as costuming can signify a desire to blend in, so too can it be simply drawing from the aesthetic to add to one's "multiplicity of stylistic identity,"[40] as subculture researcher David Muggleton notes. While Muggleton believes this multiplicity is a problem, it can be a form of fashion-able syncretism, a natural occurrence when people come into contact with each other.[41] Shohat and Stam remind us, "virtually all countries and regions are multi-cultural in a purely descriptive sense."[42] Although we may be able to see an imbalance of power in-group dynamics, apolitical individuals do not necessarily feel the same, and simply draw from what is available. This pastiche is a result of many factors—colonizers coming and going, traders exchanging cultural artifacts, individuals thinking, "that looks neat and I'd like to try it."

Image 12.3. Ay-leen the Peacemaker in Asian steampunk dress.

Outside North America, in spaces that are not predominantly white, things get more complicated. Cultural appropriation has been of great debate within North America, and we note that peoples from Eastern countries, particularly those considered "Third World," adopt Western clothing as a bid for legitimacy on the political mainstage.[43] It brings up interesting questions for former colonies: what does an SoC signify when wearing the clothes of the culture that once colonized his or her country? Perhaps it is a subtle acknowledgment that despite seceding from the shores and governments of previously colonized lands, traces of perceived Western superiority still remain, embodied in the fashion choices of its former subjects. It might also be a critique of European culture,[44] wearing the clothes of former superiors, aspiring to the same level on the hierarchy that they were forced to participate in. Perhaps steampunk fashion is something even more superficial—a consumer-driven culture isn't limited to North America, after all—it may just be another part of recreational costuming. The act of creation from available materials, old materials, even, is appealing to many steampunk participants. Recycling old fashions, re-tooling toy guns and helmets, piecing together historical bric-a-brac signifies a creative mind, even if they look odd out of context.

Thus, in the case of cultural diversity, the most relevant issues in steampunk subculture are the all-pervasive privilege and the resulting notion of Eurocentrism.

Privilege—the luxury of being able to ignore oppressive behavior and institutional systems simply because they do not affect the privileged person's experience—manifests in positive, negative, and indifferent ways as indicated in Parts I and II. While there is no need for over-policing, steampunks should be encouraged to engage in questions of racism and representation, especially when the trap of "not noticing" color exists, a mindset which does not lend SoC any power to speak for themselves politically and only pays lip service to multiculturalism by inviting SoC to participate for the sake of visual diversity.[45] Steampunks will inevitably run into conversations about race, as the inspiration for the style, subculture, and subgenre stem from a time of colonization and rampant racism. The conversations become more important while taking into account postmodern societies which purport to be multicultural while individuals negotiate racial and cultural identities on a personal level. While certainly not all SoC feel the same anxieties brought on by racial or ethnic factors, one should not assume all SoC experiences are the same based on interactions with a select few, as suggested by the Racism Bingo Card.[46] Steampunks at large are quick to denounce imperialism, yet it is telling that few ask why participants are overwhelmingly white.

So far, steampunk has also manifested itself as being Eurocentric—that is, centering the subculture on Western expressions. Merely connecting steampunk to the West is a limitation that prevents SoC from self-representation within the subculture.[47] The alternate history aspect of the steampunk ethos—reliving the past with all the knowledge of the present—can prevent this by rejecting the notion that steampunk begins and ends with Victorianism or idealization of the Victorian Era; without this rejection, the result would be a perverse Occidentalism that at best renders the imperialist era quaint, and at worst, ignores the erasure of the colonized's experiences. Lofty dreams imagine the imperialist era as it could have been, but dreams, too, are informed by reality's baggage. It is irresponsible in today's cultural mixing to shrug shoulders and say that there is none. We are tied to each other through the Internet, travel, trade, conflicts, and shared issues,[48] as well as mutual love of clockwork gears, fancy fashions, and joys of craftsmanship.

Image 12.4. Monique Poirer in native steampunk dress, by Jessica Coen.

Steampunks reclaim the Victorian aesthetic through the modification of contemporary fashions, as bricoleurs who simulate all the best things we admire of the past that binds and echoes in our lives today. Few other subcultures present such an opportunity for minorities to assert our heritages. This is not to say we should limit ourselves to fashions of ethnic origins, but also to participate and carve spaces for ourselves, where we do not wear Western fashions as the colonized, but syncretize fashions of the East and the West as equals. We steampunks may struggle to express our anti-imperialist ideals vocally, but the message does not always come through in what we wear. No matter how well-meaning, neither the clothes nor the subculture are the message. What we do, say, create, and leave behind will be the ultimate legacy that will speak for us.

Notes

1. Lavie Tidhar, "Steampunk," *The Internet Review of Science Fiction*, February 2005, http://www.irosf.com/q/zine/article/10114.
2. Waldemar Horwat, "Burning Man Treehouse," 2007, http://images.burning-man.com/
index.cgi?image=31106.
3. John Brownlee, "Meet Mr. Steampunk," June 29, 2007, http://www.wired.com/culture/design/news/2007/06/vonslatt.
4. Stillof, "Steam Wars: A New Hope," Sillof's Workshop, http://www.sillof.com/C-Steampunk-SW.htm. The steampunk artist Stillof has created several Star Wars™ figurines in the steampunk style that can be found on Stillof's Workshop blog. Stillof's work has even been recognized on *The Official Stars Wars Blog*: http://starwarsblog.starwars.com/index.php/2008/04/11/star-wars-steampunk-figures/.
5. This list of steampunk categories come from the following two sources: Lily Bulloff, "Steam Gear: A Fashionable Approach to the Lifestyle," *SteamPunk Magazine*, Issue 2 (2007), http://www.steampunkmagazine.com/pdfs/SPM2-printing.pdf; and Evelyn Kriete and G. D. Falksen, "The Steampunk Style Test," http://www.helloquizzy.com/tests/the-steampunk-style-test.
6. Damon Poeter, "Steampunk's Subculture Revealed," *San Francisco Chronicle*, July 6, 2008, http://www.sfgate.com/cgi-bin/article.cgi?f=/c/a/2008/07/06/LVL-211GOO2.DTL.
7. Bulloff, 11.
8. E. M. Collingham, *Imperial Bodies* (Malden, MA: Polity, 2001), 66.
9. Ibid.
10. Ibid., 90–91.
11. Ibid., 90. Collingham notes in his description of British head gear in India that goggles were sometimes used to protect the Anglo wearer from the harsh climate, and he includes a colonialist's reference to a Captain Ponsonby wearing "green spectacles" to shield his eyes. Though an obscure connection, this still places the steampunk's juxtaposition of utilitarian gear and everyday civilian Victorian attire within actual colonial context.

12. Edward W. Said, *Orientalism: 25th Anniversary Edition* (New York: Vintage Books, 1994), 3.

13. Abney Park, http://www.abneypark.com/2008/index.htm.

14. Examples of steampunk belly dancing can be found on the Kiss and Tell belly dancing blog, http://thegypsykiss.com/blog/2008/11/22/steampunk-belly-dance-video-collection/. Workshops using the fusion of belly dancing and steampunk have also been featured in at Belly Dance Academy in Buffalo, New York, and by participants in the steamfashion LiveJournal community.

15. Editors of the *Gatehouse Gazette*, "Victorientalism," http://www.ottens.co.uk/gatehouse/victoriental.php (emphasis added).

16. Said, *Orientalism*, 170.

17. Holly Edwards, *Noble Dreams, Wicked Pleasures: Orientalism in America, 1870–1930* (Princeton, NJ: Princeton University Press, 2000), 34.

18. Edwards, *Noble Dreams, Wicked Pleasures*, 23, 34.

19. Christine Riding, "Travellers and Sitters: The Orientalist Portrait" in *The Lure of the East: British Orientalist Painting,* ed. Nicholas Tromans (New Haven, CT: Yale University Press, 2008), 53.

20. Punk's appropriation of existing race and class divides has been noted by Daniel Traber in his study of Los Angeles punks. See Daniel S. Traber, *Whiteness, Otherness, and the Individualism Paradox from Huck to Punk* (New York: Palgrave Macmillan, 2007).

21. Celeste Olalquiaga, *The Artificial Kingdom: A Treasury of the Kitsch Experience* (New York: Pantheon Books, 1998), 28–29.

22. Cory Gross, "Varieties of Steampunk Experience," *SteamPunk Magazine* 1 (2007), http://www.steampunkmagazine.com/pdfs/SPM1-printing.pdf, 65.

23. Dru Pagliassotti, "Does Steampunk Have Politics?" *Ashen Wings,* February 11, 2009, http://ashenwings.com/marks/2009/02/11/does-steampunk-have-politics/.

24. Ibid.

25. Dru Pagliassotti, "Does Steampunk Have an Ideology?" *Ashen Wings,* February 13, 2009, http://ashenwings.com/marks/2009/02/13/does-steampunk-have-politics/.

26. Catastrophone Orchestra and Arts Collective of New York City, "What, then, is Steampunk?" *SteamPunk Magazine* 1 (2007), http://www.steampunkmagazine.com/pdfs/SPM1-printing.pdf, 5.

27. Martin McGarth, "Steaming Celluloid," June 30, 2008, http://www.matrix-online.net/bsfa/website/matrixonline/Matrix_Features_3.aspx.

28. Evelyn Kriete, et al., "steamfashion," *Live Journal,* http://community.live-journal.com/steamfashion/profile. This definition is used both on the steamfashion community Web site on Live Journal and its sister-site on Facebook, http://www.facebook.com/group.php?gid=46292697399.

29. Stolypin, comment made on the forum entry "Steampunk! A White Aesthetic Movement," *Stormfront,* September 23, 2008, http://www.stormfront.org/forum/showthread.php?t=524908&page=2.

30. While researching for a previous essay on the concept of British Colonial America in steampunk, we Googled the phrase "America in steampunk literature." We were unsettled to discover one of the first results linked was to the forums of the white nationalist group, *Stormfront*, specifically for a thread entitled "Steampunk: A White Aesthetic Movement?" that was 18 pages long and still active at the time

of the writing of this article: http://www.stormfront.org/forum/showthread.php?t=524908.

31. David Muggleton, *Inside Subculture: The Postmodern Meaning of Style* (New York: Berg, 2002), 125.

32. Edwards, *Noble Dreams, Wicked Pleasures*, 16.

33. Heather Corinna, "How Easy It Isn't," *RH Reality Check,* July 24, 2009, http://www.rhrealitycheck.org/blog/2009/07/24/how-easy-it-isnt.

34. This is a paraphrase of the definition is used both on the steamfashion community Web site on *Live Journal*, http://community.livejournal.com/steam-fashion/profile, and its sister-site on Facebook, http://www.facebook.com/group.php?gid=46292697399.

35. This statement does not refer to the conflict between what we wear and what we are, but to claims of inclusivity by white steampunks, which leads SoC to question why, if steampunk is really inclusive, we wear "white" fashions. As a marginalized group, SoC are the community audience as well as the wearers.

36. Ella Shohat and Robert Stam, *Unthinking Eurocentrism* (London: Routledge, 1994), 31.

37. Barbara Bush, *Imperialism and Postcolonialism* (London: Pearson Education Ltd., 2006), 135.

38. Shohat and Stam, *Unthinking Eurocentrism*, 254.

39. Annette Lynch and Mitchell D. Strauss, *Changing Fashion* (New York: Berg, 2007), 39.

40. Muggleton, *Inside Subculture*, 96.

41. Shohat and Stam, *Unthinking Eurocentrism*, 43.

42. Ibid., 5.

43. Carla Jones and Ann Marie Leshkowich, "Globalization of Asian Dress," in *Re-Orienting Fashion,* eds. Sandra Niesson, Ann Marie Leshkowich, and Carla Jones (New York: Berg, 2003), 11.

44. Jonathan Hart, "Translating and Resisting Empire," in *Borrowed Power: Essays on Cultural Appropriation*, eds. Bruce Ziff and Pratima V. Rao (New Brunswick, NJ: Rutgers University Press, 1997), 144.

45. Shohat and Stam use the example of Benetton advertisements in *Unthinking Eurocentrism*, 47.

46. Or any of its similar items. A complete set of -Ism Bingo Cards can be found here: http://www.flickr.com/photos/lizhenry/3185596306/in/set-72157612897466679/.

47. Shohat and Stam, *Unthinking Eurocentrism*, 342.

48. Edward Said, *Culture and Imperialism* (New York: Vintage Books, 1994), 37.

Chapter 13

DIY Fashion and Going *Bust*

Wearing Feminist Politics in the Twenty-First Century

Jo Reger

> She stands on the street posing for the Fashion Nation feature in *Bust*,
> a magazine geared toward young contemporary feminists. Her hair
> is streaked multiple colors and worn in a ponytail. Her homemade
> green dress has an overlay of dollar-bill printed material. On her feet
> are Converse tennis shoes and around her neck is a necklace made
> of brass knuckles. From her ears hang white plastic pistol earrings.[1]

Longtime feminist activist Letty Cottin Pogrebin addressed young feminists
at the 2002 Veteran Feminists of America conference by saying, "Being
able to bare your midriff . . . is fine as an expression, but it doesn't mean
things are going to change."[2] Feminist views on fashion range from adopting
dominant dress codes as a political tactic, to disavowing fashion as oppressive and patriarchal, to seeing fashion as something that can be selectively
incorporated and empowering.[3] In this chapter, I discuss how contemporary
feminists embrace and reclaim aspects of femininity and sexuality as a form
of empowerment.[4] To explore the idea of fashion and feminism, I draw on
three theoretical frameworks and related key concepts: fashion theory and
the concept of oppositional dress, feminist theory and the embodiment of the

political, and tactical repertoires as articulated by social movement theorists. Using a content analysis of *Bust* magazine, I argue that the contemporary feminists featured in *Bust* magazine are creating and embracing an oppositional fashion and reclaim femininity as empowering.

Bust runs a reoccurring section on fashion and carries a variety of articles and advertisements related to clothing, jewelry, and general issues of style.[5] I selected the magazine because of its visibility within feminist networks and its attention to fashion and dress. By adopting a style that resists mainstream consumer culture, privileges individuality, and incorporates sexuality, women profiled in *Bust* make dress and appearance a form of political resistance. However, this resistance through fashion is made problematic with the commodification of style and the perception (among some) that dress is an inadequate (and therefore controversial) form of feminist activism. I first discuss how various theories address contemporary feminist appearance and beauty norms, and then examine the relationship between feminism and fashion.

Social Movements, Protest, and Fashion

Social movements at their core are oppositional in nature, and social movement actors are seen as engaging in forms of resistance for the sake of social change. Social movement scholars have struggled to define what qualifies as a social protest.[6] Some argue that opposition to the state is what matters,[7] while others propose that changing participant identities and culture, and state policies are desired outcomes.[8] Nancy Whittier argues that political activism is legitimated on multiple levels because inequality operates at the levels of individual subjectivity, culture, and policy.[9]

Drawing on Whittier's multilevel analysis, I argue that dress as a form of political protest blends individual subjectivity and culture by signifying one's membership in a group or subculture.[10] In fact, "dress is a subculture's most powerful means of communication."[11] The importance of community building through oppositional dress has been documented in both social movement and fashion studies. Marginalized groups in society such as black Americans, members of techno culture, and particularly youth use dress as a way to "make the community stronger, thus empowering its members."[12] For example, gays and lesbians wear rainbow-colored clothing and jewelry, black triangles, or equal signs (=) as a way of signifying that they belong to a LGBTQ "family" or are "in the know."[13] Yet by these examples, if dress is clearly such an important political component of oppositional cultures and social movements, then why hasn't it been taken more seriously?

One reason is that fashion is traditionally linked to the feminine as a pursuit that engages mostly women, where "the feminine" is devalued or easily dismissed.[14] Samantha Holland argues that fashion is seen as frivolous and anti-intellectual, and historically women's dress was seen as a form of wasteful consumption.[15] Despite the view of fashion as inconsequential, dress (defined as modifications to the body), has embedded in it signifiers of power and resistance.[16] One of the most powerful ways to see the importance of dress is through the construction of anti-fashion or oppositional dress. Oppositional dress takes on mainstream society by rejecting, parodying, satirizing, or neglecting contemporary appearance norms.[17] Reinventing or creating an oppositional style has the ability to challenge all sorts of societal norms including those of propriety, class position, sexuality, racial-ethnic, and economic status. In particular, oppositional dress can challenge gender norms, both feminine and masculine. In this chapter, I focus on how feminist dress reclaims and reinvents norms of femininity.

Feminism, Femininity, and the Politics of Fashion

Many feminist scholars are concerned that traditional and often corporate-driven beauty norms disempower women by sapping their energy, time, and money. While women can gain some limited hedonic power through dress,[18] Holland's study of women and dress found many respondents concluded that to be "traditionally attractive you have to be malleable and not independent."[19] Some feminist critiques of fashion view feminine dress as primarily a form of enslavement, displaying women's bodies for a male gaze and giving them a false sense of power.[20] Part of this sense of enslavement is the idea that women are forced by social dictates to adopt certain fashions.[21] For instance, Adrienne Rich argues high heels and feminine dress are in the same categories as purdah, rape, veiling, and foot binding.[22] This perspective was reflected in the 1968 Miss America pageant protest by feminists who threw objects of female "oppression" such as high heels, bras, and girdles into a "freedom trash can."

Many of the debates within the women's movement focused on notions of political efficacy. Scholars document how more liberal feminists, represented by such women as Betty Friedan, clashed with younger or more radical feminists over the issue of appearance in the 1960s and 1970s.[23] Radical feminists often adopted a style that included jeans, loose shirts, no bras, and no makeup. This "natural" style was based on the political ideology that women were beautiful without unnecessary endeavors or patriarchal adornment. Other feminists believed this political fashion countered the goals of the movement and described it as "scruffy," wondering why women would go to lengths to make themselves ugly.[24] For feminists like Friedan, presenting oneself fashionably and attractively was a tactic reflecting the belief that the women's movement fit within dominant mainstream society. The liberal feminist goal was for women to align with cultural norms of feminine dress, (i.e., pumps, pantyhose, and suits) as a way fit into and make change within institutions.

As the media picked up on the radical feminists' politicized appearance, the idea of a feminist uniform became a part of the popular culture. Fashion scholar Kate McCarthy describes how women coming into feminism in the 1960s dealt with the matter of appearance:

> One approach to this problem [the critique of fashion by feminists], of course, is to empower women to quit making such inscriptions on their bodies. Those of us who grew into feminism in the 1970s are familiar with this effort, often caricatured as mandates, to disavow lipstick, shaving, and ideally male sexual partners.[25]

While some followed those mandates, radical feminist dress was disavowed by other feminists who felt it sent the wrong message, and by the larger public who saw radical style as evidence of the "man-hating" deviant identities of all feminists. Despite these divisions, all feminists were stereotyped as disavowing or ignoring fashion. This led *New York Times* fashion writer Ingrid Sischy to conclude that fashion will continue outside of feminism because feminists' views are "knee jerk and programmatic."[26]

Contemporary feminists continue this history of politicizing fashion. In their article, "Feminism and Femininity: Or How We Learned to Stop Worrying and Love the Thong," authors Jennifer Baumgardner and Amy Richards argue that girlie culture, one aspect of twenty-first century feminism, reclaims what past periods of (primarily radical) feminism have discarded. Girlie culture revalues femininity and embraces "girlieness as well as power."[27] Baumgardner and Richards explain that "Girlies' motivations are along the same lines of gay men in Chelsea calling each other 'queer' or black men and women using the term 'nigga.'"[28] Contemporary feminists engage in the politics of fashion through the concept of embodied politics as a creative act of resistance to disrupt power.[29] Here the female body is a site of both oppression and resistance "where cultural expectations about gender are rehearsed but also, at least, potentially, manipulated and resisted."[30] One form of embodied resistance is a process of reclaiming what mainstream culture has defined as femininity and feminine sexuality, an act that Judith Taylor describes as taking ownership of group stereotypes rather than simply conforming to them.[31] The body can therefore become a site of resisting cultural norms by reclaiming femininity through fashion. This differs from simply following cultural norms for acceptance and instead is the intentional creation and reaffirmation of femininity through dress. These politicized statements not only serve to take back the feminine in a reinvented and empowered manner, but can also serve to establish membership in a feminist community. Therefore, the relationship between fashion and femininity makes dress and appearance grounds for feminist ideology and activism.

Oppositional Feminist Fashion

So what is political about wearing a spandex dress made out of dollar-bill printed fabric, Converse tennis shoes, a necklace made of brass knuckles, and white pistol-shaped earrings? The outfit is a DIY (Do It Yourself) creation—

FASHION NATION
Kerin Weinberg
Student/Music Promoter
PHOTO BY SHANNON SINCLAIR

HOW WOULD YOU describe your style? I like to refer to myself as a biological drag queen—I dress like a drag queen even though I was born a woman. **Tell me about this outfit.** I made the money dress myself. I bought the fabric for about $12 at Spandex House, one of my favorite fabric stores in the garment district. It's two floors of spandex fabric! The dress underneath is from H&M; it was probably around $20. The shoes are Chuck Taylors. I hand-applied 2700 Swarovski crystals to them. It took me eight hours to do, over the course of a week. **How did you make the shoes?** Well, I'd rhinestoned a bunch of things—my cell phone, my iPod. Then I realized that Converse are made out of canvas and they'd make a good surface. I had to buy two ten-gross of rhinestones, and I glued them on with E6000 Adhesive. The shoes only cost $30, but the crystals cost about $165. They're spaced really close together; you can't see the shoe at all. **What about your jewelry?** The jewelry is a mixture of H&M and Girlprops. The brass knuckles [worn as pendant] were given to me as a gift from the owner of Made Clothing. The hoop earrings are either from H&M or Girlprops; they're white and plastic and probably cost about $2. I'm also wearing earrings with guns, because white plastic pistols hanging from your ears definitely lets people know you're dangerous. DEBBIE STOLLER

Image 13.1. *Looks* feature, *Bust*, Fall 2004.

a homemade dress and jewelry. At the same time this outfit refutes beauty norms (Converse tennis shoes versus high heels) and subverts consumer culture (using fabric with a dollar-bill motif). Symbols of physical power and sexuality—a tight bodice combined with a brass knuckles necklace and pistol earrings—further upend the expectations of feminine beauty. This carefully constructed outfit illustrates how aspects of femininity have been reappropriated and combined with feminism to create a look that defines the wearer as different from other women who are following dominant fashion norms. In the pages of *Bust*, the wearer is portrayed as a self-styled woman and not a fashion "don't." She plays with feminine norms without wholesale adoption (or rejection) of them. Her outfit is meant to resonate with the reader as both representing an individual *and* an identifiable collective feminist style.

Many of the contemporary feminists profiled in *Bust* use a consciously constructed look as a way to live out, on an everyday basis, their politics and ideologies.[32] As such it becomes a signifier of their feminist beliefs. Based on the content analysis, three themes emerge that incorporate these beliefs; the focus on individuality, sexualized dress, and the resistance of consumer culture.

Focusing on Individuality

One paradox of feminist fashion exemplified by *Bust*, is that while this dress creates an intentional and oppositional collective style (vintage, funky, and/or DIY); it does so in a way that values individuality. Gwendolyn O'Neal notes that oppositional subcultures on the margins often resist the status quo through clothing norms. While it may appear all members of a group are dressing the same, O'Neal argues that in fact what the members are doing is making a statement as to who they are as individuals.[33] This dynamic is captured by classical sociologists who argue it is only the collective that allows us to act individually.[34] By acting collectively, contemporary feminists complicate the dominant standards of fashion and appearance while embracing their individualism.

Feminist fashion encompasses a variety of individual styles and the women profiled in *Bust* have a wide range of style descriptors including "'70s scholar," "Dyke-alicious," "Art Nouveau punk," and "Over-the-top glamour, 1950s thrift shop, and couture." In the words of one profiled woman:

> Be comfortable in your clothes. Wear it like you own it and not the other way around. Don't be afraid to mix and match. And definitely never walk out of a store with the exact same outfit you saw in the window.[35]

This focus on individuality and dress align with scholars' descriptions of contemporary feminism as focused on everyday activism and cultural change.[36]

By prizing both collectivity and individuality through contemporary style, dress becomes a way to create community by constructing a feminist identity that seeks to unsettle dominant ways of seeing femininity. Feminist fashion is both accommodationist by accepting certain in-group community aesthetics, and resistant by refusing to completely abide by dominant femininity and fashion norms. It is interesting to note that one Asian woman describes her look as "Dragon lady disguised as Japanese bubblegum pop" claiming not only her individuality (complete with pink boa) but also reclaiming (and acknowledging) racist stereotypes of Asian women in her assertion of self.[37] What is unclear here, as many of the *Bust* outfits portray, is how the viewer understands the wearer's intent, highlighting the tension between refuting and reinforcing stereotypical dress. This tension is particularly apparent in sexualized dress.

Image 13.2. *Looks* feature, *Bust*, Dec. 2004/Jan. 2005.

Sexualizing Dress

Sexualized dress has long been a fashion staple; however it is growing increasingly more popular in the dominant culture. Stephanie Rosenbloom notes that Halloween has become a time for young women to "go bad for a day" with costumes that are more "strip club than storybook."[38] Ariel Levy points to the same phenomenon happening in women and girls' everyday fashion, and "Girls Gone Wild" antics where women bare their breasts or make out with heterosexual girlfriends in order to win a baseball cap or appear in a video.[39] However, the move toward hypersexualized clothing is more than a trend pushing women to present themselves for the male gaze. By politicizing sexuality as a part of femininity and feminism, contemporary feminist fashion is unabashedly sexual. The focus of the gaze is turned inward with women expressing their sexuality for their own gratification rather than male approval. As with individualized style, however, the intention of sexualized dress is subject to different interpretations by the wearer and the viewer. In creating sexualized fashion, there are two forces at work: reacting to perceptions of earlier feminists and reclaiming one's own sexuality from the dominant mainstream.

In *Jane Sexes It Up,* feminist scholar Merri Lisa Johnson writes that the goal for contemporary feminism is to press forward "sex-positive in a culture that demonizes sexuality, and sex-radical in a political movement that has been known to choose moral high grounds over low guttural sounds."[40] Yet Stephanie Gilmore reminds us that these struggles with conceptualizing and living out sexuality are not new. Sex and sexuality were debated issues in the so-called second wave from the infamous anti-lesbian "lavender menace" in the National Organization for Women (NOW) to the claim by Radicalesbians that women should forgo sex with men for true liberation. At the same time, Gilmore notes, NOW allowed ads for *Playgirl* and *Venus* magazines at early conventions and heterosexual members openly wrote about their desire and "kinky sex wishes."[41]

Despite the diversity of 1960s and 1970s feminist approaches to sex and sexuality, contemporary feminist activists and scholars often presume these feminist generations were anti-sex and see their own youth-oriented actions as sex-positive. To that end, many feminists in *Bust* incorporate a sense of sexiness into their dress. In the *Bust* profiles several of the women are dressed in ways that can be interpreted as sexual (e.g., fishnet stockings, camisoles, bustiers, short skirts, and shorts). For example Jamie, a designer, is profiled wearing a pair of knee-high boots, a see-through lace camisole, a pair of butt-hugging denim shorts, and white jacket tied with a bow at her neck. She says of her look, "I like to wear short shorts in the summer, together with a feminine blouse. It's professional, but fun."[42] Others describe their look with terms such as "flirty and feminine."[43] This sexualized way of dress, revealing the body and wearing lingerie as outerwear is done with a sense of play. As Kelsey, a young feminist in Johannesburg, South Africa comments, "My friends never know what I'm going to look like, because one day I'll be wearing baby dolls and the next, I'll be wearing Doc Martens."[44]

By adopting sexualized fashion, contemporary feminists incorporate sexiness into their appearances as a choice, while sidestepping the unequal sexual relationships between girls and boys, which strip girls of their own innate desires and sexuality.[45] Acting as subjects playing with being objects of sexuality, desire and sex become ways to state one's empowerment. As evidenced in the multitude of advertisements and features in *Bust*, being sex-positive through purchasing sex toys and openly discussing sexual desire and dysfunction is a part of a contemporary feminist sexual ethos.[46]

Resisting Consumer Culture

One of the main critiques of fashion is that it encourages women to consume goods, diminishes women's economic status, and supports capitalism and host of other evils including sweatshop labor and unfair trade practices.[47] One of the most evident ways oppositional fashion resists consumer culture is through buying clothes and jewelry as cheaply as possible. Frugal shopping is a mainstay of many of the women profiled in *Bust*. Almost all of the women profiled bought various pieces of clothing and shoes at thrift stores, resale shops, and street vendors. Many report that they also shop at discount or "big box" stores such as H&M, Target, and Kmart for their clothes. For example, a waitress and aspiring documentary filmmaker details where she purchased her outfit:

> I got the boots at the Salvation Army—on half price day—so they were like $2. I've had the skirt for like four years; I think I got it in Italy. The belt I've had since I was 13. The red shirt is from the 40s; a friend's mother gave it to me. The jacket I bought in a flea market on the Lower East Side for $1. I got the tights in Italy too. The bag I got at a yard sale.[48]

It is tempting to see this trend toward frugal shopping as solely the outcome of students or young women starting their careers purchasing what they can afford. While this might be the case for many of those profiled, it is important to note that many of the women also wore individual pieces of clothes that ranged from $80 to $350, illustrating how thrifty shopping is more than finding affordable clothing. Thrifty shopping only functions as political resistance when one does not have to shop frugally. By mixing expensive pieces such as a silk blouse or custom-made jewelry with articles of clothing which cost less an $10 can be viewed as a political statement against a consumer culture that encourages the consumption of high-end (and high cost) outfits, regardless of the wearer's income.[49]

Many of the items purchased in thrift or discount stores were then reinvented as part of the DIY ethic. DIY is not a new phenomenon, but grew out of punk culture and the notion that creating something oneself (e.g., earrings from safety pins or reworking a garment) is a rejection of mainstream capitalist consumerist society.[50] Ricia Chansky adds that current trends in doing needle works (i.e., knitting, crocheting) is a reaction to the standardization of goods and can be seen historically throughout U.S. culture, notably the Arts and Crafts Movement of the late nineteenth and early twentieth centuries.[51] DIY as a leisure activity is only available to social classes who have the time and resources to create goods not necessary for daily survival.

In *Bust*, women alter their clothing in a variety of ways that range from adding more decoration (e.g., rhinestones or crystals) to remaking clothing so that it fits better or expresses their own style. Chansky writes:

> In a time when many women are actively trying to work against culturally regimented ideals of feminine beauty and have healthy body images, the act of creating one's own clothes is a way to have funky, expressive clothing that fits well despite the limitations of mass produced clothing that tends to be made for specific body sizes and shapes.[52]

Two of the profiled women, one a jewelry designer and the other an illustrator, describe how they reinvented their clothing:

> *Jo:* I made the jacket from the satin of an old 1930s wedding dress. The embroidery depicts the story of P. T. Barnum, who had a traveling circus in the 1800s. He was famous because he created a fake merman—half ape, half salmon.

> *Janet:* The Hello Kitty shirt I got from Target, I just cut off the neck. Luckily I fit into a children's size large.[53]

The importance of social class is particularly evident in the Jo's description of remaking the wedding dress into a unique silk jacket. Not only does it take resources to remake the dress (i.e., purchasing the gown, sewing equipment, and embroidery supplies) but it also takes leisure time to devote to learning the skill and doing the activity.

A third way in which consumer culture is resisted is through the selection of vintage clothing. One reason is that vintage clothing is often available at thrift and resale shops and is economical and easily altered. Dirty Martini, a burlesque performer, notes:

> I have an awful habit of collecting 1950s underwear; my clos-
> ets are stuffed with the most insane lingerie. It's hard to find a
> bra in double-D that's pretty these days but back then it was a
> common size.[54]

Purchasing vintage fashions can be seen as rejecting the constantly changing nature of fashion by focusing on a particular period of dress. When asked to describe their style, many of the women highlighted styles of different periods, such as 1920s flappers, "'70s proggy-rock bands," early Lucille Ball (1940s and 1950s) or in the fashion of eighteenth century women.

In sum, through thrift shopping, reinventing clothing, and adopting vintage styles, the feminists profiled in *Bust* create a form of embodied politics that rejects some of the norms of mainstream fashion and is identifiable to other feminists. This is not to argue that adopting alternative forms of dress means one is a feminist. However, dressing with a political intent to reject mainstream fashion and cultural norms and reclaim aspects of femininity is one tactic of contemporary feminism. However, for each of the ways in which dress is made feminist, through individuality, sexuality, and anti-consumerism, there arise a series of complicated outcomes.

Complications of Politicized Fashion

Refashioning appearance through feminist ideologies has multiple, complicated outcomes. When a way of presenting oneself is associated with a movement, it can serve in a positive manner by drawing together community.[55] There may also be negative unintended outcomes such as stereotyping or labeling the movement in a way that dissuades potential members. In the earlier periods of feminism, the "natural" fashion (e.g., no makeup, unshaven bodies, and peasant shirts with jeans) was picked up by the media as the uniform of all feminists and came to be viewed as a series of stereotypes (e.g., ugly, man hating, lesbian) that still repels some women (and men) from the movement today. Feminists also deal with these stereotypes, fearing that to adopt a fashionable appearance means to disavow "true" feminist activism. In the 1990s, Jennifer Allyn wrote of the tension between feminism and fashion:

> I felt a part of a new generation of feminists. We wanted to
> make room for play in our lives—dyeing our hair, shaving our
> legs, dressing in ways that made us happy—without sacrificing
> a commitment to political activism.[56]

Yet the concern is that when any subculture creates a new way of dressing, it can be commodified, co-opted, and absorbed into the larger culture. One example is how tattoos moved from being oppositional statements by prisoners, gang members, or the modern primitives movement to becoming fashionable in the mid-to-late 1990s. Sociologist Michael Messner writes that feminism itself has been commodified through commercials for products such as Nike which exhort women to "Just do it" as a form of true empowerment.[57] Feminist DIY trends are similarly commodified. In the early twenty-first century the "handcrafted" as well as the "vintage" look became a part of mainstream fashion. Popular brands Urban Outfitters, Ugg boots, and Ann Taylor all offered crocheted or vintage-style clothing in the early 2000s. This follows a similar trend in which hip-hop, slacker, grunge, and Goth styles went from subculture dress to becoming available at any mall.

These co-opted fashion trends are without overt political statements and may diffuse the political meaning in similarly styled clothes. Further complicating the politics of feminist fashion is the way in which crafting has become an entrepreneurial endeavor for many young feminists whose goods may be purchased and consumed without a political understanding of DIY or feminism. Feminist or progressive crafting fairs are common around the country and magazines such as *Bust* run regular features on how to do certain crafts. Debbie Stoller, the editor-in-chief of *Bust*, is also the author of several books on knitting with titles such as *Stitch 'N Bitch: The Knitter's Handbook* and *Stitch 'N Bitch Crochet: The Happy Hooker*. These books, with a feminist edge, are popular with many knitters who do not claim a feminist identity. When crafts (or crafting instructions) created as aspects of feminine resistance are sold in the mainstream, the feminist political impact can become diluted.

Why, then, is fashion featured so prominently in *Bust* magazine and evident in so many contemporary feminist communities, given the potential drawbacks and complications of using fashion as a feminist statement?

Whittier argues that as repression from the state shifts in form, so does the resistance from social movements.[58] The contemporary women's movement is made up of a generation of feminists who have seen the constant chipping away of the policy and legislative gains of earlier feminists. Title IX, reproductive rights, sexual harassment, and workplace protections have been subject to attack, particularly by the presidential administrations of George Bush, Sr. and George W. Bush, although these incursions threaten to continue. Whereas U.S. feminism has always worked to change cultural norms (e.g., the Bloomer "Turkish pants" movement of the 1800s), earlier generations of feminists had periods in which the political arena was more open to institutional change.[59] In a time when the institutional avenues of making change are not as open, contemporary feminists focus on culture as one way of making change. Fashion addresses in significant cultural ways the manner in which we understand femininity and masculinity in society. When women begin to alter their presentations of femininity, as represented in *Bust*, it has cultural significance. In examining the ways in which fashion is being constructed by some young feminists it is clear that a feminist identity is being asserted and ideologies on issues such as sexuality are being elaborated. The body becomes the location where larger issues are played out (i.e., sweatshop labor and anti-consumerist values) and where connections to other social movements are made.

By drawing on three theoretical frameworks seldom used together, feminist-, fashion-, and social-movement theory, this essay illustrates that dress is one of the most evident aspects of a cultural tactical toolbox that activists use.[60] The concepts of oppositional fashion and embodied politics are important in understanding movements that engage in lifestyle, culture-focused politics. Adding these concepts to a social movement vocabulary opens new directions of study, challenging the way in which we define political protest as well as how we understand the dynamics of tactics, innovation, cooptation, and commodification. By narrowly defining movement tactics and politics as focused only on policy efforts, scholars miss the opportunity to see how micro-level, personal action functions within social movement contexts. Vibrant debates about the current state and strategies of contemporary feminism continue, yet the evidence is clear that contemporary feminists present a form of social resistance written on the body and expressed both communally and individually, dynamics of social movement protest that are informative to scholars and important to activists.

In conclusion, I return to the feminist concerns exemplified by Letty Cottin Pogrebin's statement that opened this chapter: Does fashion create social change? Is contemporary feminism more than "baring one's midriff?" When a group of people articulates the norms of the status quo and seeks to reclaim definitions of themselves through cultural means, does this alter society? Is this forging social change? To many who view social movements as only collectively making change through direct engagement with the state, contemporary feminism's focus on fashion, as illustrated by *Bust* magazine, falls short. However, if we open the definition of the political to encompass work to bring about cultural shifts, I argue that by dressing in a way to reclaim femininity and sexuality as powerful, while working to negate the forces of overconsumption, contemporary feminists enact a form of social change. However, this argument is tempered by the knowledge that mass social change is difficult when a primary tactic of social movement actors is individual choice. When individual agency, as in feminized and politicized dress, is done in a culture of commodification, the impact of the tactic is often diluted and misunderstood in the larger culture and within the movement.

Notes

1. *Bust*, "Fashion and Booty," Fall 2004, 37.

2. As cited in Stephanie Gilmore, "Bridging the Waves: Sex and Sexuality in a Second Wave Organization," in *Different Wavelengths: Studies of the Contemporary Women's Movement*, ed. Jo Reger (New York: Routledge, 2005), 97.

3. While there are many definitions of "feminist" and "feminism," I identify *Bust* magazine and its contents as feminist for several reasons. First, *Bust* is often referred to as a contemporary feminist magazine because of the philosophy of the founders (among them Debbie Stoller, who often appears in the media and documentaries as a voice of feminism and is the author of several knitting books). Second is the magazine's overall philosophy of self empowerment and the critique of patriarchy. Evidence of this is in the magazine's tagline, "For Women with Something to Get off Their Chests." Third, the fashion focus of the magazine often refers specifically to feminism, such as the cover headline "Be a Feminist or just dress like one," *Bust*, August/September 2006, cover.

4. See Jennifer Baumgardner and Amy Richards, "Feminism and Femininity: Or How We Learned to Stop Worrying and Love the Thong," in *All About The Girl: Culture, Power And Identity*, ed. Anita Harris (New York: Routledge, 2004), 59–68; Beth Kreydatus, "Fashion," in *The Women's Movement Today: An Encyclopedia of Third-Wave Feminism*, ed. Leslie Heywood, vol. 1 (Westport, CT: Greenwood Press, 2006), 59–68.

5. The analysis was conducted using the Fall 2002 to Oct./Nov. 2007 issues with the magazine increasing its publications from four times a year to bimonthly publications in 2005. The magazine was founded in 1993 as a feminist 'zine (self-produced magazine). A standard feature of the magazine is called "Looks—Fashion and Booty." The feature is similar in each issue with women describing their outfits, where they got individual pieces, why they put them together the way they did, and how it made them feel. I coded each issue by analyzing the hair, outfit, race-ethnicity, occupation, style descriptors used, the reworking of the clothing, and the adjectives in the copy. A total of twenty-two features were analyzed.

6. See Verta Taylor and Nella van Dyke, " 'Get Up, Stand Up': Tactical Repertoires of Social Movements," in *The Blackwell Companion to Social Movements*, eds. David Snow, Sarah Soule, Hanspeter Kriesi (Malden MA: Blackwell Publishing, 2004), 262–293.

7. Charles Tilly, *Social Movements, 1768–2004* (Boulder, CO: Paradigm Publishers, 2004).

8. David Meyer, "How Social Movements Matter," *Contexts* 2, no. 4 (2003): 30-35; Suzanne Staggenborg, "Can Feminist Organizations Be Effective?" in *Feminist Organizations: Harvest of the New Women's Movement*, eds. Myra Marx Ferree and Patricia Yancey Martin (Philadelphia: Temple University Press, 1995), 339–355.

9. Nancy Whittier, *The Politics of Child Sexual Assault: Emotions, Social Movements and the State* (Malden, MA: Oxford University Press, 2009).

10. Verta Taylor and Nancy Whittier, "Collective Identity in Social Movement Communities: Lesbian Feminist Mobilization," in *Frontiers in Social Movement Theory*,

eds. Aldon D. Morris and Carol McClurg Mueller (New Haven, CT: Yale University Press, 1992), 104–129.

11. Gwendolyn O'Neal, "The Power of Style: On Rejection of the Accepted," in *Appearance and Power*, eds. Kim K. P. Johnson and Sharron J. Lennon (New York: Berg, 1999), 127–137; 141.

12. O'Neal, "The Power of Style: On Rejection of the Accepted," 129. Also see Suzanne Szostak-Pierce, "Even Further: The Power of Subcultural Style in Techno Culture," in *Appearance and Power*, 141–151; Samantha Holland, *Alternative Femininities: Body, Age and Identity* (New York: Berg, 2004).

13. Jane Ward, "Diversity Discourse and Multi-Identity Work in Lesbian and Gay Organizations," in *Identity Work in Social Movements*, eds. Jo Reger, Daniel J. Myers, and Rachel L. Einwohner (Minneapolis: University of Minnesota Press, 2008), 233–255.

14. Shari Benstock and Suzanne Ferriss, "Introduction," in *On Fashion*, eds. Shari Benstock and Suzanne Ferriss (New Brunswick, NJ: Rutgers University Press, 1994), 1–17; Holland, *Alternative Femininities.*

15. Holland, *Alternative Femininities.*

16. Kim K. P. Johnson and Sharron J. Lennon, "Introduction: Appearance and Social Power," in *Appearance and Power,* 1–10; O'Neal, "The Power of Style: On Rejection of the Accepted."

17. Holland, *Alternative Femininities.*

18. See Ariel Levy, *Female Chauvinist Pigs: Women and the Rise of Raunch Culture* (New York: Free Press, 2006); Nancy A. Rudd and Sharron J. Lennon, "Social Power and Appearance Management among Women," in *Appearance and Power*, 153–172.

19. Holland, *Alternative Femininities,* 81.

20. Kate McCarthy, "Not Pretty Girls?: Sexuality, Spirituality, and Gender Construction in Women's Rock Music." *The Journal of Popular Culture* 39, no. 1 (2006): 69–94; Adrienne Rich, "Compulsory Heterosexuality and Lesbian Existence," in *Bread, Blood and Poetry* (New York: W. W. Norton, 1994), 23–75; see also discussion in Linda Scott, *Fresh Lipstick: Redressing Fashion and Feminism* (New York: Palgrave MacMillan, 1994).

21. Baumgardner and Richards, "Feminism and Femininity."

22. Rich, "Compulsory Heterosexuality and Lesbian Existence."

23. See Rachel Blau DuPlessis and Ann Snitow, *The Feminist Memoir Project: Voices from Women's Liberation* (New York: Three Rivers Press, 1998); Karla Jay, *Tales of the Lavender Menace: A Memoir of Liberation.* (New York: Basic Books, 1999); Scott, *Fresh Lipstick;* Deborah Siegel, *Sisterhood Interrupted: From Radical Women To Grrls Gone Wild* (New York: Palgrave Macmillan, 2007).

24. As cited in Siegel, *Sisterhood Interrupted,* 85.

25. McCarthy, "Not Pretty Girls?," 71.

26. Ingrid Sischy, "Will Feminism's Fourth Wave Begin on the Runway?" *New York Times Style Magazine*, February 25, 2007, http://www.nytimes.com/2007/02/25/style/tmagazine/25tbody.html?ex=1173330000&en=1506c56f789e38fd&ei=5070

27. Baumgardner and Richards, "Feminism and Femininity," 59.

28. Ibid., 61.

29. Patricia Hill Collins, *Black Feminist Thought: Knowledge, Consciousness, and the Politics of Empowerment* (Boston: Unwin Hyman, 1991).

30. McCarthy, "Not Pretty Girls?," 70; See also M. Evans and C. Bobel, "'I am a Contradiction:' Feminism and Feminist Identity in the Third Wave," *New England Journal of Public Policy* 1 and 2 (2007): 207–222; Natalie Fixmer and Julia T. Wood, "The Personal is Still Political: Embodied Politics in Third Wave Feminism," *Women's Studies in Communication* 28, no. 2 (2005): 235–257.

31. Judith Taylor, "The Problem of Women's Sociality in Contemporary North American Feminist Memoir." *Gender & Society* 22, no. 6 (2008): 705–727; Chris Bobel, "'Our Revolution Has Style:' Contemporary Menstrual Product Activists 'Doing Feminism' in the Third Wave." *Sex Roles* 54 (2006): 331–345; Ricia Chansky, "A Stitch in Time: Reclaiming the Needle in Third Wave Feminist Visual Expression" (paper presented at the National Women's Studies Association meeting, St. Charles, IL, 2007).

32. Because of their inclusion in a magazine that focuses on feminism and links feminism and fashion, I am assuming that the people profiled are feminists even though the limited copy does not identify them as so. Even if some do not choose to identify as feminists, they are clearly being presented as feminist fashion models.

33. O'Neal, "The Power of Style: On Rejection of the Accepted."

34. I thank David Maines for this insight.

35. *Bust,* Dec./Jan. 2007, 33.

36. Bobel, "'Our Revolution Has Style;'" Evans and Bobel, "'I am a Contradiction;'" Fixmer and Wood, "The Personal is Still Political."

37. Illustration 2, *Bust,* Dec. 2004/Jan. 2005, 39.

38. Stephanie Rosenbloom, "Good Girls Go Bad, for a Day," *New York Times,* October 19, 2006, http://www.nytimes.com/2006/10/19/fashion/19costume.html?scp=8&sq=stephanie%20rosenbloom&st=cse.

39. Levy, *Female Chauvinist Pigs.*

40. Merri Lisa Johnson, "Jane Hocus, Jane Focus," in *Jane Sexes It Up: True Confessions of Feminist Desire,* ed. M. L. Johnson (New York: Four Walls, Eight Windows, 2002), 9.

41. As quoted in Gilmore, "Bridging the Waves," 106.

42. *Bust,* April/May, 2005, 33.

43. *Bust,* October/November, 2005, 33.

44. *Bust,* April/May, 2007, 42.

45. See Deborah Tolman, *Dilemmas of Desire: Teenage Girls Talk about Sexuality* (Cambridge MA: Harvard University Press, 2002).

46. See also Jo Reger and Lacey Story, "Talking About My Vagina: Two College Campuses and the Vagina Monologues," in *Different Wavelengths: Studies of the Contemporary Women's Movement,* 139–160.

47. Kreydatus, "Fashion."

48. Transcribed as written, *Bust,* Winter 2002, 27.

49. For example consider the designer jean fad of the 1980s in the United States with the designer label prominently displayed on the back pocket as a status symbol.

50. Bobel, "'Our Revolution Has Style.'"

51. Chansky, "A Stitch in Time," 6.

52. Ibid., 5.

53. *Bust,* Aug./Sept. 2007, 37 and Dec./Jan. 2004/2005, 39, respectively.

54. *Bust,* Oct. /Nov., 2006, 37.

55. Staggenborg, "Can Feminist Organizations Be Effective?" 339–355.

56. Jennifer Allyn and David Allyn, "Identity Politics," in *To Be Real: Telling the Truth and Changing the Face of Feminism,* ed. Rebecca Walker (New York: Anchor Books, 1995), 144.

57. Michael Messner, *Taking the Field: Women, Men and Sports* (Minneapolis: University of Minnesota Press, 2002).

58. Whittier, *The Politics of Child Sexual Assault.*

59. For example see Karla Jay's memoir *Tales of the Lavender Menace* for a description of the rush of accomplishments of the movement in the 1970s.

60. Ann Swidler, "Culture in Action: Symbols and Strategies," *American Sociological Review* 51 (1986): 273–286.

Chapter 14

Stylish Contradiction

Mix-and-Match as the
Fashion of Feminist Ambivalence

Marjorie Jolles

Looking Like a Feminist

"This is What a Feminist Looks Like." So says the T-shirt—a basic cotton-poly blend, utilitarian in style and cut, made in Nicaragua for Gildan Activewear Mexico and sold by the Feminist Majority Foundation.[1] Worn on the bodies of diverse feminists, the T-shirt's rhetorical force derives from the provocative tension between the utterly *general* "This" of the printed slogan and the utterly *specific* body to which it is attached. As a free-floating signifier, the "This" not only makes feminism instantly available to anyone who wears the shirt, it also communicates to everyone that feminism is a big tent, capable of accommodating anybody. The T-shirt comes in all shapes, sizes, and colors—just like feminists.

This all-inclusive ethos performs multiple rhetorical functions at once. It self-consciously responds to the assumption, borne out in hostile cultural stereotypes, that there is a singular way a feminist looks. The T-shirt both defends feminism and invites others in. Its slogan gestures toward ongoing debates within feminism, by acknowledging mainstream feminism's troubled history of placing the needs and interests of privileged women at its center while denying crucial differences (of race, sexuality, class, age, region, religion, physical ability) among women, thereby marginalizing the needs and interests of women outside that normative frame. Indeed, the T-shirt stands for difference writ large, due precisely to the indeterminacy of the "This" of the slogan, which seems to promise that all aspects of the self can be contained under the sign of feminism, suggesting that "This" captures the entirety of the self. As both a fashion statement and a political statement, the shirt affirms that feminism—to quote bell hooks—"is for everybody."[2]

Along with the T-shirt, the Feminist Majority Foundation's Web site hosts a short video, also entitled "This Is What a Feminist Looks Like." The video features men and women of varying ages, races, shapes, and styles, speaking in enthusiastic and deadpan tones, each of whom utters for the camera, "This is what a feminist looks like." The video contains repeated references to a broad range of fashions and personal styles as compatible with feminism. Actress Christine Lahti tells the viewer, "It doesn't mean that you hate men . . . it doesn't mean that you have hairy legs." Pop singer-songwriter Lisa Loeb smiles into the camera and says, "Sometimes I choose to wear short skirts. Sometimes I choose to wear pants. I don't think I'm less of a feminist when I wear a super-short skirt."[3] Again and again, in popular debates concerning what feminism is and is not, fashion is invoked as a practice for both commenting on and enacting one's feminism.

This welcoming embrace of the full self into feminism via fashion reflects the profound influence that so-called third-wave feminism[4] has had on popular discourses of female subjectivity. Specifically, the indeterminacy of "This is what a feminist looks like" shares a rhetorical link with the contemporary feminist emphasis on the notion of contradiction as an essential feature of feminine, and feminist, selfhood.

Contradiction as Feminist Ethos

Contradiction is a common theme in contemporary feminist discourse, especially among those who identify as "third-wave" feminists. Stacy Gillis, Gillian Howie, and Rebecca Munford, the editors of *Third Wave Feminism: A Critical Exploration*, observe that "third wave feminists tend to consider second wave feminism as triangulated in essentialism, universalism and naturalism and as having reaped the political consequences. Having learnt the lessons of history, they prefer contradiction, multiplicity and difference."[5] Gillian Howie and Ashley Tauchert describe this emphasis on internal contradiction as stemming from a more general poststructuralist rejection of the notion of a self with a stable, unified inner core. "The critique of the subject," they argue, "led to an investigation of the differences *between* men and women, differences *within* the group 'women,' and differences embodied in *one* woman."[6] In their book, *Third Wave Agenda*, Leslie Heywood and Jennifer Drake explicitly acknowledge this when they claim, "because our lives have been shaped by struggles between various feminisms as well as by cultural backlash against feminism and activism, we argue that contradiction—or what looks like contradiction, if one doesn't shift one's point of view—marks the desires and strategies of third wave feminists."[7]

In the introduction to her now-classic text, *To Be Real*, Rebecca Walker also identifies contradiction as an important theme in contemporary feminist thought seeking to critique and distance itself from earlier feminist logics. Walker describes her early adulthood as marked by a fear of doing feminism "wrong," of being "horribly unfeminist, and so, horribly bad."[8] Walker writes: "[my] existence was an ongoing state of saying no to many elements of the universe, and picking and choosing to allow only what I thought should belong. The parts of myself that didn't fit into my ideal were hidden down deep, and when I faced them for fleeting moments they made me feel insecure and confused about my values and identity."[9] These parts of herself, Walker reflects, "represented contradictions that [she] had no idea how to reconcile."[10] In her effort to rethink a feminism that can respond to this conflict, she describes third-wave feminism as "help[ing] us continue to shape a political force more concerned with mandating and cultivating freedom than with policing morality."[11] Walker envisions a feminism in which we can "demand to exist whole and intact, without cutting or censoring parts of [our]selves."[12] This emphasis on a self made up of irreconcilable fragments that all deserve embrace bears an uncanny resemblance to the total self who is captured by the "This" of "This is what a feminist looks like." For Walker, the trouble is not her inner contradiction, but rather the shame that caused her to say "no" to the contradictory parts of herself. Walker inverts her shame, insisting that she has not failed feminism, but that feminism has failed her by not permitting those inner contradictions to exist. She neither laments contradiction nor proposes to resolve it. Instead, she acknowledges an inner incoherence while simultaneously demanding that feminism allow her to "exist whole and intact."

Likewise, Gloria Anzaldúa famously advocates understanding oneself in contradictory terms as a useful *mestiza* response to the limited and limiting logics of the modern Western self, claiming that "the new *mestiza* copes by developing a tolerance for contradictions, a tolerance for ambiguity."[13] In the best-selling *Where the Girls Are*, feminist media critic Susan J. Douglas aligns herself with this same understanding of contemporary female subjectivity, describing American women as a "bundle of contradictions,"[14] and explicitly linking contradiction to feminism by observing that "contradictions and ambivalence are at the heart of what it means to be a feminist."[15] In a move that resembles the rhetoric of "This is what a feminist looks like," Douglas acknowledges that the feminist self is a complex whole—jumbled and occasionally torn, not always unified. In this same zeitgeist, Donna Haraway's canonical text of early postmodern feminism, "A Manifesto for Cyborgs," celebrates the cyborg as a figure of subjective hybridity and collage, "a kind of disassembled and reassembled, postmodern collective and personal self. This," Haraway asserts, "is the self feminists must code."[16]

The Fashion of Contradiction

Feminists have coded this self so effectively in recent years that the notion of the contemporary American feminine self as a collage of contradictory bits and pieces has been absorbed into mainstream popular fashion trends and discourses of personal style. The self whom Walker, Anzaldúa, Douglas, Haraway, and others describe as having difference at her core expresses this internal chaos vividly in the hugely popular trend of ironic mix-and-match fashion. While mix-and-match has a rich history as a sartorial strategy ever since the advent of women's separates—historically, it has served decorative, utilitarian, and subcultural goals, and has long been celebrated as a way to stretch one's wardrobe in hard economic times—I focus here on a distinctive, early twenty-first century revival of a mix-and-match aesthetic in American mainstream women's fashion, described by fashion journalist Anita Leclerc as a "parade of patterns [that is] like watching seven rival marching bands converge at a four-way intersection—talk about your clash of symbols."[17] This latest iteration of mix-and-match style takes as its goal something other than utility or wardrobe-stretching, appearing instead to serve the expressive, rhetorical goal of announcing the wearer's contradictory nature. Through a style of deliberate clashing, the contemporary American woman visually comments on her hybridized inner self by wearing multiple highly referential looks, juxtapositions of formerly unmixable, unmatchable styles. In contrast to subcultural styles such as punk that seek cultural disruption through sartorial disruption, the commentary in contemporary mainstream women's mix-and-match is far more normative. It deploys the rhetoric of contradiction not to lodge a complaint but to announce one's comfort—a playful engagement with both feminism and femininity.

In a feature called "Best Dressed Girls in America," *Seventeen* magazine selected a small group of readers who exemplify what the feature editor calls "bold style."[18] Eight out of the seventeen girls featured describe their personal style as some form of deliberate *bricolage,* using words like "eclectic," "eccentric," "odd and experimental," and "a little bit of everything." Catherine from New Orleans, age thirteen, describes her personal style as "edgy punk mixed with glam prep;" Tory from Concord, Massachusetts, age fifteen, calls her personal style "'60s mod and '70s boho."[19] In the "Looks" column in *Bust* magazine, the featured fashionable feminist Cynara Geissler describes her fashion sense as "pull[ed] from a lot of seemingly disparate places. There's a lot of tough, Springsteen, working-class stuff going on and also a Claudia Kishi from *The Baby-sitter's Club* kind of whimsicality."[20] What is most striking about the girls and women featured in these magazines is not only the immense popularity and mainstream embrace of mix-and-match style, but their reflexive awareness of themselves as participating in an aesthetic of contradiction closely linked to changing notions of what constitutes both modern feminine style and modern feminine subjectivity. In their self-constructions, these *bricoleurs* situate themselves in many eras—each with historically specific gender ideologies and attendant looks of femininity—at once, acknowledging their engagement in a deliberate citational practice that produces a polysemic subject. They speak in terms of constructing themselves out of preexisting styles that add up to something new, whose essential feature is its inherent undefinability, due to its inherent multiplicity.

This trend is not simply a result of the consumer's own creative take, DIY-style, on the contents of her closet; the message that a clashing mix-and-match style best captures the mood of today's woman comes from the corporate top down, too. Jenna Lyons, Creative Director for American retailer J. Crew, says she is "obsessed with unexpected pairings" that distinguish the Fall 2009 women's collection.[21] When British retail phenomenon Topshop opened its flagship American boutique in New York City, its promotional press materials defined the Topshop look as impishly contradictory. In a feature on the Topshop Web site as well as in an interactive advertisement on the *New York Times* Web site, users were introduced to Topshop Style Advisers, a team of young experts who function as "brand ambassadors" for the retailer, offering lessons for achieving distinctive personal style.[22] Their declarations of fashion savvy affirm this trend conflating eclecticism with individuality, implicitly linking contemporary femininity with a sexy form of bricolage. Style Adviser Gabriela Langone assures the shopper that "your style is your fashion footprint, so always let it be individual," while Daniela Gutmann promises that "we're not judging anybody. It's O.K. if you want to wear a million prints at a time." Gemma Caplan, one more from the Style Advisor team confesses, "sometimes I feel like being all girly and cutesy, sometimes I feel like being rock-y."[23]

This refusal of singularity in terms of feminine style reads like refusal of singularity in terms of feminine subjectivity—the fashion equivalent of Susan Bordo's notion of "gender skepticism," a rejection of gender as a stable ground of experience in favor of radical difference and indeterminacy.[24] The Style Advisor tip on Topshop's Web site for Autumn/Winter 2009: "Clash your silhouettes to create a show-stopping look."[25] Such suggestions to sartorially manifest a fragmented, clashing self echo Haraway's cyborg, whom Lisa Walker reads as a figure of the "politics of heterogeneity . . . marked by a resistance to self-identity."[26]

This gesture linking a contradictory subjective life with a contradictory fashion sense extends beyond fashion retailers. The emergence of Michelle Obama as a fashion icon has been duly covered in the popular press, with special attention paid to her skill as a "mix-and-match master."[27] Known for her talent at mixing high and low, classic and trendy, and strong and soft, Obama is considered to have a singular, quirky style that conveys a sense of self-possession.[28] At the 2009 Council of Fashion Designers of America awards ceremony, Michelle Obama was honored with the Board of Directors Special Tribute, in recognition of a distinctive style described by Council president Diane von Furstenberg as "a unique look that balances the duality of her lives," invoking the notion of a multiple self so familiar to feminists versed in theoretical work on the shifting self.[29] While the duality of Michelle Obama's life is heavily covered in the press, such coverage avoids political or materialist analysis that might expose that dualism to examination. Analytical attention is rarely devoted to understanding the particular normative forces that give style and shape to the duality of her life; instead, the perception of Michelle Obama as a successful modern woman is communicated through her clothes, which seem to speak to the cultural command that women "multi-task" and "balance" the multiple aspects of their lives, in the sense of juggling the various demands generated by women's expected roles. This gendered political and moral imperative to "balance" appears unconsciously reinforced through a mix-and-match aesthetic.[30]

In descriptions of her life (and lifestyle) during her husband's first year in office, Michelle Obama is repeatedly described in rhetoric that celebrates—rather than problematizes—her multiplicity, with such observations as, "There she is, this Harvard-educated lawyer and former executive, digging up sweet potatoes on the back lawn of the White House,"[31] and "She's Michelle . . . great-great-great-granddaughter of a slave . . . Michelle the devoted mom . . . Michelle the wife of Barack . . . Michelle the glamorous style icon . . . Michelle the political player."[32]

This conception of Michelle Obama as having so many component parts—some of them, were they to be examined, potentially in conflict with each other—is mirrored in coverage of her fashion sense. To her fans, the very appeal of her look is in its vaguely ironic assemblage of multiple fashion references. This signature of stylistic self-consciousness suggests a playfully defiant resistance to normative codes, suggesting the triumph of the individual over social forces that threaten—but fail—to normalize her (see Image 14.1). Sally Singer, at the time the Fashion News and Features Director of *Vogue*, singled out Obama's unconventional mix of purple sheath dress by Maria Pinto with a black patent leather, metal-studded Azzedine Alaïa belt at the 2008 Democratic National Convention, claiming, "the combination of that dress with that belt was amazing. Her clothes said that she was authoritative and appropriate, yet also very accessible and very refreshing."[33] Obama herself acknowledges this is her trademark look, describing her fashion sense in her June 2008 appearance on *The View* as "I do a little bit of everything."

Just as she does not claim a singular look, Michelle Obama does not claim a singular political ideology. When pressed, she has resisted identifying as a feminist. In an interview during her husband's presidential campaign, she expressed her feminist ambivalence as a more generalized reluctance to identify with "labels," stating, "You know, I'm not that into labels. . . . So probably, if you laid out a feminist agenda, I would probably agree with a large portion of it . . . I wouldn't identify as a feminist just like I probably wouldn't identify as a liberal or a progressive."[34]

Image 14.1. April 2009, Michelle Obama wearing her much-editorialized Moschino oversized bow blouse and Azzedine Alaïa metal-studded leather belt—equal parts girlish frill and edgy punk.

If Michelle Obama promotes a highly visible image of ironic mix-and-match as mirroring an ideological ambivalence in the political arena, Carrie Bradshaw is the figure who best exemplifies it in the popular imagination. The protagonist of the *Sex and the City* franchise is famously ambivalent toward much that feminism has wrought: eschewing yet craving marriage, cynical yet hopeful about romance, adamant yet anxious about self-sufficiency. The character of Carrie is in many ways a meditation on late twentieth-century feminism (as it intersects with late twentieth-century capitalism), a figure who attempts to "have it all" and often comes up short. Stella Bruzzi and Pamela Church Gibson speak directly to the cacophonous fashion sense of Carrie Bradshaw, whose "violent yoking together of clashing sartorial styles,"[35] "jarring styles," "pastiche . . . and wacky personal style"[36] became Carrie's signature look. Indeed, Bruzzi and Church Gibson acknowledge that this self-conscious aesthetic of mix and collage aptly describes not only Carrie's fashion sense, but the very character of Carrie herself, whom they describe as "a composite of multiple, conflicting personae, a layered performance" reflecting often contradictory aspects of her feminine self: "her romantic tendency, her child-like exhibitionism and her professional obligation to reconfigure herself repeatedly in her work."[37] Carrie *is* collage—internally, and thus, externally

Contradiction as Retreat

One gets the sense that it is downright unfashionable to claim allegiance to a stable fashion style or a stable feminine identity. The third-wave celebration of contradiction as an essential feature of selfhood has made "having it all"—which, in discourses of subjectivity, amounts to "*being* it all"—not only possible, but hegemonic. In her trenchant analysis of queer female style, Rebecca Ann Rugg has observed that privileging "fluid or changeable identity has become, ironically, extremely rigid . . . I am uncool because I am full-time in one identity."[38] Instead, she "must somehow mark [her]self to be seen as a member of the pomo crowd that doesn't 'limit themselves' by taking gender/identity seriously."[39] Rugg finds the expectation of relentless self-reinvention—and the attendant, relentless visual commentary on it through fashion—actually a constraint on self-expression. Likewise, Susan Bordo has identified "plasticity" as the guiding "postmodern paradigm," a cultural mandate of self-stylization that favors ambiguity and multiplicity over definition and locatedness.[40] Michelle Obama's claim that she "does a little bit of everything" and her resistance to "labels" (including the label "feminist") may be understood as participating in this phenomenon of locationlessness. In a similar vein, Bordo has observed the postmodern preference for instability and multiplicity to be motivated by a "dream of everywhere," in which the self occupies all possible positions, locations, and subjectivities, thereby enabling a retreat from a committed position.[41]

Indeed, it is the very taking up of a committed position—and expecting the same of others—that many self-identified third-wave feminists find so limiting about so-called second wave feminism.[42] (Recall Rebecca Walker's plea for a *new* feminism that would eschew "policing morality" and "cultivat[e] freedom" instead.) Thus, precisely because a putative second-wave feminism is thought to insist upon what a feminist looks like, third-wave feminism insists only that "This" is what a feminist looks like, whatever "This" turns out to be. Unpredictable juxtapositions that constitute mix-and-match ensembles may be read as forms of feminist *jouissance,* vigorously defying definition. In making multiple fashion references at once, a contradictory style names its historical and ideological roots, yet through such genealogical reflexivity, an exaggeratedly eclectic style simultaneously avoids being wholly determined by history and ideology. Rejecting a single, stable, or non-ironic look, mix-and-match seems to promise transcendence of a specific cultural location by nodding to, while not quite claiming, so many locations at once. That is, this form of referentiality appears to express not so much an identification with, but rather a *mastery over,* histories of feminine style. In fashion terms, this "dream of everywhere" manifests as stylistic contradiction, or "eclectic chic," in the words of one *Vogue* model.[43]

When it comes to both Michelle Obama and Carrie Bradshaw, their ambivalent stances toward feminism—the ways they have not "had it all" but remain nonetheless representatives in the popular imagination for this brand of ambiguously feminist agency—are expressed in sartorial indeterminacy, dressing "traditional" one day, "modern" the next, and even more often, both at once. The notion of modern-woman-as-collage is never registered as a feminist complaint, nor is it situated in a context of political critique in which we might understand those alienated and competing aspects of subjectivity as indicative of a culture out of joint. Rather, the rhetoric of contradiction in both fashion discourse and so-called third-wave discourse is used only to describe the inner life of the individual subject, and as a result, serves to obscure contradictory social relations that could stand to be illuminated.

When Contradiction Reveals

The strongest argument for the analytic utility of contradiction can be found in the work of Karl Marx and feminists working in the Marxist tradition. The foundation of Marxist analysis is that "it is not the consciousness of men that determines their existence, but their social existence that determines their consciousness."[44] During times of social transformation, in which material changes produce ideological changes, emergent revolutionary "conscious-ness must be explained from the contradictions of material life . . . from the conflict existing between the social forces of production and the relations of production."[45] Daniel Bell describes contradiction as a "disjunction of realms" and "adversary relations" in which ideological and political conflict occur,[46] and Fredric Jameson has called contradiction "the very motor power of the dialectic itself."[47] Scott Meikle describes the Marxian sense of contradiction as an "active incompatibility," a particularly apt description for capturing the appealing clash of jarringly juxtaposed looks in women's mix-and-match fashion.[48]

Illuminating what contradiction means for feminists, Sandra Lee Bart-ky explains that being a feminist requires undergoing a transformation of consciousness, of *becoming* feminist through active epistemic and ethical reorientation. Bartky identifies two "necessary conditions for the emergence of feminist consciousness. . . . [first], . . . the existence of what Marxists call 'contradictions' in our society and, second, . . . the presence, due to these same contradictions, of concrete circumstances which would permit a significant alteration in the status of women."[49]

For Bartky, as for Marx, feminist consciousness can only emerge when there is some dissonance between representations of reality and one's mate-rial experience of it, when one perceives "the ways in which some parts of the social whole are out of phase with others."[50] Examples Bartky provides of such conflict include the existence of millions of women in the workforce in the postwar era with the contemporaneous existence of cultural ideolo-gies locating womanhood in the domestic sphere. The lived, material expe-rience of contradiction during a time of possibilities for change is marked by deep discomfort, "an anguished consciousness, an inner uncertainty and confusion."[51] Out of this discomfort and confusion comes an awareness that change both should *and actually can* occur. This awareness is the hallmark of feminist consciousness.

Importantly for both Marx and Bartky, contradictions signal a potential moment for revolutionary change. As Marx writes, "mankind . . . inevita-bly sets itself only such tasks as it is able to solve . . . the problem itself arises only when the material conditions for its solution are already present or at least in the course of formation."[52] To refer again to feminism, under these terms, we could say that feminism is only able to emerge at histori-cal moments in which material reality makes it practicable and conceivable. The reason to pay attention to contradiction, then, is because of what it can reveal, simultaneously, about both what is wrong and what is possible.

In a powerful example of the use of contradiction for diagnosing social injustice, Deirdre Davis describes African American women's experiences as objects of street harassment. She claims that by

embracing the multiplicitous self, African American wom-
en . . . have learned how to handle the multiple forms of oppression, including gender and racial oppression. . . . By embracing
the multiple parts of the self and moving away from a binary
construction of 'self,' we also recognize the possibility for internal
contradiction. African American women have historically and
consistently existed in a zone of dissonance.[53]

Davis locates this dissonance in the contradictory fact that "African American
women, as society's 'other,'" are simultaneously disenfranchised and necessary members of a society built on hierarchy.[54] Thus, this contradictory feature
of African American female experience is an index of a larger contradictory
reality, in which African American women are invisible and visible, marginal
and central, unnecessary and essential. Exposing this contradictory state of
affairs between ideology and practice exposes social injustice, and moves
forward both discourse and praxis regarding transformation of gender, racial,
sexual, and class oppressions.

The concept of contradiction is especially useful for theorizing the oppositional push-pull of a complex system like feminism. Feminism, which has
historically tended to rely on a fixed and knowable category—"women"—
shows its contradictory nature in its confrontation with difference that threat-
ens to unravel the very category for which it stands. When feminists of
color, working-class feminists, Third World feminists, transgender feminists,
and others who stand outside of the normative center challenge feminism
to reckon with its own denials of difference, feminism can be said to be
propelled by contradiction in productive ways. In their article, "Liberal Irony,
Rhetoric, and Feminist Thought: A Unifying Third Wave Feminist Theory,"
Valerie Renegar and Stacey Sowards propose to construct a feminist rhetorical theory that honors the irony and contradiction they claim are central to
third-wave feminism. "When the contradictions of the past are viewed from a
different perspective," they argue, "a dialectic arises to connect the members
of the various feminist factions."[55]

Neither this dialectic nor its predicted progressive outcomes are guaranteed, however, if contradiction is cause for retreat rather than struggle.
Consider what popular writer Katha Pollitt said in a 2007 interview with the
New York Times. When asked, "Do you think feminism has been disfigured by
consumerism? To certain women out there, feminism seems to mean buying
what you want instead of being what you want," Pollitt responds: "Young
women live these contradictions and everyone's down on them because their
skirts are too short. I don't blame them if sometimes they just want to go
shopping."[56] In the same interview, when Pollitt confesses to obsessively
Googling an ex-lover who left her for a much younger woman, the int-

erviewer wonders what "all this girlish confession . . . say[s] about the current state of feminism," to which Pollitt responds, "Not a thing. It says that people are complicated and everyone has a mysterious inner life."[57]

While I absolutely agree—sometimes people *are* complicated and *do* have mysterious inner lives—I wish to draw attention to the swift foreclosure performed by Pollitt's response: "not a thing." Certainly no movement or theory like feminism can capture and regulate every voluntary and involuntary moment of one's inner life, but we *can* expect feminism to speak to the very issues raised by the interviewer. Examining the relationship between feminism and consumerism could lead to productive insights about one's own implication in material systems of self- and world-making that may or may not be in the service of one's values. Questioning the ways a woman struggles with abandonment by a lover might illuminate the limits of women's agency within still-patriarchal patterns of heteronormative coupling that rank women's desirability in terms of age. Thus, at issue is not whether we are or are not contradictory subjects—clearly, we are. Rather, at issue is wasting contradiction's *utility.* Contradictory subjects—with their contradictory fashions—are in a position to grapple with the very ideological and historical dissonances they stylistically enact, if such critique is encouraged.

Contradictory Collectives

The question is whether styles of personal contradiction are, on their own, equivalent to political critique. Cultural theorist Kaja Silverman observes that in contemporary culture, "imaginative dress has become a form of contestation—a way of challenging not only dominant values, but traditional class and gender demarcations."[58] Especially in the case of vintage clothing, Silverman argues that ironic fashion can provide a way for the feminist to announce her own historicity, thereby providing a commentary on past, present, and post-feminisms. Likewise, Daniel Traber, in his work on the "punk preppy," argues that stylistic hybridity that "permit[s] subjects to reinvent themselves through endless combinations of disparate elements" creates possibilities for "a degree of freedom allowing them to develop new identities and new ways of knowing."[59] Indeed, for Traber, contradiction *is* freedom, revealed by his observation that "the shuffling of ontologies is the form agency takes."[60]

I am not convinced that the fashion mash-up always represents an effort at meaningful political agency. The contradictions brought to life by feminine and feminist bricolage are not equivalent to a meditation on oneself as caught up, in an anguished way, in contradiction—nor do they represent a reflection on feminism's failures to enable a less conflicted subjectivity. By committing to everything and nothing at once, fashions of self-conscious collage can be read as a celebration of contradiction for contradiction's sake, without complaint, and without attention to the potential uses of contradiction. In the examples I provide of contemporary mix-and-match, the poststructuralist notion of a contradictory self described by Haraway and others is gestured toward, but ultimately, the self is represented as reconciled, her conflicting fragments of subjectivity ultimately resolved with each other, living together harmoniously under the sign of the third wave. This description of contradiction has the rhetorical effect of expressing a *unity*, not a contradiction. Contradiction is described as a happy—even sexy—state of affairs, devoid of the persistent anguish and debilitating ambivalence Bartky describes so movingly. This is contradiction absent the struggle, contradiction as a static fact of feminine experience, evacuated of its political force and thus a failed catalyst for collective consciousness-raising.

Kathy Miriam attributes this gap between the individual and the collective to the effects of expressivist feminist rhetoric on feminist politics. Specifically, Miriam charges the expressivist turn with directing political energy away from remaking the world and toward the aesthetics of self presentation. For Miriam, "a politics of identity is expressivist when expressions of identity and recovery of an authentic self come to define praxis. . . . The expressivist approach to politics begs the question of how practices of expression interrelate with concrete practices of social transformation. We ask *Who am I?* but not *To what ends?*"[61] Miriam here echoes a similar sentiment expressed by queer theorist Riki Wilchins who, remarking on the language of identity politics, asks, "this rings true, but does it also ring useful?"[62] The distinction that both Miriam and Wilchins highlight between expression and utility is precisely the distinction I wish to highlight between contemporary feminist connotations of contradiction—as a feature of individual selfhood to express—and more analytically grounded connotations of contradiction as a feature of collective reality that, once illuminated, can indicate social disjunctions and inequities, and, once harnessed, can activate positive change.

Let us use our consciousness of ourselves as contradictory beings, then, toward political ends. I am not suggesting that all contradictions are ultimately reconcilable, but rather, that feminism ought to be lived as an unfinished and agonistic project, in which contradictions direct our attention to areas where renewed feminist work is needed. As a fashion statement, an aesthetics of contradiction might be marshaled alongside an agonistic, analytic feminism that responds productively to the frustration and alienation of self that often accompanies living at the fraught nexus of ideology and practice. As Naomi Scheman has observed, "subversive playfulness is not enough" to do away with the unified subject so many feminists find anachronistic. We still need "concrete political struggle to effect the material changes that would actually make the unified subject an anachronism."[63]

I began with the example of the "This is What a Feminist Looks Like" T-shirt to underscore my observation that the third-wave feminist ethos of contradiction is being vociferously played out in contemporary fashion and style trends. The "disassembled and reassembled" female self whom Haraway tasks feminists with coding *is* being coded, in the visual rhetorics of fashion and style in which women enact, historicize, and comment on their own subject positions. Ascribing new value to contradiction—along with increased skepticism toward a notion of the self as unified and coherent—represents an important contribution to feminist discourse. But our work must entail a rigorous linkage of individual subjectivity with collective change, and this process will inevitably include fearless dialogues about what, exactly, a feminist looks like. An apolitical celebration of contradiction risks softening the ethical challenges of feminism, thereby limiting its transformative potential for both the self and her world. "If," as Silverman observes, "clothing not only draws the body so that it can be seen, but also maps out the shape of the ego, then every transformation within a society's vestimentary code implies some kind of shift within its ways of articulating subjectivity."[64] Our task, then, is to map this emergent subjectivity into a larger project for a future in which the alienation of contradiction is a cause for renewed feminist struggle.

Notes

1. The Feminist Majority Foundation is a large, influential American non-profit organization and, since 2001, the publisher of *Ms.* magazine.

2. bell hooks, *Feminism is for Everybody: Passionate Politics* (Cambridge, MA: South End Press, 2000).

3. Feminist Majority Foundation, Videos: "This Is What a Feminist Looks Like," http://feminist.org/news/videos.asp.

4. I acknowledge serious problems with using "wave" terminology to capture the history and ideological complexity of feminism in the United States. Compelling cases have been made by both academic and popular feminist writers to abandon the "wave" terminology and to classify iterations of feminist thought less in generational terms and more in ideological terms. I share this view. My interest, when using the terms "third wave" and "second wave," is not to perpetuate a cultural narrative of feminist waves but to identify individuals by the terms they themselves use to actively signal their distance from what they perceive as rigid, "second wave" feminism.

5. Stacy Gillis, Gillian Howie, and Rebecca Munford, introduction to *Third Wave Feminism: A Critical Exploration,* 2nd ed., eds. Stacy Gillis, Gillian Howie, and Rebecca Munford (New York: Palgrave Macmillan, 2007), xxiv.

6. Gillian Howie and Ashley Tauchert, "Feminist Dissonance: The Logic of Late Feminism," in *Third Wave Feminism,* 51.

7. Leslie Heywood and Jennifer Drake, "Introduction," in *Third Wave Agenda: Being Feminist, Doing Feminism,* eds. Leslie Heywood and Jennifer Drake (Minneapolis: University of Minnesota Press, 1997), 2.

8. Rebecca Walker, "Introduction," in *To Be Real: Telling the Truth and Changing the Face of Feminism,* ed. Rebecca Walker (New York: Anchor Books, 1995), xxx.

9. Ibid.

10. Ibid.

11. Ibid., xxxv.

12. Ibid.

13. Gloria Anzaldúa, *Borderlands: La Frontera* (San Francisco: Aunt Lute Books, 1987), 101.

14. Susan J. Douglas, *Where the Girls Are: Growing Up Female with the Mass Media* (New York: Times Books, 1994), 9.

15. Ibid., 20.

16. Donna Haraway, "A Manifesto for Cyborgs: Science, Technology, and Socialist Feminism in the 1980s," in *Feminism/Postmodernism,* ed. Linda J. Nicholson (New York: Routledge, 1990), 205.

17. Anita Leclerc, "Print Mixology," *New York Times,* April 14, 2010, http://www.nytimes.com/2010/04/15/fashion/15PRINTS.html?ref=fashion.

18. Zandile Blay, "Best Dressed Girls in America." *Seventeen,* August 2006, 108.

19. Ibid., 98.

20. "Looks." *Bust,* October/November 2009, 31.

21. J. Crew, "Jenna Lyon's Picks—Jenna's Favorite Women's Clothing, Shoes, Jewelry & Accessories," http://www.jcrew.com/AST/Browse/WomenBrowse/Women_Feature_Assortment/Jennaspicks.jsp.

22. Eric Wilson, "Trust Me. You'll Look Cool in This," *New York Times,* April 8, 2009, http://www.nytimes.com/2009/04/09/fashion/09TOPSHOP.html?scp=2&sq=eric%20wilson%20%22trust%20me%22&st=cse.

23. *New York Times,* "Topshop Style Advisers," http://www.nytimes.com/slideshow/2009/04/08/fashion/20090409-topshop-slideshow_index.html.

24. Susan Bordo, *Unbearable Weight: Feminism, Western Culture, and the Body* (Berkeley, CA: University of California Press, 1993), 215–218.

25. Topshop, "Style Advisor: Build Your Perfect Wardrobe for AW09 With These Four Key Pieces," http://us.topshop.com/webapp/wcs/stores/servlet/StaticPageDisplay?catalogId=32051&storeId=13052&brdcrmb_trail=&identifier=tsus1%20style%20advisor%20video&intcmpid=FEATURE_HP_US_WK2_STYLEADVISOR#.

26. Lisa Walker, "How To Recognize a Lesbian." *Signs* 18, no. 4 (1993): 870.

27. Michelle Obama: Power Fashion," *Harper's Bazaar,* April 6, 2009, http://www.harpersbazaar.com/fashion/fashion-articles/michelle-obama-fashion.

28. "Point of View: Barack Obama, 44th President," *Vogue,* January 2009, 88.

29. Samantha Critchell, "Michelle Obama Gets Fashion Honor at NYC Ceremony," *Associated Press,* June 16, 2009, http://abcnews.go.com/Entertainment/wireStory?id=7848507.

30. I am grateful to Shira Tarrant for this insight.

31. Associated Press, "Michelle Obama: It's tough to stay grounded." January 19, 2010, http://today.msnbc.msn.com/id/34935966/ns/today-white_house/.

32. Katie Couric, "Michelle Obama Looks Back on her Big Year—And Answers *Your* Questions," *Glamour,* December 2009, 224.

33. Marcia Froelke Coburn, "High-Low Chic," *Chicago Magazine*, http://www.chicagomag.com/Chicago-Magazine/February-2009/The-Making-of-a-First-Lady/High-Low-Chic/.

34. Anne E Kornblut, "Michelle Obama's Career Time-Out," *The Washington Post*, May 11, 2007, http://www.washingtonpost.com/wp-dyn/content/article/2007/05/10/AR2007051002573_pf.html.

35. Stella Bruzzi and Pamela Church Gibson, " 'Fashion is the Fifth Character:' Fashion, Costume and Character in Sex and the City," in *Reading Sex and the City,* eds. Kim Akass and Janet McCabe (New York: I. B. Tauris, 2004), 117.

36. Ibid., 119.

37. Ibid., 118.

38. Rebecca Ann Rugg, "How Does She Look?," in *Femme: Feminists, Lesbians, and Bad Girls*, eds. Laura Harris and Elizabeth Crocker (New York: Routledge, 1997), 186.

39. Ibid.

40. Bordo, *Unbearable Weight*, 245.

41. Ibid., 225–229.

42. I am similarly ambivalent about the term "second wave" for the constraints it imposes on conceptualizing the history and complexity of American feminism. Therefore, I use the term "second wave" in the same spirit in which I use the term "third wave," to enter the very discourse I wish to critique, and not to communicate my comfort with these terms on their own.

43. Lily Robinson, quoted in "*Vogue* Index," *Vogue*, October 2009, 281.

44. Karl Marx, "Toward a Critique of Political Economy: Preface," in *Marx: Selections*, ed. Allen Wood (New York: Macmillan, 1988), 135.

45. Ibid., 136.

46. Daniel Bell, *The Cultural Contradictions of Capitalism* (New York: Basic Books, 1996), 14.

47. Fredric Jameson, "Rousseau and Contradiction," *South Atlantic Quarterly* 104, no. 4 (2005): 700.

48. Scott Meikle, "History of Philosophy: The Metaphysics of Substance in Marx," in *The Cambridge Companion to Marx,* ed. Terrell Carver (Cambridge: Cambridge University Press, 1991), 316.

49. Sandra Lee Bartky, *Femininity and Domination: Studies in the Phenomenology of Oppression* (New York: Routledge, 1990), 12.

50. Ibid., 13.

51. Ibid., 14.

52. Marx, "Toward a Critique of Political Economy," 136.

53. Deirdre E. Davis, "The Harm That Has No Name: Street Harassment, Embodiment, and African American Women," in *Critical Race Feminism: A Reader*, ed. Adrien Katherine Wing (New York: New York University Press, 1997), 199.

54. Ibid.

55. Valerie R. Renegar and Stacey K. Sowards, "Liberal Irony, Rhetoric, and Feminist Thought: A Unifying Third Wave Feminist Theory," *Philosophy and Rhetoric* 36, no. 4 (2003): 335.

56. Katha Pollitt, quoted in "Woman's Studies: Questions for Katha Pollitt," *New York Times Magazine,* September 23, 2007, 17.

57. Ibid.

58. Kaja Silverman, "Fragments of a Fashionable Discourse," in *On Fashion,* eds. Shari Benstock and Suzanne Ferriss (New Brunswick, NJ: Rutgers University Press, 1994), 193.

59. Daniel Traber, "Locating the Punk Preppy," *The Journal of Popular Culture* 41, no. 3 (2008): 500.

60. Ibid.

61. Kathy Miriam, "Liberating *Practice:* A Critique of the Expressivist Turn in Lesbian-Feminist and Queer Practice," *NWSA Journal* 19, no. 2 (2007): 35.

62. Riki Wilchins, "Deconstructing Trans," in *GenderQueer: Voices from Beyond the Sexual Binary,* eds. Joan Nestle, Clare Howell, and Riki Wilchins (New York: Alyson Books, 2002), 61.

63. Naomi Scheman, *Engenderings: Constructions of Knowledge, Authority, and Privilege* (New York: Routledge, 1993), 189.

64. Silverman, "Fragments of a Fashionable Discourse," 193.

About the Authors

Kathryn A. Hardy Bernal is the Fashion Theory Coordinator and Senior Lecturer in Contextual and Theoretical Studies for the School of Art and Design at AUT University, New Zealand. In 2007, she curated *Loli-Pop* (Lolita + Pop), an exhibition for Auckland War Memorial Museum, which explored the Japanese Gothic & Lolita movement and its relationship with popular culture. Kathryn's research background is in art, design, and literature of the Victorian period, with an emphasis on Medievalism, Pre-Raphaelitism, Aestheticism, Japonisme, Art Nouveau, and Mourning. Her most current focus is on cross-cultural engagements between the Neo-Gothic and Japan, and contemporary Japanese fashion subcultures. Kathryn would like to acknowledge and thank her friends and colleagues, Bevan Chuang, James Percy, Angie Finn, and Vivien Masters, for their support and contributions.

Renée Ann Cramer is Associate Professor and Director of the Law, Politics, and Society Program at Drake University. Trained as a political scientist, she is an interdisciplinary scholar who uses interpretive methods to understand issues surrounding birth, autonomy, and dignity from a critical race and critical feminist perspective. She teaches course on Reproductive Law and Politics, American Indian Law and Politics, and Critical Race and Feminist Theory. Her first book: *Cash, Color, and Colonialism* was recently reissued in paperback by the University of Oklahoma Press. She is currently writing a book on the celebrity baby bump, *Pregnant with the Stars*, as well as a book on the regulation of homebirth midwifery. She is a wife and mom, a runner and yogini; and her soundtrack for writing this chapter included lots and lots of Gwen Stefani and Ani DiFranco.

Justin R. Garcia is an evolutionary biologist at The Kinsey Institute for Research in Sex, Gender and Reproduction at Indiana University, Bloomington. His primary research focuses on the evolutionary and biological foundations of human love, intimacy, and sexual behavior. He is currently co-editing *Evolution's Empress* (Oxford University Press), and coauthoring a book with Peter Gray, tentatively titled *Evolution and Human Sexuality* (Harvard University Press).

Jaymee Goh is a writer of speculative fiction and a scholar/blogger of critical theory. She has contributed to *Tor.com, Racialicious.com*, the Apex Book Company blog, *Beyond Victoriana.com*, and *Steampunk II: Reloaded* (Tachyon Publications). Her fiction is published in *Expanded Horizons* and *Crossed Genres*. She graduated from Saint Mary's University (Halifax, Nova Scotia) with an Honours degree in English and received her MA in Cultural Studies and Critical Theory at McMaster University. Her blog (http://jhameia. blogspot.com) explores marginalization and culture, and she analyzes steampunk literature from a postcolonial perspective at *Silver Goggles* (http:// silver-goggles.blogspot.com).

Evangeline (Vange) Heiliger is Visiting Assistant Professor and ACM-Mellon Postdoctoral Fellow in Gender Studies at Coe College. Her chapter in this anthology is based on her dissertation, *Shopping Our Way to a Better World? Redefining Gender, Sexuality and Moral Citizenship Under Ethical Consumerism* (Women's Studies, University of California, Los Angeles). Her current research includes *Weird Bodies and Weedy Economies: Feminist Ecological Possibilities in Queer Economic Bodies*—a project investigating trash, class, embodiment, and queer sustainable economies; and a forthcoming essay, "When 'The Economy' Isn't Enough: A Queer Feminist Desire for Economic Bodies." Vange would like to thank Grace K. Hong and UCLA's 2007 Graduate Summer Research Mentorship program for mentorship and financial support; and Ellen Broidy, Loran Marsan, Jenny Musto, Katie Oliviero, Saru Matambanadzo, Chris Heiliger, Anna Ward, and Van Ngoc-Thanh Nguyen for their insightful feedback on various drafts of this essay.

Astrid Henry is Associate Professor of Gender, Women's, and Sexuality Studies at Grinnell College in Iowa. She is the author of *Not My Mother's Sister: Generational Conflict and Third-Wave Feminism* (Indiana University Press), a book examining contemporary generational conflicts as they have developed between feminism's third and second waves in the United States over the last two decades; excerpts from *Not My Mother's Sister* have been reprinted in *The Women's Movement Today: an Encyclopedia of Third-Wave Feminism* (Greenwood Press) and *Gender Inequality: Feminist Theories and Politics* (Oxford University Press). Henry's articles on third-wave feminism and generational relationships within U.S. feminism appear in *Women's Studies Quarterly* and *PMLA*, as well as in the anthologies *Catching a Wave: Reclaiming Feminism for the 21st Century* (Northeastern University Press),

Different Wavelengths (Routledge), and *Reading "Sex and the City"* (I. B. Tauris), among others. She is currently working on a study of memoirs by U.S. feminists since the 1970s, and serves as secretary of the National Women's Studies Association.

Leslie Heywood is Professor of English and Creative Writing at SUNY-Binghamton. Interdisciplinary in focus, her areas are creative writing, gender studies, sport studies, science studies, and environmental studies. Heywood is the author of the poetry books *The Proving Grounds* (Red Hen Press) and *Natural Selection* (Louisiana Literature Press) and the memoir *Pretty Good for a Girl* (The Free Press). She is the creative nonfiction editor of *Ragazine: http://ragazine.cc/*, and the literary editor of *The Evolutionary Review*. Her academic work includes *Built to Win: The Female Athlete as Cultural Icon* (University of Minnesota Press), *Dedication to Hunger: The Anorexic Aesthetic in Modern Culture* (University of California Press), *Bodymakers: A Cultural Anatomy of Women's Bodybuilding* (Rutgers University Press), and *Third Wave Agenda: Being Feminist, Doing Feminism* (University of Minnesota Press). Heywood also edited *The Women's Movement Today: An Encyclopedia of Third Wave Feminism* (Greenwood Press).

Marjorie Jolles is Assistant Professor of Women's and Gender Studies at Roosevelt University, where she teaches courses in fashion theory, global feminist ethics, feminist philosophy, and philosophy of the body. She has published articles on style, the body, and rhetorics of feminine authenticity in *Hypatia: A Journal of Feminist Philosophy*; *Critical Matrix: The Princeton Journal of Women, Gender, and Culture*; and *The Oprah Phenomenon* (University Press of Kentucky). Her articles on feminist pedagogy appear in *Feminist Teacher* and *The American Philosophical Association's Newsletter on Feminism and Philosophy*. Her current research is on class antagonism in postfeminist fashion culture. She received her PhD in Philosophy from Temple University.

Jan Kreidler is an independent scholar who holds a PhD in Literature and Criticism from Indiana University of Pennsylvania. Her academic interests include topics such as women's studies, minority voices, multiculturalism, and American southern literature. With over twenty years of teaching experience, she now travels extensively, particularly in the United Arab Emirates.

Elline Lipkin is a scholar, poet, and nonfiction writer who holds an MFA from Columbia University and a PhD from the University of Houston in Creative Writing with a concentration in Women's Studies. Her books include *Girls' Studies* (Seal Press) and *The Errant Thread*, which was chosen by

Eavan Boland to receive the Kore Press First Book Award. Her nonfiction writing appears in *Salon.com*, the *Ms. Magazine Blog*, *Girl w/Pen: Bridging Feminist Research and Popular Reality*, and a range of other contemporary sources. Lipkin has been a Postdoctoral Scholar with the Beatrice Bain Research Group on Gender at the University of California, Berkeley where she also taught for the departments of Gender and Women's Studies, Comparative Literature, and College Writing. Since 2008 she has been a Research Scholar with the Center for Study of Women at the University of California, Los Angeles.

Diana M. Pho has been involved with the steampunk communities in the New York metro area and New England and has traveled the country as a convention speaker and general rabble-rouser using the "steamsona" stage name Ay-leen the Peacemaker. She is the founding editor of the award-winning blog *Beyond Victoriana* (beyondvictoriana.com), which focuses on multicultural steampunk and retrofuturism. She has been interviewed about steampunk and its evolving subculture for multiple science fiction and pop culture Web sites, documentaries, and for the books *The Steampunk Bible* (Abrams Image) and *Steampunk: Reloaded* (Tachyon Publications). She currently lives and works in New York City.

Jo Reger is Associate Professor of Sociology and Director of the Women and Gender Studies Program at Oakland University in Michigan. Reger is the author of *Everywhere and Nowhere: Contemporary Feminism in the United States* (Oxford University Press) and editor of *Different Wavelengths: Studies of Contemporary Feminism in the United States* (Routledge). Her work on the U.S. women's movements has appeared in a variety of journals including *Gender & Society* and *Qualitative Sociology*. Jo Reger thanks Rachel Einwohner, Judy Taylor, and Nancy Whittier for their comments on earlier versions of this chapter and the editors of the volume for their comments and assistance.

Catherine Spooner is Senior Lecturer in English Literature at Lancaster University, UK. She is the author of *Fashioning Gothic Bodies* (Manchester University Press) and *Contemporary Gothic* (Reaktion), as well as numerous articles on Gothic literature, fashion and popular culture. She is the co-editor, with Emma McEvoy, of *The Routledge Companion to Gothic*. Her next book will be *Post-Millennial Gothic: Comedy, Romance and the Rise of Happy Gothic* (Continuum).

Jayne Swift is a graduate of the University of Iowa (BA, MA, Women's Studies) and the University of Washington (MA, Cultural Studies). She is currently in the Feminist Studies PhD program at the University of Minnesota. A recent example of her work in the field of commercial sex studies, "Behind the Marquee: A Worker's Eulogy for the Seattle Lusty Lady Theatre," was featured on *Sexuality & Society* (http://thesocietypages.org/sexuality/), a social science blog hosted by The Society Pages. When not in school she spends her time kicking both her stripper and femme heels on multiple stages.

Shira Tarrant is Associate Professor in the Women's, Gender, and Sexuality Studies Department at California State University, Long Beach. Her books include *When Sex Became Gender* (Routledge), *Men Speak Out: Views on Gender, Sex, and Power* (Routledge), and *Men and Feminism* (Seal Press). Her writing on masculinity, feminism, pop culture, and sexual politics appears in various publications including *Bitch Magazine*, *AlterNet.org*, the *Ms. Magazine Blog*, *Women's Studies Quarterly*, *Fix Me Up: Essays on Television Dating and Makeover Shows* (McFarland), the *Encyclopedia of Gender in Media* (Sage), and *The Women's Movement Today: An Encyclopedia of Third-Wave Feminism* (Greenwood Press). Shira Tarrant received her PhD in political science from the University of California, Los Angeles. Read more at http://shiratarrant.com.

Denise Witzig teaches feminist theories, popular culture, media, and writing in the Women's Studies Program and the English Department at Saint Mary's College of California, where she is the Coordinator of the Women's Studies Program and Associate Professor in Women's Studies. Her research interests include fashion theory, gender and consumerism, and popular representations of sexualities and feminist politics in image culture. She has written on shopping and marketing to youth cultures, as well as on representations of sexual authority and female identity in literature. Her work on the writer Edith Wharton has appeared in the *National Women's Studies Association Journal* and two critical anthologies. Witzig has recently written on feminist histories and representations of masculinities in the TV show *Mad Men*, and she plans further critical explorations into the popular mythological past of "The Sixties."

Index

Can I quote KBS?
sewn-to-the bone.